All Things Wild and Wonderful

Wildlife Imagery in Yorkshire Churches

by

M. Jill Lucas

ISBN 978-0-9544035-1-5

Published by Northern Bee Books, 2013
Scout Bottom Farm
Mytholmroyd
Hebden Bridge HX7 5JS (UK)

Front cover:
St Martin of Tours with his pet hares.
Window, 1437. St Martin le Grand, York.

Design and artwork
D&P Design and Print
Worcestershire

Printed by
Lightning Source, US

All Things Wild and Wonderful

Wildlife Imagery in Yorkshire Churches

by

M. Jill Lucas

For Brian
God blessed me with you.

CONTENTS

FOREWORD

Christian churches often swarm with animal life, carved into wood and stone, gleaming in windows, embroidered into hassocks and twisted into ironwork. Such a delight belongs to buildings of every period, and searching them out is one of the pleasures these sacred places give. Sometimes their depiction rests on ancient lore about animal life, once current among our forebears. Often enough, depicting the animal creation shows a sheer pleasure in its variety and beauty.

A church building is an act of praise, in which human life joins with all creation in giving thanks to God for our "creation, preservation and all the blessings of this life", to quote the General Thanksgiving of the Book of Common Prayer. This book will enhance our pleasure, and deepen our sense of the whole of life brought together with human and angelic worshippers in acknowledging the glory of God.

Keith Jones
Dean of York

ACKNOWLEDGEMENTS

I would like to thank Dr David Barker for his encouragement in the writing of this book; Michael Denton for reading and correcting inaccuracies in the section on birds; Albert Henderson for his help with the hares and rabbits; Rita Rothery for her comments and helpful suggestions on the grammar and punctuation; Professor Kenneth Varty for his support throughout the writing of this book and for providing useful information on a variety of subjects; to the staff of the Huddersfield Reference Library who were very good at tracing and confirming details of obscure references, and particularly to the Dean of York the Very Reverend Keith Jones for writing the Foreword. Special thanks to my husband Brian who photographed the flora and fauna, (not always very enthusiastically when the subjects were in awkward places) and for acting as chauffeur and general dog's body for a long number of years. Sadly he died before seeing the book published. The images taken in Beverley St Mary and Beverley Minster are reproduced by kind permission of the Vicar and churchwardens; those in St Mary, Bolton on Swale and All Hallows, Harthill with permission of their PPC's, All Saints, Silkstone and Holy Trinity, Acaster Malbis by kind permission of their respective Vicars, St Stephen, Lindley pictures used by permission of Ann and John White. Studley Royal photographed by permission of English Heritage. Rothwell with permission of Holy Trinity Church and Selby Abbey with permission from the churchwardens.

I am indebted to the incumbents of the many churches we visited who gave us permission to photograph subjects in their churches. I am grateful to the churchwardens, vergers, guides and the many parishioners whom we met who were so very helpful and informative. If I have omitted any one, the omission is unintentional and I offer my sincere apologies.

INTRODUCTION

Question: What do an otter; a pelican and a six-legged spider catching a fly have in common?
Answer: They are all found in Yorkshire churches.

Many articles, books and guides have been written and published on churches, their architecture, history and furnishings. On a day's outing, coach, car trips and walks 'take in' the local church, abbey, cathedral or minster. Postcards and pamphlets specifying details of particular interest in the church are usually available, but sadly wildlife imagery is often neglected by the authors of such publications. Rarely do they mention the vivid depictions, the variety of subjects or the workmanship which can be seen. Yet birds, plants, animals and other creatures are found carved in wood and stone, painted or stained on glass and embroidered on church vestments and other ecclesiastical textiles.

This book is the work of many people, not just the author. Architects, builders and craftsmen and women from a bygone era to the present day have, through their artistry, imagination and skill, given us a rich cultural heritage. Not all churches are town or village centred; many were built before the advent of proper roads and are accessible only by a lane or steps. Others were built by the lord of the manor in the grounds of his estate. However, all are worth searching out for the superb wildlife treasures which may be contained within them. From the large and imposing abbeys, cathedrals and minsters to the smallest of parish churches, the atmosphere in these places of worship is a tribute to the devout and their devotions both in the past, in the present and one hopes in the future. The book is intended primarily for the tourist who likes looking round churches, for the layman with an interest in church art and iconography, for the incumbent who doesn't always know what his or her church contains and for the naturalist who may be encouraged to look for and find more than bats, dry rot and death watch beetles. In all approximately 110 churches out of the 1000 or more visited are described or mentioned. The area covered is the real Yorkshire before the boundary changes took place.

The majority of the population in the Middle Ages and earlier were unable to read or write, this privilege being confined to the wealthy and to some of those in Holy Orders. The latter said the services in Latin and the aristocracy spoke and read in French. Only the uneducated spoke English, and stories, myths and legends were handed down orally.

The people learnt about the Bible by well-known characters and episodes from it being portrayed in stained glass windows, these becoming an ever present reminder to the congregation of their Christian faith. Quite how this could be I don't know, as many of the windows were and are too high to be seen properly without binoculars and/or a step ladder: the inscriptions are usually written in Latin and in many cases are far too small to be read. The same argument applies to stone carved capitals except where they are at eye level as in Selby Abbey. Wood carvings are a little different, but even then some of the most interesting are on misericords in the chancel where the congregation would certainly not have access. It was forbidden to sit in the medieval church and when praying one stood with uplifted hands. Later, kneeling to pray became the norm. When canons were elderly or infirm a certain amount of relaxation was permitted and this took the form of a T-shaped stick upon which the aged and infirm leant. It was known as a reclinatoria and was followed later by the misericord as a concession to the aged clergy who had to attend the obligatory seven services throughout the day and Matins at midnight. Also a lot of misericord carvings do not have a religious theme. The subjects were sometimes chosen for their symbolism and sometimes for their realism, as when they illustrate the wildlife of the countryside. Some portray the attributes and emblems of saints and royalty, whilst others depict characters found in contemporary literature. Some are purely decorative or may represent a tradesman's mark, e.g. a mouse for Robert Thompson. Many of the subjects chosen have a secular rather than a sacred theme. The wildlife and the context in which it is found provide a fascinating area of study concerning the myths, legends, literature, sports, pastimes and domestic life from the Normans to the present day. It is a study which will repay the enthusiast with endless hours of pleasure, from plotting which church to visit next to the visit itself, and always there is the possibility of discovering a hidden gem.

My interest in the subject originated from an article which I read many years ago about owl holes. Many barns have 'owl holes' built into them, allowing the birds easy access to food and nesting sites, but below and behind the clock face in a church tower in Lincolnshire is a chamber specially built to accommodate owls, to encourage them, one assumes, to take up residence in the hope that they would rid the church of vermin. When I retired after thirty years as a veterinary nurse, I decided to look in our local churches (all 72 of them) not that I expected to find owl holes, but just to see what I could discover. A long number of years previously because of my interest in plants and animals, one of my neighbours referred to me 'as yon queer lass' (we are in Yorkshire after all!). I think some incumbents had the same impression. A simple request to look in their church for wildlife brought a variety of responses, from a stunned and disbelieving silence vibrating down the telephone wires, to what can only be described as the ecclesiastical version of raucous laughter and in one case in particular, a very offended "we have nothing like that in our church, Madam". I think this vicar had unholy visions of me finding bats in his belfry, fungi in his floorboards and wood-boring pests in his pews.

My late husband, to whom this book is dedicated, thought I was wasting time, money and most important of all film! I found and photographed sufficient subjects to give an illustrated talk which proved to be one of the most popular of all our talks. When Brian retired he decided that if I was to continue then I should have decent slides and extend the search to counties other than Yorkshire. He disposed of most of my slides, planned routes and suggested that in future I carry a duster and a paint brush with me wherever we went – those spiders and their cobwebs get everywhere! For an avowed atheist he took up the search with unbridled enthusiasm. It didn't take long to go from just looking and photographing to wanting to know more, why the subjects were chosen, what they illustrated, who were the designers etc.? I owe my thanks to those authors whose books were consulted on these subjects. One thing leads to another, and this book is the result of nearly thirty years of reading and researching churches in God's own County of Yorkshire.

Before leaving any church, please say a prayer and put some money in the donation box.

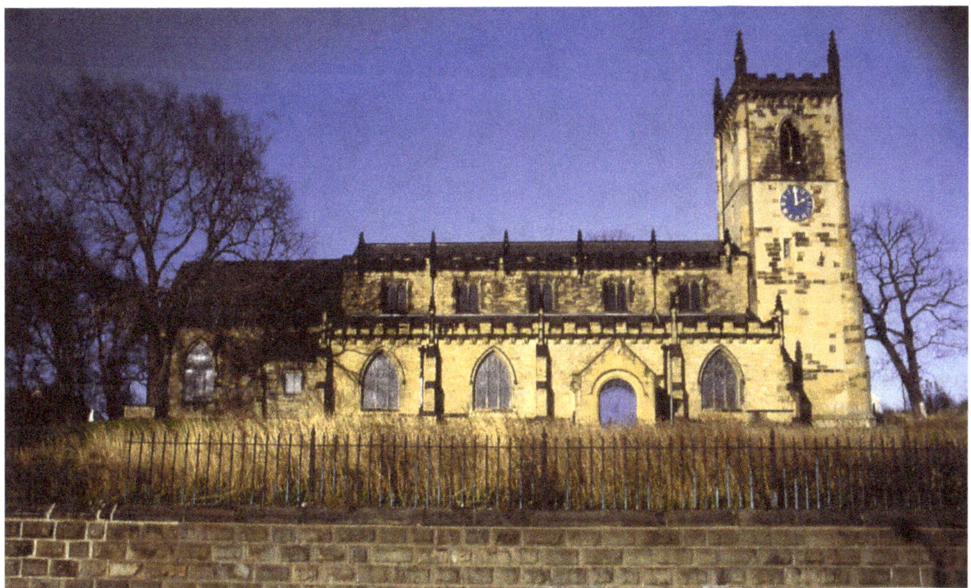

Holy Trinity, Rothwell.

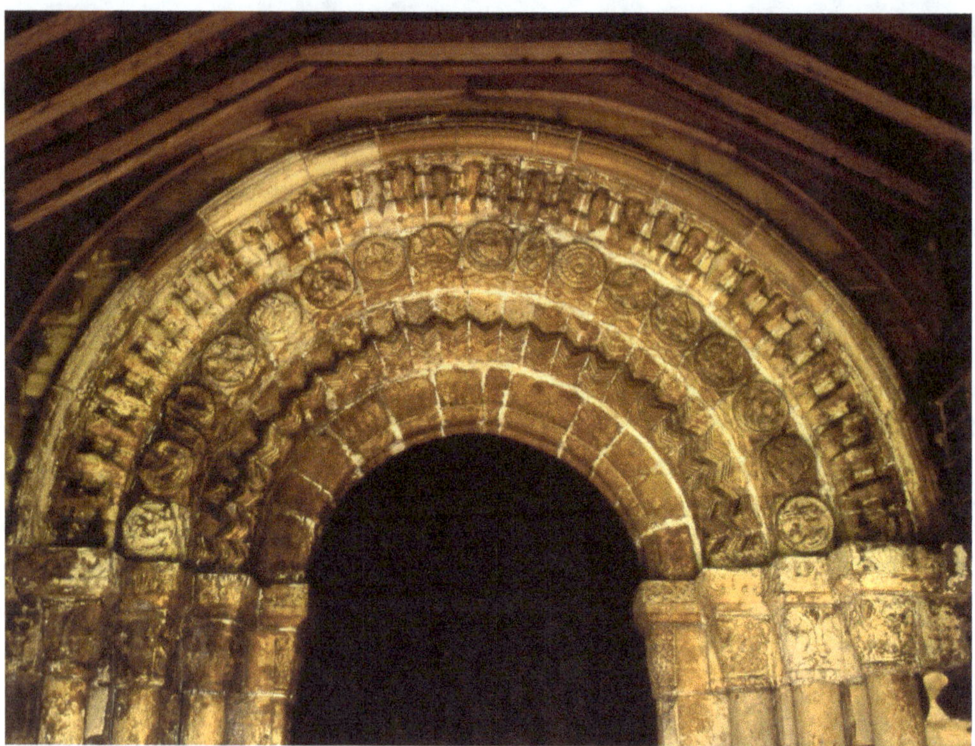

Norman Arch, Brayton.

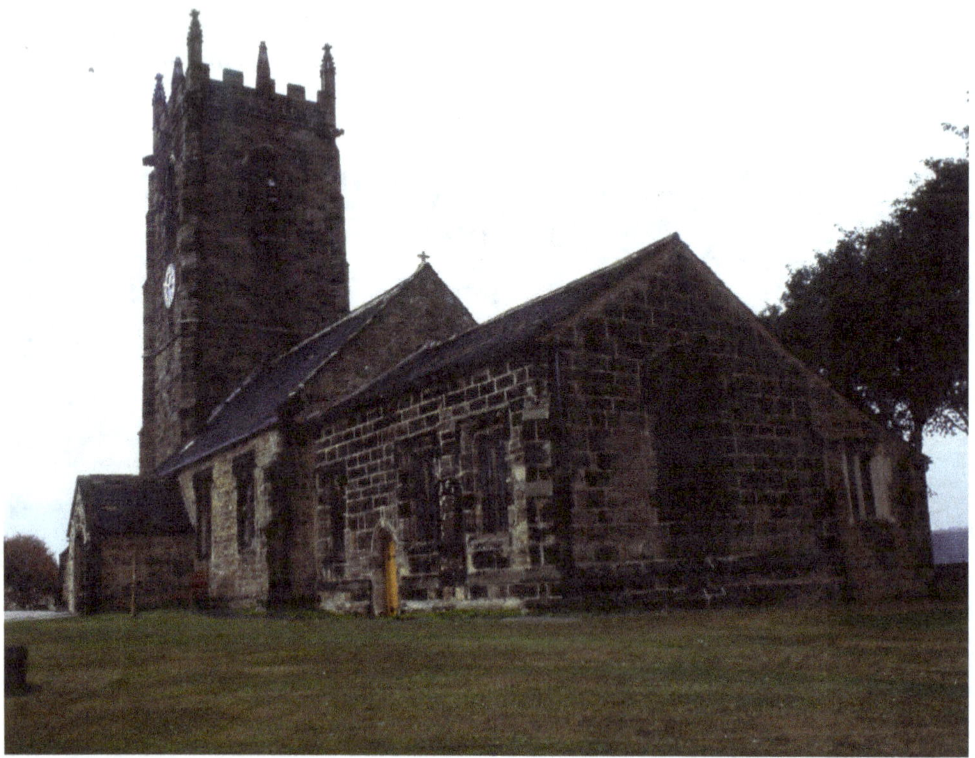

St Michael, Emley.

YORKSHIRE CHURCHES

Acaster Malbis Holy Trinity

Holy Trinity is an early 14th century church situated by the River Ouse.

Pulpit. Pomegranates are illustrated being pecked by birds. They are normally seen pecking grapes.

Window, circa 1320. Quarries containing bramble leaves and blackberries, holly and ivy leaves and berries, and oak leaves and acorns are portrayed.

Adel St John the Baptist

This is a Grade one Listed Building. Dating from the mid 12th century it is one of the finest Norman churches in Yorkshire.

As you enter the church there are two steps down into the nave. This is said to be common in ancient churches dedicated to John the Baptist. It symbolises his stepping down into the River Jordon for baptism.

Capitals, Norman. A centaur is fighting two dragons, and pagan and Christianised salamanders are carved on opposite pillars, the Christianised ones are distinguished by the incised cross on their backs.

Chancel arch, Norman. The outermost arch of the chancel illustrates thirty seven different heads including those of a rabbit, an owl, a cat, a fish said to be a pike, and on a 'triple' face, a fox is the third or bottom face. The third capital on the opposite side of the arch depicts a boar above a hunting dog.

Sanctuary, Door-knocker or Closing ring in bronze, 13th century. This is shaped like the head of a bear with a man's face taking the place of nostrils. A fugitive could claim the sanctuary of the church if he reached the closing ring even if the church was closed. Unfortunately the original ring was stolen.

Window, 1933. Designed by F. C. Eden, an owl bellman and a cellarer bird are shown in characteristic pose but the latter lacks the dish and keys (cf. Marsden). Surrounding them is a border of bluebells, mallow, pansies, pinks, snowdrops and thistles.

Window, 1955. Known as the 'Bright and Beautiful', it was designed by Harry Stammers of York and placed in the 16th century window frame. (cf. Masham and Scarborough). Charming birds and animals in fantastic and weird patterns and colours are depicted. There is a green mole, a white mouse and a purple rabbit with deep purple lines on its body, a red and orange pheasant, bluebells, a red and yellow butterfly, a blue frog with white spots and a blue and white bird.

Ancient stonework and modern glass blend very happily in this delightful little Norman church. The naïve carvings of the stone work are complemented by the outrageous colours of the animals and birds in the windows.

Aldborough St Andrew
The present church was built around 1330 and is the third church on this site.

Windows, 19th and early 20th centuries. The former has a background of oak leaves and acorns. The latter was designed by Hemmingway and portrays a rabbit, squirrels; bullfinch, a heron, mallard, an owl, a parrot, partridge, pheasant, and both Wood and Pouter pigeons, a robin, swan, teal and woodpecker; fish and a lizard. Holly leaves and berries are in the tracery, and variously coloured oak leaves and acorns are in the background and on the borders.

Alne St Mary
In the Norman arch of the south porch, which dates from 1150, are carved medallions and lunettes, (some badly eroded), with signs of the zodiac, Labours of the Months and bestiary animals; fortunately some of the latter are labelled e.g. *Vulpis, hyena, panthera* etc. Some of the carvings were replaced in the 18th century. but still discernible are birds pecking at a fox lying on his back feigning death whilst two other birds approach; a panther with its mouth wide open being observed by a smaller animal; a hyena and a Caladrius hovering over a dying man. Some of the carvings show a bestiary influence. The inner order features the Agnus Dei, a bear, and a camel, a goat (probably), a horse, Aspido chelone, an eagle renewing its youth, and a pelican vulning to revive a child lying beneath it. This is unusual in that the bird is normally seen reviving its own young.

Ampleforth The Abbey Church of St Lawrence.
The Roman Catholic Church was designed in the Gothic style by Sir Giles Gilbert Scott. Building started in 1922 and was completed in 1961.

Capitals. Octagonal capitals also designed by Sir Giles Gilbert Scott and dating from 1924 are carved on each face to show numerous animals, birds, fishes and insects. Curiously, no flowers are depicted. Animals include a bat, beaver, dog, fox, goat, hedgehog, hyena, kangaroo and mouse, rabbits in profusion, a rhinoceros, seal, squirrel, weasel and wolf. Identified birds are a cock, flamingo, heron, lapwing, an ostrich, a penguin, pheasant and a turkey. Also carved are an alligator or crocodile, a crab, flying fish, swordfish, frog, slug, tortoise, butterfly, cockchafer beetle and dragonfly.

Aysgarth St Andrew
This 12th century church was rebuilt in the reign of Henry V111 and rebuilt again by James Green of Portsmouth to open again in 1866. Only part of the medieval tower remains.

Bench end, circa 1480. This was formerly part of the Abbot's stall at Jervaulx and is now made into the Vicar's stall. It illustrates the rebus of William de Heslington who became Abbot in 1472. It depicts a hazel twig in a tun (barrel) with the letter W above.

Poppyheads to the stall show a lion, thistle, wheat and, as far as is known, a unique example of a chained antelope whose chain is held by a seated man.

Chairs. There are two chairs: one has bosses of hawthorn and ivy, the other bosses of roses.

Choir stall front. This is part of the rood screen from Jervaulx. It was carved in 1506 by the Ripon School of carvers and brought to Aysgarth in 1536 at the dissolution of the monasteries. Painted in blue, gold and red, small birds are carved in the narrow border.

Choir stall ends. An antelope in hazel and a fabulous beast also in hazel, copied from the rood screen cornice, are featured.

Cornice to the rood screen. Animals portrayed include a dog, an elephant bearing a howdah, a lion, a dragon and a griffin.

Embroidered modern kneelers illustrate an elephant, an eagle, a dragon and other creatures copied from the rood screen.

Pulpit. This has a border of vines and grapes.

Window, 1905. Illustrated are a number of squirrels each one differently posed.

Badsworth St Mary the Virgin

Window. Saint Hubert is featured with a dog, and also with a representation of his attribute which is a stag with Christ crucified between its antlers. Also pictured is Saint Giles with his attribute of a hind. The saint has an arrow through his hand; normally it is the animal which has been pierced by the arrow.

Baildon St John

St John's was built in 1848 with the addition of the south tower in 1928.

Window, 1930. Shown in the glass is a bat, either a hare or a rabbit and a squirrel; a bluebird, a Chinese Pheasant, a hawk or a parrot; a fig tree, flowers, an oak, purple iris and water lily. A frog, a snail, a dragonfly and fish are also featured.

Bainton St Andrew

The church built in the 1330s to 40s has animal carvings on the outside.

Barton le Street St Michael and All Angels

Described by Nikolaus Pevsner as a 'sumptuous small Norman church rebuilt without restraint in 1871'. Parts of the original Norman stonework have been incorporated into the new building.

Corbels on the outside of the church depict a pointer, a ram's head, a squirrel, an eagle, an owl, a pelican, and a crane eating either an eel or a snake.

Bedale St Gregory

Situated at the northern end of the main street this 13th/14th century church is said to be one of the truly outstanding North Yorkshire churches.

Font, 14th century. Carved are a bat, squirrel, a pig eating acorns and a pelican-in-her-piety. The latter is the earliest portrayal observed and the bird is clearly restoring life to the nestlings as three heads are visible and there are red paint spots on the bird's breast.

Beverley The Minster

This is the largest of all the parish churches in England. Parts of it date from 1230 and it was completed in 1450. It is a mixture of Early English, Decorated and Perpendicular styles.

Misericords dating from 1520. Scenes include an ape nursing a child, a second ape with a flask, another ape on horseback, a fourth ape in foliage, an ape with a staff chasing a cat, and apes robbing a peddler. Five bears are portrayed: - a bear tied to a wheelbarrow, another being muzzled, a third licking its paw, one dancing or wrestling with a man, and a bear dancing to bagpipes. There is a camel, a cat being combed by a monkey, a second cat catching mice, and one playing a viol to mice; a cow lying down, another cow being milked; a deer browsing, a doe scratching her head, and a stag hunting scene. Also pictured are a fox ridden by an ape, a fox nursed by an ape, another standing over a bird, a fourth with sleeping geese, another preaching to geese, two seated foxes facing each other, a fox hunting scene with the fox chased into an earth by three dogs, an archer aiming an arrow at the fox, a woman with a distaff chasing after a fox which is making off with one of her geese whilst four more geese are seen in the background; a fox hanged by geese and in another scene the rope is removed from the dead fox's neck by an ape, and finally a hare riding a fox. There are leopards' heads with protruding tongues, a lion, a monkey being trained by a man, a monkey using a dog as bagpipes, a pig playing bagpipes to dancing piglets, a second pig playing a harp, a saddled pig, another pig ridden by a boy; two sheep butting each other, and hawking and stag and fox hunting scenes.

Birds depicted include a crowing cock, two cocks quarrelling, a cock scratching its head; a hen with five chicks, another sitting on chicks with one on her back; a dove, an eagle; a goose scratching its head and another one preening, and a man shoeing a goose. The latter is symbolic of man's folly. However, geese were either shod in leather or had their feet tarred when being walked to the market. A hawk preying on a partridge, an owl with a mouse, a second owl mobbed by four birds (signifying the Jews who preferred the darkness of ignorance to the light of Christian knowledge), a pelican feeding six young, a pelican picking up a serpent; two storks or cranes eating from a sack of corn, and a swan swimming are illustrated. Bramble fruit and foliage, roses, and vines and grapes are represented.

Also seen is a large fish seizing a smaller one, dragons, a dragon and a lion fighting, a griffin, a unicorn scratching its head, a wodehouse fighting a dragon, and a wyvern.

Elbow. A fox with a goose slung over his back.

Choir screen designed by George Gilbert Scott in 1876. Foliage and a sow suckling her litter are found in a spandrel.

Statue, probably early 14th century. A fox shown dressed in a shift and carrying a staff, is followed in procession by a duck, a hen and a cock.

Label stop. Good and evil are portrayed as two nuns, one with a rosary the other with a cross, beneath a goat's head.

Beverley St Mary

Built in the 14th/15th centuries with fragments of Norman work, this is one of the most beautiful of all parish churches in the whole of England.

Misericords, circa 1445. An ape parodying a physician is holding a bag towards an ecclesiastic who holds a coin. There are bear baiting and hunting scenes, dogs sitting on foliage, a stag lying beneath a tree, and an elephant and castle. Fox carvings include a fox shot by an arrow consulting an ape, a fox preaching to a friar and a nun whilst two cowled apes sit below holding scrolls, two foxes holding a book up to an eagle lectern and two more foxes dressed as friars receiving their instructions from a Franciscan monk.

An eagle, a pelican-in-her-piety, birds on leaves, oak leaves, and vine and grapes are depicted. Other carvings include dragons on foliage, griffins standing on dragons, and a griffin either side of the Tree of Life with a rabbit beneath each one, a wodehouse between two lions, a wyvern attacked by a knight, and a knight attacking a wild boar.

Roof bosses, 1520-25. A fox with a cock in his cowl preaching to ducks, and a fox running away with a goose are illustrated.

Statue, 1330. A rabbit with a pilgrim's staff and scrip stands above a lovely, little benign-looking lion's head corbel. This carving is thought to have been the inspiration for Tenniel's drawing of the White Rabbit in Lewis Carrol's book.

Birstwith St James

Standing guard over the church's entrance is a Wellingtonia tree.

Capitals. Plants featured are lily and oak.

Corbels. Huge corbels on either side of the chancel arch show passion-flowers and vine and corn.

Bishop Wilton St Edith
Parts of the church are Norman with additions from the 13th/14th centuries. Restoration of the church was undertaken between 1858-9 by J. L. Pearson for Sir Tatton Sykes.

Doorway arch, Norman. Carved animal heads include a monkey banging a tambourine and, in new stone, a monkey blowing pipes.

Tiles. Dating from the last quarter of the 19th century, a mosaic of black and white marble in the form of birds by Salviati can be found. The design is a copy of that in the Vatican which was originally in the palace of the Caesars of Rome. Identification of the birds is difficult.

Bolsterstone St Mary

Window, 1869. Saint John with a chalice from which a tiny dragon is emerging. A snake is the usual beast depicted.

Bolton Abbey The Priory Church of St Mary the Blessed Virgin and St Cuthbert
The west tower was started in 1520 and the Early English nave was restored in 1880 by G. E. Street.

Wall painting, 1880, by R. A. Bottomly. Adorning a wall are Madonna Lilies, barley, olive and palm trees, passion-flower, wild rose and vine. The Madonna Lily is the traditional symbol of Saint Mary, to whom the church is dedicated. Barley represents the bread whose significance Jesus used many times during His ministry. He went to His Passion from the Mount of Olives. On Palm Sunday He rode in triumph into Jerusalem. The passion-flower is symbolic of Our Lord's Passion. The Crown of Thorns is symbolised by the wild rose and the vine was used to teach the relationship between Him -the vine - and the believers - the branches.

Bolton on Swale St Mary
This is mostly Victorian with a south arcade which is possibly 13th century, and a late 16th century tower.

Woodwork circa 1859.

Pews. Hawthorn, and ivy foliage and fruit decorate the pews.

Pulpit. Carvings of hawthorn, ivy, oak with acorns, and pomegranates are portrayed.

Reading Desk. Hawthorn, oak and acorns are depicted.

Window, 1905. Birds and a gull with clawed not webbed feet, bluebell, lily, marguerite, passion-flower, violets, fish, cuttlefish and a lobster can be seen. Borders in other windows show bryony, hawthorn, ivy, vine and grapes.

Boynton St Andrew
This church has a 15th century stone tower, and a brick nave and chancel rebuilt in 1768-70 by John Carr.

Lectern. A turkey cock is the emblem of the Strickland family. In 1526 the bird was introduced into this country from Mexico by the then Lord of the Manor, Sir William Strickland, hence the turkey lectern.

Bramham All Saints
There is a Norman tower, a late 12th century north arcade, a 19th century chancel and chapel and 20th century screen and panelling.

Cornice Decorating the cornice are flowers, vines and a snake twining around an apple tree.

Stalls, late 19th /early 20th centuries. Honeysuckle and berries, oak and ivy, strawberry and clover, tulips and daffodils ornament the stalls.

Bridlington (old) The Priory Church.
The nave which originally came from the Augustinian Priory dates from the 13th/14th centuries. Sir George Gilbert Scott refurbished the west tower in the 1870s. On an 11th century coffin lid (or more likely a bread stone) is a carving of the Aesopian fable of The Fox and Stork. A fox is watching as a stork drinks from a jug.

Brompton by Sawdon All Saints
Most of the church dates from the 14th/15th centuries. A memorial to Sir George Cayley, 'the father of aeronautics' is the porch built in 1895. In 1802 William Wordsworth was married here.

Window, 1907. Pictured are a horse, a pig, a mallard, an owl, a swallow, flax and pansy.

Window by Rosemary Rutherford and dated 1970 depicts twenty one birds including Blue Tit, gannet, hoopoe, pheasant, robin, swallow and woodpecker.

Bubwith All Saints
There are a few Norman remains, otherwise the church dates from the 13th -16th centuries.

Altar frontal. Modern embroidery depicts animals, birds, flowers and insects:- a mouse, a stoat in ermine, a Blue Tit and a wren, apple, bramble, corn, currants, daffodils, hazel, horse chestnut, ivy, nuts, poppies, primroses, roses, snowdrops, Winter Aconites, Wood Anemones, Yellow Flag, a butterfly and a snail.

Burgwallis St Helen
Herringbone masonry can be found in the outer walls of the Early Norman nave.

Screen, 16th century, restored. Vines, grapes and Tudor roses bedeck the cornices.

Windows, Victorian. There are daffodils, daisies, roses, snowdrops and possibly a bee in a heraldic shield.

Copgrove St Michael
The chancel and small window within it are both Norman.

Window. Saint Francis is painted with both domestic and wild creatures including a cow, a dog, a fox, a horse, an otter, a squirrel and a cock and pheasant.

Coxwold St Michael
For the last eight years of his life, Laurence Stern, author of *The Life and Opinions of Tristram Shandy,* was the incumbent here. He died in London in 1768 and his remains were brought back to Coxwold 200 years after his death. There is a uniquely T-shaped Communion rail.
Thompson mice are carved in the Lady Chapel, on the altar and on the Bible case.

Croft St Peter
Lewis Carroll's father, Charles Dodgson was rector between 1843-68. Lord Byron whilst on honeymoon with Annabella Millbanke attended services at Croft.

Sedilia 14th century. Bears fighting or playing, a pig suckling two piglets whilst eating acorns, lion's heads and a ram's head are depicted.

Window. Designed by Carl Edwards and dated 1981, the window has representations of a horse, a pig, mallard and a swallow.

Dewsbury All Saints
There are fragments of an Anglo-Saxon cross from the early 9th century and medallions dating from the 13th century of what represent two of the monthly labours.

Window, mid 14th century. Roundels with two of the 'Occupations of the Months' are featured, harvesting representing August and a man beating down acorns for his pigs representing either October or November.

Quarries, 15th century. Much of the glass is in very bad condition and is partially hidden behind a modern toilet block! There is a border of dolphins and squirrels surrounding a lion; a porcupine, birds, foliage and a snail.

East Rounton St Laurence
Built in 1884 by Robert James Johnson. The North Window, circa 1926, is dedicated to the explorer, naturalist and archaeologist Gertrude Bell.

A memorial tablet to Sir Hugh Bell has carvings of English flowers round the border - bluebell, daffodil, daisy, ivy, narcissi, periwinkle and primrose.

Window, circa 1926 illustrates a camel, acorn and pomegranate.

Ebberston St Mary the Virgin
The church is situated in the grounds of Ebberston House. There is a Norman nave and chancel, 12th century ironwork on a modern door and a 16th century tower.

The top hinge of the South doorway is in the shape of a dove with an olive leaf above its head.

Lectern. This is in the form of an eagle facing sideways with its feet further forward than is usual making the bird appear to be falling over. The bird's feathers are more detailed than is normally seen.

Ecclesfield St Mary
Known as the Minster of the Moors, the church contains 15th/16th century furnishings and medieval glass fragments.

Window, 19th century. Birds in cages of all shapes and sizes are hung up or rest on the ground, whilst the bodies of other birds are hung on hooks. The inscription from Matthew 10:1 reads 'so don't be afraid; you are worth more than many sparrows'.

Filey St John or St Oswald
The parish church appears to be cut off from the town and until 1889 it was in the North Riding. The windows dating from 1896-1906 are by Herbert W. Bryans and have his trademark of a running greyhound.

Poppyheads. A dolphin, a bird and an owl are carved on three poppyheads.

Fishlake St Cuthbert
Begun by the Normans this church is famous for the south doorway with its carvings of animals, humans and birds.

Elbows. Beech mast and foliage, bramble and blackberries, lily, and oak and acorns are depicted.

Folkton St John
The nave and chancel are Norman and are thought to have been built prior to 1150.

Capitals. Carved on one capital is either a hare or a rabbit.

Fylingthorpe St Stephen

Capital. Hawthorn, ivy, vine and grapes are to be seen.

Gargrave St Andrew

Window, 19th century by Jean Capronnier. This shows a swan-like pelican-in-her-piety. The artist has given her clawed instead of webbed feet.

Greenfield St Mary

Embroidery. Passion-flowers are beautifully worked on an altar frontal.

Window. Crows on their nest are shown bringing food to their nestlings, a Green Woodpecker, a heron and butterflies are also present.

Guisborough St Nicholas

The tomb-chest or Brus Cenotaph is the church's treasure. It features a rebus on the name of Prior Cockerell. Saint James with a scallop shell and a cock on a reel connecting them to Prior James Cockerell who ruled the Priory from 1519 to 1534. It contains niches in one of which is a carving of Saint Ambrose with a beehive at his feet. It was removed from the Augustinian Priory in 1539 after its dissolution.

Pulpit. Around the top is a border of passion-flowers.

Window. A medieval fragment depicts an open-mouthed dog-like animal with a ridged back, a bird, oak leaves and acorns.

Guisley St Oswald

The ancestors of the American poet Henry Wadsworth Longfellow worshiped here and in 1812 the marriage between Maria Bramwell and Patrick Bronte was celebrated here.

Capital. A squirrel is carved sitting in hazel.

Halifax St John

There is a life-size figure with his alms box of a beggar known as Old Tristram.

Misericords, 15th century. Five misericords depict a lion's mask, a pelican-in-her-piety, roses, vines and grapes, and a mermaid with a comb and mirror.

Harrogate St Peter

Temple Moore began building the nave and chancel between 1905-14. The chancel was completed by his nephew in 1935.

Capitals, circa 1876. Examples of fruit and flowers are to be seen: - apple, bluebell, buttercup, hawthorn, ivy, polypody, roses, sycamore, vine and barley.

Pulpit. Illustrated are clover, daisy, a fern, hawthorn, ivy, lily, maple, possibly mulberry, oak, primrose, rose and vine.

Harthill All Hallows

Parts of the church date from the 13th, 15th and 17th centuries. The church celebrated its 900th birthday in 1979.

The lectern and pulpit were carved by the Italian wood carver, Carlo Scarselli between 1877 and 1880. On the lectern are birds on ivy pecking berries and on vines pecking grapes.

Pulpit. This is ornamented with birds on brambles, on figs and on juniper berries. There is an owl on fir cones and a partridge on wheat. Filling the spaces are ivy leaves and berries.

Headingly St Chad

Designed by Lord Grimthorpe and W. H. Crossland the nave, tower and spire were finished in 1868. In 1910 the chancel was added.

Pulpit, circa 1915. There is a snake, a bat chained to ivy, and an eagle pecking the eye of a moon-faced man.

Window, circa 1918 designed by Margaret Edith Aldrich Rope. Flora and fauna of the world are illustrated:- a camel, cattle, a deer and her fawn, a dolphin, an elephant, hart, hedgehog, a lion and lioness, Long-haired Dachshund, rabbit, seal, sheep, squirrel, tiger and zebra. Birds include a crow, duck, flamingo, heron, ostrich, peacock, a swan and cygnets, and thrush. There are also crocus, fungi, horse-chestnut, water-lily and Yellow Flag. A crocodile, fish, newts and a tortoise are represented. The latter is the artist's mark of M. E. A. Rope and refers to her family nickname of 'Tor'.

Hemingbrough St Mary the Virgin

From the 11th century the church was owned by the prior and monks of Durham. In 1427 it became a collegiate church but this was suppressed in 1548. The spire was built in the 15th century by a prior named Washington or Wassingtorn of Durham who held the office 1416-46. A row of washing tubs carved at the top of the tower is a pun on the prior's name. What is thought to be the oldest misericord in the country is found here. It is dated circa 1200.

A wooden panel circa 1525 is beautifully carved depicting four monsters.

Stool, 15th century has a scene of a bear blowing the bagpipes.

Heslington St Paul

This is an estate church built 1857-8 by J.B. and W. Atkinson.

Floor mosaic, 1858. A roundel in red, white and black mosaic portrays a pelican-in-her-piety with three chicks.

Howden St Peter

In 1267 St Peter's was made a collegiate church and from then until the late 14th century building was on going. The tower was built 1388-1406.

Statue, 14th century. The Virgin with a dove near her ear.

Poppyhead, Jacobean? Hop, thistle.

Window, 15th century. A small monkey is seen praying.

Hunsingore St John the Baptist

Brasses contain lilies and roses.

Corbels show a bird in a vine, ivy leaves and berries, lily, mallow, passion-flower, and wheat and grapes.

Label stops are decorated with hop, ivy, oak, passion-flower, rose and vine.

Window. A beautifully coloured fish with its mouth wide open to show its tongue is situated at the top of a window. Do fish have tongues, or is this an example of anatomical inaccuracy?

Kilburn St Mary

A memorial to Robert Thompson the 'Mouseman of Kilburn' is the refurbishment in 1958 of the medieval chapel of Saint Thomas.

Lectern, modern. Carvings of an alligator or crocodile and a mouse can be seen. The mouse is the maker's mark of Robert Thompson and it is also carved on the reading desk and on the pulpit.

Kirkburn St Mary

Probably built circa 1130, Pevsner states 'probably the best Norman church in the East Riding after Newbold'.

Font, Norman. This depicts a cat with a long tail and its paws on a mouse, also a bird with a small snake beside it.

Kirkby Malham St Michael the Archangel

Oliver Cromwell witnessed a wedding here and a copy of his signature is in the vestry.

Screen. In the spandrels are the following plants:-daisy, hawthorn, maple, oak, pine cones, pomegranate, primrose and rose.

Window, modern. Saint Cuthbert is shown holding an otter and standing among birds. In the border is an Eider Duck.

Kirkby Malzeard St Andrew

After a fire in 1908 the church was rebuilt by J. Oldrid Scott, son of Sir George Gilbert Scott.

Window. Saint Cuthbert with otters is represented.

Kirkby Wharfe St John the Baptist

There is a 17th century door and the nave and north chapel are Early English, and Perpendicular.

Window, 17th century. A fox in clerical garb is preaching from a pulpit.

If human activity can be allowed in a book on wildlife imagery in churches, the Jacobean screen has beautifully carved panels which illustrate a jester with his bauble; a baker with an oven and a tray of cakes; an archer shooting at a bird in a tree; a man with a dipper standing beside a barrel; a man washing and men playing cards

Kirk Leatham St Cuthbert

The medieval church was replaced in 1763 by the present building designed by Robert Corney.

Window. The church commemorating the saint has a window illustrating Cuthbert holding an otter, one of his attributes, with Eider drakes at his feet - another of his attributes - and Black-headed Gulls flying above his head. Saint Hilda with a goose at her feet is standing amongst crocus, iris and tulips.

Ledsham All Saints

The lower part of the tower, the nave and chancel are 8th century Saxon, the belfry is Norman.

Window, medieval. A man wearing a short tunic is carrying a hawk on one wrist and holding what may be jesses in the other hand. This is possibly illustrating hawking as June's 'Occupations of the Months'.

LEEDS

St Aidans has an apse at both the east and the west. Built of red brick in 1891-4, it contains work by Sir Frank Brangwyn undertaken in 1916.

Font cover. Roses.

Window. Harebells and tulips, and geese with a dog are illustrated.

St John the Evangelist

This church dates from 1634 and was built by John Harrison.

Pulpit, Animals are carved on a ledge of the pulpit.

Panels in the roof show flowers and birds.

Window, 1869 by Ward and Hughes. A House Martin is visiting its nest.

Window, circa 1870. Acorns, daisies, pomegranate, snowdrops and Wood Avens are portrayed.

Windows, 1894 and 97 by C. E. Tute contain within squares, birds, whimsical owls which are the symbol of Leeds, daisies and tulips.

Marsden St Bartholomew

The church was built in 1895 with the tower added in 1911. The table-tomb of Enoch Taylor, a machine maker, is in the graveyard, now a park. The giant hammers used by the Luddites to wreck machinery were known as Enochs. 'Enoch did make them and Enoch shall break them'.

Window, 1895. An owl bellman without the dish and keys is portrayed (cf. Adel).

Masham St Mary the Virgin

A painting attributed to Sir Joshua Reynolds, of part of the Nativity is above the chancel arch.

A memorial tablet dated 1750 portrays a crab.

Window designed by Harry J. Stammers in 1958, (cf. Adel and Scarborough) of Saint George and Saint Francis. The latter is preaching to predominantly vivid green, white and red birds with splashes of lurid yellow. A cock, heron, owl, peacock and pheasant etc. can be recognised.

Micklefield St Mary

Window. An extraordinary looking pelican, with what appears to be a halo around its neck, is feeding three chicks with very long bills in a nest of twigs. The whole is enclosed in a shield.

Middleton Tyas St Michael and All Angels

In the south wall of the chancel is a brass to the Reverend John Mawer who was descended from King Coyl and who according to Pevsner, knew twenty two languages.

Capital, circa 1300. Hawthorn, ivy, oak, sycamore and vine and grapes ornament the capitals.

Window, 1925. Saint Francis is featured with an owl, two robins and other birds.

Monk Fryston St Wilfrid

The base of the tower is Anglo-Saxon and the chancel 14th century.

Bench ends, Victorian. Heraldic shields portray a cat and the heads of three stags; another cat with three greyhounds; a third cat and a lion's head; three birds and a dragon, and lions.

Poppyheads. Marguerite, pomegranate, vine and grapes are depicted.

Pulpit. Featured are a bird, marguerite, pomegranate, rose and a serpent.

Reredos, 1905. Pictured are daffodil, daisy, fir cones, hop, ivy, lily, Lily-of-the-valley, oak, olive, primrose, rose and hips, strawberry, sycamore, vine and grapes and a snake with two birds.

Window, circa 1900. This contains roses in quarries.

Nether Poppleton St Everilda

This is a small Norman church with fragments of medieval glass, 17th century monuments and a modern rood by Henry Harvey.

Window. 15th century quarries illustrate medieval birds.

Normanton All Saints

This is a Gothic church with Decorated and Perpendicular styles.

Pews. The pews are ornamented with carvings of flowers: - bramble, cinquefoil, convolvulus, geranium, hawthorn, holly and berries, maple, oak, primrose and rose.

Reading Desk. Carvings of grapes, pomegranate and a rose are shown.

Reredos. A pelican-in-her-piety and other birds, lily, acorns, pomegranate, rose, vine and grapes and butterflies are featured.

Window. A Red Squirrel eating a nut is portrayed.

Old Malton The Priory Church of St Mary

It was originally founded by Eustace Fitz-John circa 1150 as a retreat and seminary house for canons only. It later belonged to the monastic Order of Gilbertines.

Misericords, late 15th early 16th centuries and 19th century copies. Represented are a kneeling Bactrian Camel, a hare or rabbit, a heraldic lion, an eagle, an owl, a pomegranate or pineapple and a griffin.

Riccal St Mary the Virgin

Dating from 1160 it has a magnificent south doorway.

Doorway arch, Norman circa 1160. Depicted are an animal, possibly a dog plucking a harp, a goat, a sleeping lion, a wolf, a dragon and a mermaid or siren.

Richmond St Mary

Built 1130-1200 and with the tower added circa 1400. It was restored by G. G. Scott in 1859 and again in 1892 by Hodgson Fowler. Early 16th century stalls with misericords are from Easby Abbey. The church is home to the Green Howards Regimental Chapel furnished by Robert Thompson.

Misericords from 1515 said to have come from Easby Abbey, depict a gorged and chained hart, a pig blowing bagpipes to two dancing piglets, foliage, pine cones, roses. An amphisbaena, basilisk, wyvern, and a dragon with a mouthful of 'tombstone' teeth can be seen.

Elbow. A wyvern is represented.

Ripon The Cathedral of St Peter and St Wilfrid

In the 7th century Ripon was a cathedral for five years then reverted to being a parish church. Building commenced in the mid 12th century and continued until the reign of Henry V111. The west front is described by Pevsner as the 'finest in England'. In 1836 it became a cathedral for the second time in its history. Restoration was carried out by Sir George Gilbert Scott and others.

A mixture of architectural styles can be seen here, there is a Norman transept, Gothic nave and choir and an Early English west front. The father of Lewis Carroll whose real name was Charles Lutwidge Dodgson, was a canon of the Cathedral and some of the characters in the 'Alice' books are thought to have been inspired by some of the cathedral carvings. One such carving is to be seen, with some difficulty, under the roof of the south transept. It features a lady in a turret with a sword in front of her and a cat's face beneath her. Is this perhaps the Red Queen and the Cheshire cat? Another carving is believed to illustrate a greedy mayor of Ripon and is in the form of a seated monkey.

Misericords, 1489-94. A Ripon man, William Bromfleet was the Master Carver. There are two antelopes, an ape attacked by a lion, a duck and a cock forming the congregation for a preaching fox, a fox running off with a goose, another fox caught by two dogs, a hart gorged and chained, a lion attacked by two dogs and a pig playing the bagpipes to two dancing piglets are portrayed. Birds to be seen are a pelican-in-her-piety, a hawk catching a rabbit and two birds feeding on fruit. Flowers are represented by columbine, hart's-tongue fern, the back and front views of a rose, sycamore leaves (?), and vine and grapes. Fabulous and mythical beasts include a blemya, a dragon attacked by two dogs, two fighting dragons, a dragon and a lion fighting, a griffin devouring a human leg, a second griffin catching a rabbit, a mermaid with a brush and mirror, a unicorn, and a wyvern.

Elbow. Decorating an elbow are a centaur and an elephant bearing a castle within which are either the disciples or soldiers.

Window in the library, circa 1540. There are two quarries, one depicting a bird and the other an animal, possibly an ass.

Window, 1873. An otter is holding a scroll in its mouth on which is written the word DERN which stands for Deus Evangel Rex Nazareni.

Chapter House. Hanging in the Chapter House is the original charter of James 1. Around the border are illustrations of some of the flowers which may be found growing in the district.

Rothwell Holy Trinity

Delightful scenes from nature are carved on 126 poppyheads dating from 1858. They are the work of Edmund Bates a wood carver from Leeds with assistance from William Gibson, and as far as is known they are unique in the county for the design, number and quality of the carvings. Animals, birds and flowers abound. There is a duck quacking at two foxes who are looking up at it, an owl sitting in ivy is looking down at a mouse peeping through foliage, another owl sits on top of ivy, a Short-eared Owl is perched in ivy, and parrot is seen among vine leaves, a pelican in iris leaves, a partridge in vines, a vulture, possibly a hornbill, a dodo and a worm. The rebus of Vicar Bell, a bell with vicar written across it, is hidden in vines, and there are vines and a wheatsheaf, oak leaves and acorns, passion-flowers and strawberry leaves and fruit.

Ryther All Saints

The west window, circa 1325, has its original glass.

Window, late 15th/ early 16th centuries and circa 1830 Victorian quarries.

Squirrels and birds appear in the border and there are quarries showing a thistle, trefoil and a rose bush with a crown around its stem and two initials which may be N K. As yet I have found no explanation for this.

Scarborough St Mary
A monument from 1728 is by the French sculptor Louis Francois Roubiliac. Anne Bronte was buried here in 1849.

East Window. Dated 1958 and designed by Harry J. Stammers this window contains five lights. The bottom part is a glorious mixture of sea creatures, insects, animals, birds and the occasional flower. First light from the north: - bat, horse, leopard, shrew, crane, penguin, crocodile, fish, frog, newt, snake, sea horse, beetle, butterfly, caterpillar, grasshopper, moths and shells. Second light:- beaver, boar, Bactrian Camel, deer, giraffe, kangaroo with a baby in her pouch, seal, harebell, pineapple, chameleon, frog, tadpole, sting-ray, jellyfish, sea anemone, beetle, caterpillar, dragonfly and moth. Third light: - moose, the heads of a sloth and a walrus, heron, parrot, chameleon, newt, crab, jellyfish, moth and spider. Fourth light:- bison, bull, fox, lion, monkey, Polar Bear, porcupine, rabbit, rhinoceros, a whale spouting or blowing, an egg, ostrich or crane, fowl, petrel and other birds, a conker, fungi, strawberry, beetle, bug, mayfly, mite, moth, starfish and shells. Fifth light: - goat, mole, mouse, squirrel, birds, fish, stickleback, sea anemone, turtle, butterfly, moth and worm.

Selby The Abbey of St Mary and St Germaine
Originally a Benedictine Abbey, the building of the present church began circa 1100. The central tower collapsed in 1680 and had to be rebuilt. In 1906 a disastrous fire badly damaged the nave, but a number of roof bosses were saved.

Capitals, 13th century. At eye level on both north and south arcades are lovely pictures in stone, for example, a cow chewing its cud, a pig eating acorns, a rabbit running among- of all things - fig leaves and figs, a fish with a wonderful mouthful of teeth swimming in seaweed, the head and forelegs of a deer, passion-flowers and roses.

Roof Bosses. Painted in gold is an elephant, a pig and the most delightful little mermaid with long flowing tresses and a curved tail.

Window, 13th century, restored. Portrayed is a border of pink, purple and grey coloured Red Squirrels.

Window, 14th or 15th centuries. This tells the story of Saint Germanus. There is Germanus as the hunter with the heads of dead animals strung on trees; standing near a dead stag, then later as the saint blessing the cock's corn.

Window, probably 15th century. Depicted are two monkeys standing by a table. One holds a knife the other a bowl, hung above them is the carcass of a pig. This is probably a parody of November's 'Occupations of the Months'.

Sherburn St Hilda
This is a largely Norman church which was restored and added to in 1912 by Charles Hodgson Fowler.

Organ case. Hawthorn, holly, rose and vines are depicted.

Poppyheads, 1912. Carvings of a bear, dachshund, birds, and an eagle with a snake, butterflies, and other animals can be seen.

Sherburn in Elmet All Saints
The church is situated on a hill outside the village. Much of it is late Norman and intact.

Corbels. Foliage and flowers are illustrated.

Elbows. Clover, hawthorn ivy and maple decorate the elbows.

Window, 1875. A fish is being roasted beside a fire.

Skelton Christ the Consoler
Situated in the grounds of Newby Hall and designed by William Burgess, the church was built between 1871-2 by Lady Mary Vyner in memory of her son who was murdered by Greek bandits. The sculptor was Thomas Nicholls.

Choir stall fronts. Lizards and butterflies may be observed.

Lectern. Featured are a bird with wheat in its beak, another with a caterpillar, a further two birds, and butterflies.

Embroidery.

Altar frontal designed by William Burges and worked by Lady Mary. Birds and butterflies are embroidered with gold thread and coloured beads/stones.

Lectern fall. An embroidered and fringed edging with birds as on the altar frontal.

Chancel. On the north and south walls carved in stone are amphisbaenas and wyverns.

The outside stonework includes shields depicting a bull, three bulls, three stags, heads of three boars and a dog in the centre of three what are thought to be spiked dog collars. There are various gargoyles and two dogs possibly pointers above the stone rain water outlets.

Stocksbridge St Matthias

Window. Saint Francis is preaching to a congregation of birds in a modern (1950) window. Among the birds is an owl, a flock of geese, a heron, thrush, woodpecker and a nest with three chicks in it.

Studley Royal St Mary
The church described as 'one of the most perfect churches in the kingdom', was

built by the Victorian architect William Burgess at the request of the Marchioness of Ripon whose brother, Frederick Grantham Vyner was murdered in 1870. A foundation stone was laid in March 1871, but the church was not consecrated until 1878. The sculptor was Thomas Nicholls and the stained glass designers were Lonsdale and Weekes. The church was made redundant in 1970 and since 1984 has been in the care of English Heritage and managed by the National Trust.

Choir stalls. Subjects carved on some the choir stall fronts are a lizard eating another lizard, an amphisbaena and a wyvern.

Cornice of the choir screen. There is a row of eight painted parrots or parakeets differently posed.

Embroidery. A butterfly is worked on the altar frontal.

Poppyheads. Representations of a bird, a caterpillar and butterfly; a butterfly and a worm; a bird and a fly, and a bird and a dragonfly decorate the poppyheads.

Spandrels. Within the choir stall spandrels are snails and mythical beasts.

Misericords. An unusual assortment of creatures is found on the misericords including a bat, frog, lizard, snail, cockchafer, butterfly, dragonfly, fly, and crayfish.

Pillars. A stone pillar on the south side of the chancel has a pencil drawing of a swallow. This is a cartoon for the swallow carved in stone. Above the bird are carved six individual flies. On the North side are six carved butterflies.

Wall painting. On the south wall of the chancel is a tree with fruit representing the Tree of Life with its twelve kinds of fruit. A bird is catching a dragonfly and one is pecking at something on the ground.

Side chapel. There is a stone mouse at the angle between the east and north walls.

Screen, marble. This has depictions of clover, rose and hawthorn flowers.

At the west end of the church is a boar carved in stone. There are nineteen stone doves all in different attitudes on the archway to the west door whilst on the ironwork outside the door are more birds.

Thirkleby All Saints

Designed by Edward Butler Lamb in 1850. There is a monument to four of the children of Sir Thomas Frankland by Flaxman.

Capitals. Carvings of hawthorn, ivy, lily, oak, rose, thistle, vine and wheat can be seen.

Thirsk St Mary

Pevsner describes this church as 'the most spectacular Perpendicular church in the North Riding'. Building commenced circa 1460 and continued in to the 16th century.

Heraldic shields and some woodwork depict asses.

Wakefield All Saints Cathedral

The tower with its spire is the tallest in Yorkshire and was built in the early 15th century. It is about 247 feet high. Between 1858 and 1874 the church was restored by Sir G. G. Scott.

The parish church of All Saints became a cathedral in 1888.

Window possibly by Charles E. Kempe in the 1870s. There is a delightful silvery coloured fox's head, the rear view of a hare and a pheasant also in silver.

Wensley Holy Trinity

There is the banner of the Loyal Dales Volunteers raised against Napoleon.

Stalls, 16th century. Illustrated are an antelope, a bear, and a dog gnawing a bone, a lion, a rabbit, a dragon and a fabulous beast.

West Tanfield St Nicholas

There is a late 13th century tomb of a knight and his lady still with its original wrought iron hearse with sconces for holding seven candles.

With the exception of the stools, all the delightful woodwork in this church is thought to be by R. L. Boulton of Cheltenham.

Altar, circa 1927. A mouse, the head and feet of a bird, an owl's face, a bee and a grasshopper are featured.

Choir stall fronts, circa 1927. Carvings include a snake with a beetle and a worm, a lion with a protruding tongue, a Red Squirrel, cock, and a hen with chicks one of which is on her back, an eagle and roses, also a fabulous beast chewing its own forked tail.

Elbows to the choir stalls. Shown are a lion, dove, eagle's head, pelican and a bird with a snake. There is also a fabulous beast and a long-haired, moustached and naked man.

Medallions on the choir stalls contain an owl's face and a hawk, a wyvern and a man in vegetation, a wyvern and flowers and a fabulous beast and a human face.

Communion rail. On the underneath, out of sight, are a chameleon, crocodile, lizard and a snake. On the communion rail gates are medallions with the Agnus Dei with birds and butterflies, a dove with an olive branch, and a pelican with three young. There are smaller medallions showing leaves, roses and a thistle.

Corbels. Ivy and other leaves are depicted.

Stools, circa 1933. Lion's, ox and ram's heads, a 'Thomson' mouse, an eagle's head and a 'Green man' decorate the stools.

Poppyheads. A dove, an owl's face, a large and a small ape in foliage and a hen on her nest.

The pulpit, dating from 1933, has a carving of a shield. On two of the quarters of the shield a stag is seated in a sheepfold.

Reading desk This shows a tiny mouse in a niche, hazel and nuts.

Poppyheads to the desk depict on one side, a monkey in vegetation, and on the other side, an animal in a tree and a bird on its nest. Hawthorn and vines are also featured.

Reredos, 1928. Hidden among roses and leaves is a mouse; birds including cockatoos, a crowing cock, lovely Crested Tits, an owl's face, a parrot and perhaps a waxwing. There are butterflies and a bee. On the gallery rail to the reredos are birds in and among lilies.

Window. In restored 14th century window glass is a border of stylised butterflies.

Look outside the porch at the stone dog-tethers.

Wintringham St Peter

Bench ends. Carved on the bench ends are an antelope, greyhound and griffin.

Stall fronts. These illustrate a pelican-in-her-piety and vine and grapes.

YORK

All Saints North Street

Since the 11th century there has been a church on this site the first reference to it being in 1089. In medieval glass, circa 1420 are two windows depicting the Pricke of Conscience and the Corporal Acts of Mercy.

Misericord. A late 15th century misericord portrays a pelican-in-her-piety with three chicks.

Window. A cock standing on a globe represents the rebus of Bishop Alcock.

Window. The Pricke of Conscience window shows people rising from the dead not from graves but from rabbit burrows.

All Saints Pavement This church is mentioned in the Domesday Book.

Window, 1420. A lamprey is portrayed.

St Cuthbert

Window. Saint James is illustrated with a spider on his hat and a scallop shell in the background.

St Denys Walmgate The church was built in the mid to late 12th century.

Window, 14th/15th centuries and Victorian replacements have quarries of butterflies with each insect having two pairs of antennae!

St Helen This was declared redundant in 1548, the church was partially demolished in 1551 to be rebuilt in 1534. Restoration took place in 1857.

Window, late 17th century Flemish roundels and quarries picture a mouse, a tulip and a female figure riding a unicorn. The latter may be illustrating the bestiary story of the virgin and unicorn. If it is, it is most unusual in that the virgin is sitting sideways on the animal instead of the creature laying its head in her lap.

St Luke A lizard can be seen indicating the family crest of the architect Ernest Walker. There is also a mouse.

St Margaret A redundant church used by the Theatre Royal for storage.

Doorway arch. Norman. This portrays two fighting stags, and a fox and stork with a pitcher between them. The latter is probably illustrating one of Aesop's fables. The stone work fox is badly eroded.

St Martin le Grand

Dating from circa 1170, the church was badly damaged in the Second World War. It was partly rebuilt by George G. Pace in 1961-68.

Window, 15th century and restored lozenges. There are two lozenges each containing a small marten in whose mouth is a scroll with the legend 'mart' written on it. This is a reference to the saint to whom the church is dedicated. A roundel features an antelope, gorged, chained and tushed (the badge of Henry V1).

Another window dating from 1437 shows Saint Martyn of Tours with his pet hares.

St Mary

There was a church on this site before the Norman Conquest. It is another church to be mentioned in the Domesday Book. It was refurbished in 1974-75 to become the York Heritage Centre.

Window, 14th century. Saint James is depicted with a six-legged spider on his hat.

Window, modern. This features a representation of Saint Cuthbert with three of his attributes, otters, eagles and a rook with a piece of bread in its beak. This is an allusion to the story whereby the birds were pecking thatch from the saint's shelter and when he rebuked them they brought him food.

The Minster The Metropolitan Church of St Peter

Bosses in the south transept have a natural history theme from the ancient hymn "Bless the Lord, all created, sing His praise and exalt Him forever" Drops of water falling on the leaves and plants represent "O ye showers and dew", A fire-breathing dragon is "O ye fire and heat", a tree with and without leaves is " O ye winter and summer", whilst a nightingale and a bat with the sun and moon is "O ye night and days. "O ye light and darkness" is depicted by an owl and a cockerel, "O ye wells" is illustrated by children looking into a well head. Whales in the sea portray "O ye whales and all that move in the waters". Birds and animals are "O all ye fowls of the air" and "O all ye beasts and cattle" respectively. Other bosses depict national symbols – thistle for Scotland, leek and daffodil for Wales and shamrock for Northern Ireland

Capitals in the choir crossing circa 1400 depict a fox preaching to a lamb which is holding a crosier, a monkey twisting a pig's tail; a man attacked by two animals; a man shoeing a goose, and a mermaid holding a mirror in one hand whilst clutching a fish to her breast with the other hand. The mirror represents vanity and the fish a soul (sole) caught for Satan.

Capitals on The Screen of Kings, circa 1500, feature a cat and mouse, a fox and goose, lion and lamb, a ram in a thicket, a 'Green' man etc. A hind carving beneath Henry 111 is believed to be the rebus of William Hindley, who took more than twenty five years to complete the work,

A stone carving above the west door is composed of three individual scenes with a common theme - that of dissension. The central carving is of two hounds attacking either a boar or a fox whilst a man to the left appears to be blowing a horn and one on the right holds a very long stick. The carving to the left shows a domestic quarrel in progress and one sees on the right two apes or men wrestling.

Kneelers. Embroidered kneelers designed by Joan Freeman in 1981 and worked by members of the Guild of York Minster Broiderers, depict some of the wild flowers found in Europe, the Middle East, Russia, the Arctic, North America and Canada, Australia and New Zealand, Central and South America, India and the Far East, Africa, England and Wales, Scotland and Ireland.

Window. The borders of the 14th century Pilgrimage window illustrate a parody of the funeral of the Blessed Virgin Mary. Monkeys carry the coffin which has a smaller monkey attached to the coffin cross bearer. A fox preaches to a cock from a lectern, and another fox, this one making off with a goose, is chased by a woman wielding a distaff whilst a monkey and an owl watch. A hound chased by a stag is attacked by a smaller hound and there are squirrels, monkeys holding owls and monkeys inspecting urine flasks.

St Stephen's window which is 15th century has a canopy of eagles and a border of wolves' heads and oak leaves. Other borders in the north transept windows show vine leaves, lion's heads, and the wheat sheaf monogram of Kempe.

Window. Monkeys playing a variety of musical instruments are to be seen in the early 14th century Bell-Founders' window. Other nave window borders contain leopards, lions, eagles, falcons, and oak and vine leaves. Maple foliage and roses are represented in the Clerestory windows.

The Chapter House vestibule

Bosses in the vestibule have 'Green' men with various leaves issuing from their mouths, for example, buttercup, ivy or oak foliage.

Capitals, circa 1290, depict a procession of animals: - a hare, hound, the winged bull of Saint John, a fox carrying a bird, a dog, a pig suckling her young, an owl and a bird eating an acorn.

Chapter House

A label stop, 1260-85, portrays a pig on top of a man's head. Quite what this stone carving is symbolising has not yet been discovered.

Capitals, 1260-85, show two birds with their beaks up a man's nostrils, a fox, monkey, squirrel and snail among oak leaves, a boar fighting, a cat and mouse, a lion, a monkey on a dog's back, a pig eating acorns, and another snail and a squirrel. Birds are represented by an eagle clawing at a woman's eye, and a falconer. Also featured is a lizard.

The Dean's door surround illustrates a dog chasing a hare, a pig with her litter, a squirrel, and, like one of the capitals in the vestibule, an owl and a bird eating an acorn.

Dean's Chapel.

Spandrel, 13th century. Reynard the fox looks up at a cock perched in a tree. An amphisbaena and a centaur are also present.

Zouche Chapel.

Windows containing quarries from the 14th/15th centuries show an eagle, finches, game birds, a hawfinch, hawk, heron, a Long-eared Owl with a mouse, an osprey and young, an owl with young, a peacock, pheasant, wagtail, woodpecker, and a wren facing a spider which has six instead of eight legs. A bear being stung by a bee, a performing bear, deer feeding, a dog, pony and a procession of monkeys are portrayed.

Window by Ervin Bossanyi (1891-1975) a Hungarian who immigrated to England in 1934. The window designed by him shows an assortment of peculiar looking birds.

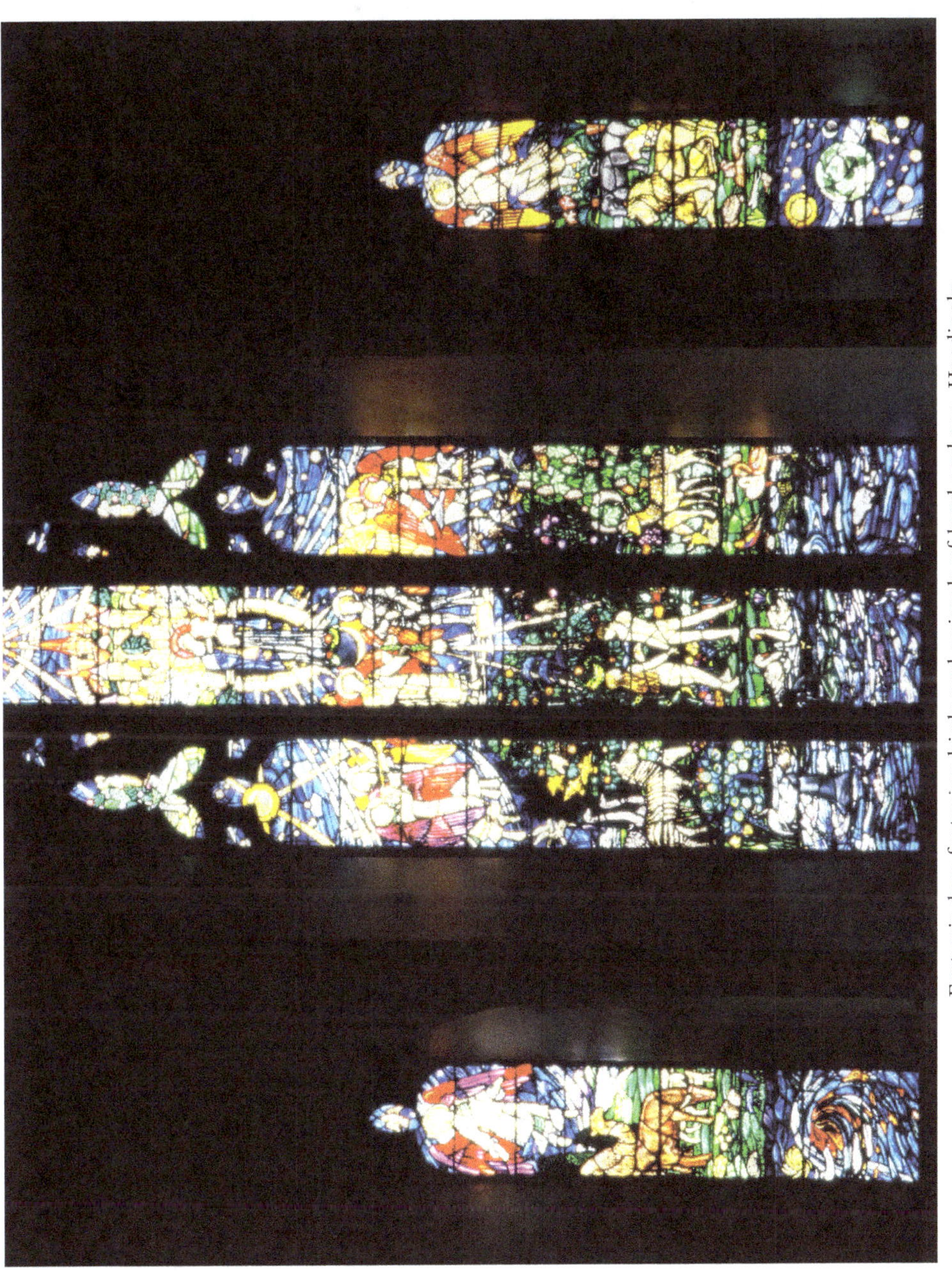

East window featuring birds and animals of land and sea. Headingly

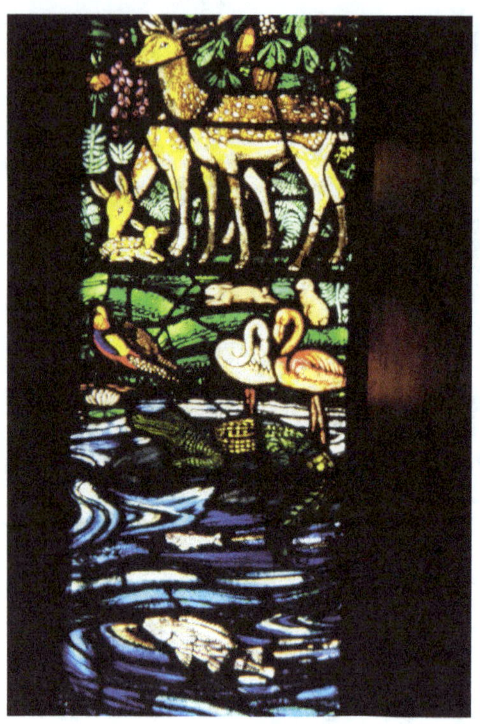

Detail from light of Creation Window.
Animals, birds, fish etc. Headingly.

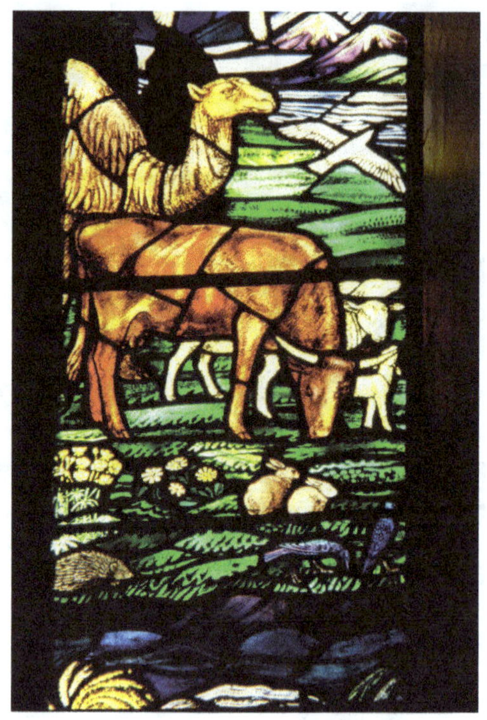

Detail from light of Creation Window.
Hedgehog, rabbits, flowers etc. Headingly.

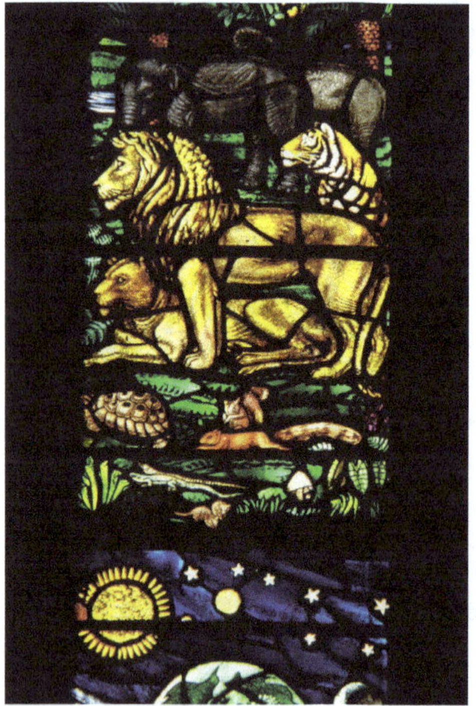

Detail from light of Creation Window.
Jungle beasts, tortoise, fungi etc. Headingly

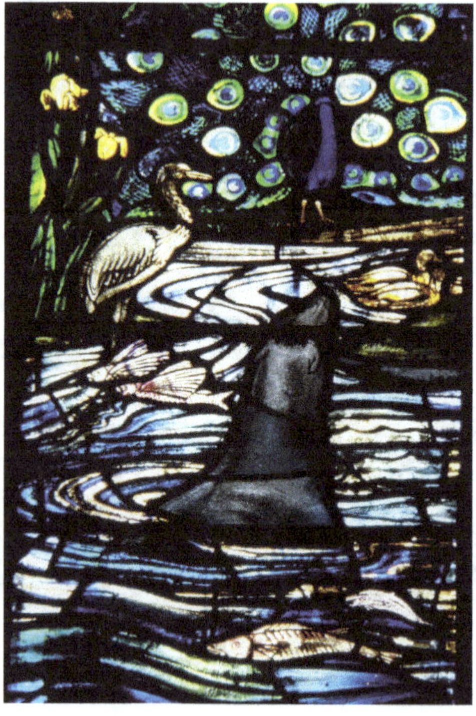

Detail from light of Creation Window.
Seal, peacock, iris etc. Headingly.

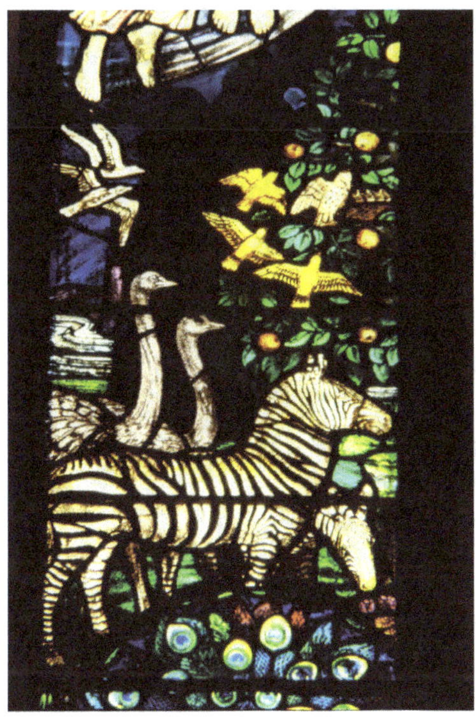

Detail from light of Creation Window. Zebra, ostrich etc. Headingly.

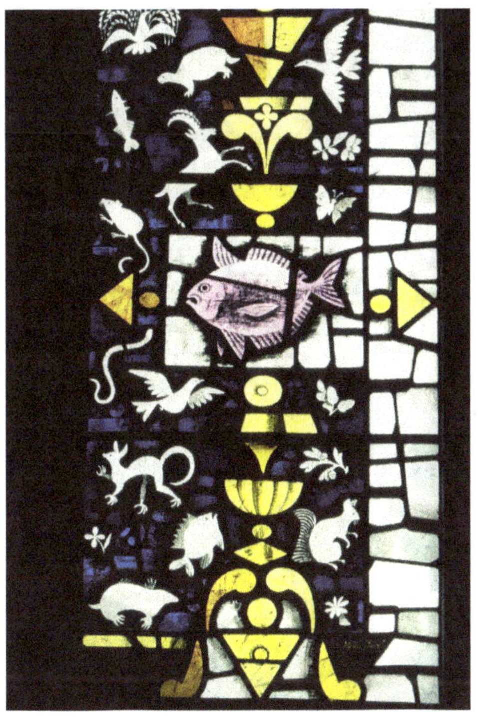

Detail from light of Creation Window. Animals, birds, fish, etc. Light, 1958. Scarborough.

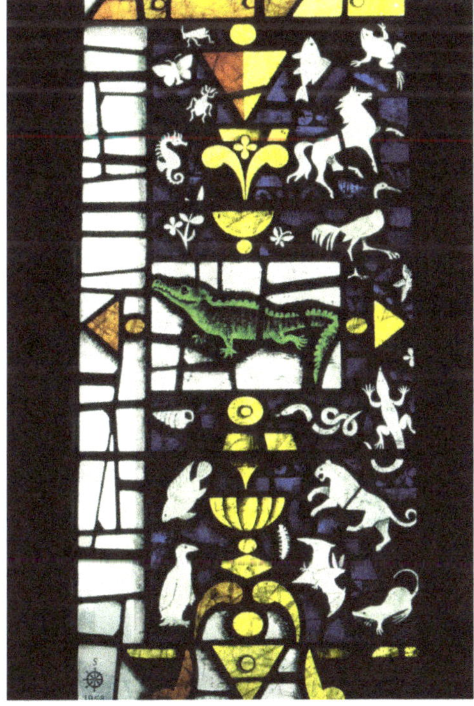

Detail from light of Creation Window. Animals, birds, fish, shells etc. 1958. Scarborough.

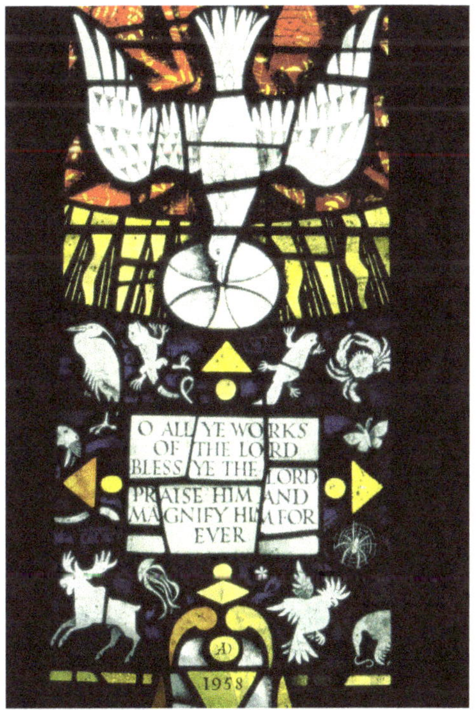

Detail from light of Creation Window. Animals, crab, spider, jellyfish etc. 1958. Scarborough.

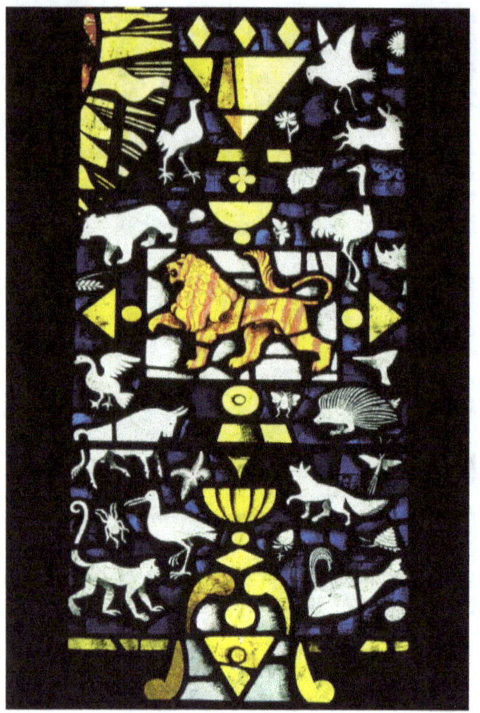

Detail from light of Creation Window.
Whale spouting, insects, animals, birds, etc.
1958. Scarborough.

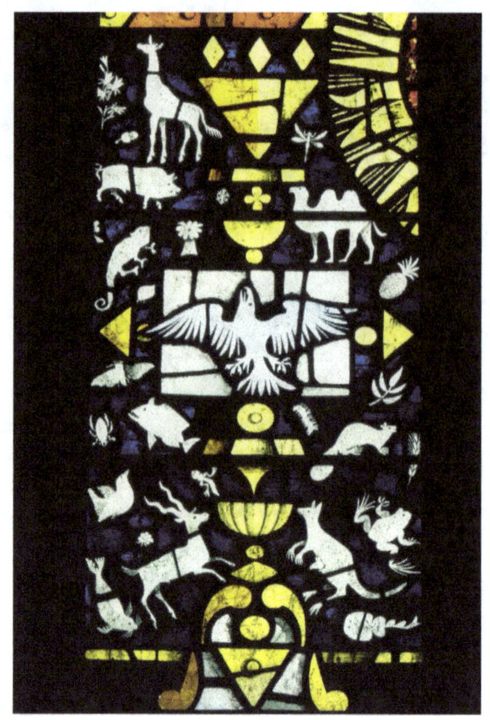

Detal from light of Creation Window.
Jellyfish, dragonfly, chameleon etc. 1958.
Scarborough.

BIRDS in YORKSHIRE CHURCHES

Bullfinch	Lapwing	Pigeon, Pouter
Cock and Hen	Mallard	Wood
Cockatoo	Martin, House	Robin
Crane	Nightingale	Rook
Crow	Osprey	Stork
Dove	Ostrich	Swallow
Eagle	Owl, Barn	Swan
Eider Duck	Little	Teal
Falcon	Long-eared	Tit, Blue
Flamingo	Short-eared	Crested
Gannet	Tawny	Thrush
Goose	Parrot	Turkey
Gull, Black-headed	Partridge	Vulture
Hawk	Peacock	Wagtail
Hawfinch	Pelican	Waxwing
Heron	Penguin	Woodpecker, Green
Hoopoe	Pheasant	Wren

In ancient Egypt birds were a symbol of the soul and they also symbolise air which is one of the four elements. Like fishes they were made on the fifth day of creation, and the first bird protection law is found in the Bible (Deuteronomy 22:6-7). This law specifically forbids the taking of the parent bird and its offspring. Birds of prey and those eating carrion were classed as 'unclean' and could not be eaten.

Birds are now a common decorative motif in church imagery, but early Christians strictly observed the second of the Ten Commandments, i.e. 'Thou shalt not make thee any graven images, or any likeness of any thing that is in heaven above, or that is in the earth beneath, or that is in the waters beneath the earth'. By the end of the second century however, Christians were proclaiming their faith in artistic ways with representations of biblical scenes and Christian symbols; the dove as the Holy Spirit is one such symbol. Early paintings appear as funeral decorations. The motifs on funeral urns and coffins vary from the dove as a symbol of peace, to the peacock representing immortality. In addition to symbolising spiritual, heavenly things, birds may be used as heraldic devices and some may appear as attributes of saints; they are frequently naturalistic and the stork may sometimes illustrate Aesop's fable of the Fox and Stork. Birds may also be found which modern ornithologists would have difficulty in identifying. The dove, eagle and pelican are the three most commonly found birds with religious significance. Doves are sometimes carved on fonts and painted on windows where they are emblematic of the Holy Spirit which descended on Jesus when he was baptised, but are also found elsewhere in churches, particularly on pulpits and screens where they are pecking grapes thus symbolising the Eucharist.

Lecterns invariably feature the eagle of Saint John although a turkey lectern is found in one Yorkshire church and a pelican in Durham Cathedral. The pelican is usually, but not always, found depicting the bestiary story and is therefore seen in 'its piety' (see Pelican below) with the number of chicks varying from one to five. It is rarely correctly carved and generally looks more like an eagle or a swan than a pelican, having clawed feet and a hooked beak. Modern carvings of the bird however tend to be anatomically correct.

Birds as emblems of the nobility include the ostrich, swan and falcon. The swan emblem was worn by the family of de Bohun; Henry of Lancaster, who married Mary de Bohun, used the swan emblem as a badge. The Prince of Wales used the swan as a livery badge after Henry became king. The falcon features in scenes of hawking which is June's occupation in the 'Labours (or Occupations) of the Months' cycle.

The iconography of many saints illustrate birds. Probably the most frequently encountered are the cock of Saint Peter, Saint Cuthbert's Eider Ducks and the pet Whooper Swan of Saint Hugh of Lincoln. Windows which depict Saint Francis often have representations of familiar birds of the countryside. In Selborne, home to Gilbert White the eighteenth century naturalist vicar, eighty six species can be identified in the window dedicated to him, and some of the birds of Clay marshes (Norfolk) are painted on window borders in Clay village church. Owls were a popular subject for the medieval carvers and thrushes with or without a snail appear to be favourite birds with a modern carver, a number of pulpits in Cornish churches displaying these birds.

Birds of no known species are found on medieval quarries (diamond-shaped pieces of glass) where they are usually painted or stained yellow and have a pattern of black dots or stripes across the wings. Nineteenth century floor tiles in black and white mosaic in Bishop Wilton also depict birds whose identity would be difficult to establish.

Blackbird Kevin, who was a 7th century Irish saint went into retreat during Lent, and whilst he was reading, praying and contemplating in his hut in the wilderness, he put his hand out of the shelter and raised it to heaven. A hen blackbird, mistaking it for a nesting site, laid her eggs in the palm of his hand

and Saint Kevin, who was both patient and compassionate, held his hand aloft until the bird hatched her young and they flew away. From the sweetness of the male's song, the Blackbird typifies the Grace of God, but he can also be the personification of temptation. The Colly birds mentioned in the *Twelve Days of Christmas* carol represent the four disciples. Colly is an old name for the Blackbird.

Blue Tit This bird is associated with preachers as it was considered to be eloquent and to have the gift of prophesy.

Bullfinch In addition to the goldfinch and robin, the bullfinch symbolises sacrifice, especially the Passion. An early legend states that a little bird plucked a thorn from Christ's brow whilst He was on His way to Calvary carrying the Cross. The Sacred blood tinged the bird's feathers and it has worn the mark ever since.

Crane According to a legend mentioned by Aristotle and repeated in medieval bestiaries, one crane standing guard for the flock holds a stone in an uplifted claw. If the bird drowses or falls asleep the falling stone will wake it up. Hence it is a symbol of vigilance and watchfulness. It may also represent charity. In Japan it is a symbol of longevity.
Cranes are migratory birds and this fact was known in Biblical times (Jeremiah 8:7). They were still wild in England in the Middle Ages.

Crossbill After all the others had left Him, crossbills were said to have tried to remove the nails from Christ's hands and feet as He hung on the Cross.

Crow All black birds were associated with the devil, but the crow is a model of hospitality, Christian constancy and devotion. It was thought that if the mate was lost the remaining partner lived a life of solitude. There is a Japanese proverb which states 'The filial duty of feeding one's parents is known even to the crow.'

Cuckoo No symbolic significance.

Diver These birds were thought to bring rain and in Orkney the Red-throated Diver is called the 'Rain-Goose'

Dove Doves and pigeons are often referred to in the Bible. Noah first sent out a raven from the ark and when it did not return, he sent out a dove. When it came back to the ark, he sent it out again. The second time the dove returned it held a sprig of olive in its beak. It was sent out a third time but did not come back. The symbolism associated with this story is interpreted as follows: - to Christians, the sprig of olive brought back by the dove was the making of man's peace with God. The dove could find no rest for the soles of its feet except on the ark and so the Christian soul can find neither safety nor peace outside the Church.

When a dove is seen drinking from a chalice it can denote either souls in Paradise or it can be a symbol of the Eucharist. A dove pecking grapes is another symbol of the Eucharist.

The dove of Noah means rest; of David, peace, and of Christ, salvation. The dove separates the wheat from the chaff and so the preacher should separate the pure grains of Christian doctrine from the husks of Judaism. The dove's two wings signify the love of man and of God, solicitude and contemplation; the active life and the passive, meditating life. The ring around its neck is the encircling sweetness of the Divine Word; the gold and silver of its feathers represent purity and innocence and its whiteness and coloured tints signify the spirit of chastity in conflict with passion. The blood of the martyrs staining the feet of the church is represented by the Dove's red feet, whilst the past and future are surveyed by its eyes which by their yellow lustre indicate maturity and reflection. In the Old Testament, the poor made an offering of Turtle Doves or two young pigeons, one for a sin offering and the other for a burnt offering (Leviticus 5:7). Christ's conception was effected supernaturally through the Virgin's ear. A statue in Howden of a dove with its beak directed towards the ear depicts this. Mohammed had a pet dove which he fed with wheat out of his ear. Like the crow, the Turtle Dove is an example of Christian constancy, chastity and devotion and a symbol of peace and forgiveness. The two Turtle Doves of *The Twelve Days of Christmas* carol represent the Old and New Testaments.

See Dragon under Fabulous/Mythical Beasts

Duck Saint Cuthbert's chickens were Eider Ducks. When he was a hermit on the Farne Islands these birds were much loved by the 7th century saint and he made his island the first bird sanctuary. In the Middle Ages the tameness of the ducks during the breeding season was attributed to the holiness of the saint. In the 12th century one of the Durham monks wrote of the saint 'he had assured the Eiders a continuity of peace and quiet, allowing no one to touch them, slaughter them or molest them with any mischievous intent'. In China the Ruddy Shelduck is a symbol of conjugal fidelity.

Eagle The eagle is an ancient symbol of power and victory and was considered to be the king of all the birds thus symbolising Christ. This was later interpreted as God's kingdom on earth. An eagle with its wings open in flight signifies the bird carrying the Word and the Light of the Gospel. It became the emblem of an empire and the badge of Charlemagne. It is stated in the bestiary that the eagle renews its youth by flying towards the sun until its old plumage and its cataracts are burnt away, 'then at length, taking a header down into the fountain, he dips himself three times in it and instantly he is renewed with a great vigour of plumage and splendour of vision' (cf. Psalm 103:5). The bird renewing itself in the fountain became a medieval symbol of both Christ's Ascension and of regeneration by baptism. In another tale, when the eagle grows old its beak becomes so long it is liable to starve to death, but the bird breaks off a piece of its beak against a stone enabling it to eat again. Christians therefore, should break off all carnal thoughts upon the rock of salvation. Yet another story tells how the bird looking up to the sun, then down to the sea, sees a fish and plunging into the water, seizes the fish which it then takes up to its eyrie. In this story the eagle is Christ, the sea the world and the fish the elect whom He saves. The bestiary also claims that an eagle presents its young to the sun and the eaglet, when stricken by the sun's rays, will gaze fearlessly into the light, but if it turns its head away the parent bids consider that it is not worth bothering about. There may be some foundation in fact for three of the bestiary statements, the cataracts probably refer to the nictitating membrane, captive hawks and falcons cock their heads and have an unblinking stare, and the moult is probably meant by the renewal of youth. The eagles quoted in the Bible are most likely to be various species of vulture. 'Enlarge thy baldness as the Eagle' (Micah 1:16), suggests the Griffon Vulture and 'there will be eagles gathered together' (Matthew 24:28), clearly describes vultures flocking to a carcass. The Lathom legend states that an eagle flew off with the Lathom heir. However, he grew up to claim his inheritance. Another version of the same legend says that the aged and childless Lord Lathom was eager to adopt an heir and a swaddled infant was brought to him by an eagle. An eagle nurturing a child is the badge of the Stanley's.

Falcon The personal badge of Richard, Duke of York (1411-60) was the falcon with fetterlock. Legend tells us that Saint Francis was woken to pray each morning by a falcon.

Flamingo No symbolic significance.

Goldfinch The goldfinch in common with the sparrow represents the soul, and like the swallow, linnet and other birds it signifies the resurrection. Sacrifice, especially the passion, is indicated by the goldfinch, robin and bullfinch. The red feathers on either side of its head are said to be stained with the blood of Christ as the bird attempted to remove the thorns from His brow. A caged bird was a symbol of the soul imprisoned in the body. Leonardo da Vinci stated that ' it is said of the goldfinch that if its young are imprisoned, it will carry spurge to them, preferring to see them dead, than alive and in captivity'. The bird is therefore a bringer of death. It was a bird beloved by Jesus and there is a legend telling us how, after God had coloured all the other birds only the goldfinch was left a plain, ashy grey. He asked God for a speck of red, a dash of white and a patch of yellow, eventually asking for most of the colours, which God then painted on the feathers in a mood of amused tolerance. This was later interpreted as, no matter how unimportant an individual may be if he holds on to his piety and takes his worries to God he is certain of spiritual raiment. The bird sings beautifully and yet obtains its food amongst the sharp spines of thistles, and this was explained as the Good Preacher on earth who has to endure greatly, and although living among the thorns of this world, cheerfully serves God. In the 13th century, the goldfinch became associated with the Caladrius, and was an anti-plague and fertility symbol. In the late Middle Ages, a parallel between the twelve young of the goldfinch and the twelve disciples of Christ was identified by religious mystics. The fruitfulness of the bird was equated with the spreading of the Gospel by the disciples. The colour of fertility is yellow and the bird has bright yellow patches on its wings. It is generally true that the bulkier an animal the less prolific it needs to be. For example, the camel, elephant and horse normally produce a single offspring, whilst a very small bird lays many eggs. A goldfinch actually lays five to six eggs in a clutch and a goldcrest seven to ten.

Goose The symbol of vigilance is a goose and the bird is an attribute of Bishop Martin of Tours. The saint's feast-day is November 11th which coincides with either the migration of geese or the season in which they were killed and eaten in olden times. The custom of dining on roast goose at Martinmas is connected with, and the survival of, the pre-Christian practice of animal sacrifices on festival days. The goddess Freya was goose or swan-footed, Eros rides a goose or drives a swan chariot, and geese, sparrow and partridge were sacred to Aphrodite. The goose was supposed to be an oracle. So much importance was attached to it that it is thought that a goat and a goose led the first crusade in 1096. The Celts held the bird to be sacred and Saint Werbergh granted her protection to a flock of geese. She resuscitated a goose which had been killed and cooked in breach of her promise of protection.

Barnacle geese were believed to grow on trees by the sea. With the aid of their beaks, they hung from branches and when fully feathered they fell. If they reached water they swam and lived, but if they landed on dry ground they perished. They are an illustration of the saving efficacy of baptism. This species was also thought to hatch from barnacles, so it was permitted to eat them as fish during Lent. A fox with a goose symbolises man who is an easy victim of the devil and his minions (monkeys), geese listening to a fox preaching signify credulity, and shoeing a goose is an example of man's crass stupidity, although when geese went to market they were frequently walked there and had their feet either tarred or booted for protection. A goose can be a pointed warning against the followers of Wycliffe and the Lollards, a warning lest the foolish are seduced by false doctrine. In the well known Christmas carol *The Twelve Days of Christmas* the 'six geese a-laying' represent the six days of creation.

Hawk A hawk represents evil and the devil stooping on the unwary. The bird is illustrated in Manuscripts, Psalters and Breviaries, and in the twelve monthly occupations June maybe represented by hawking. The hawk was the emblem of Horus, one of the Egyptian deities.

Hen, chicken and cock The 'fatted fowl' of the Old Testament may have been domestic poultry although geese were probably the first birds to be domesticated, and in Egypt were kept as early as 1530 B.C. In the New Testament, hen and chickens symbolise Christ's love for His children (Matthew 23:37, Luke 13:34). The cock is the herald of the day after a night of darkness. It is an attribute of Peter the Apostle, alluding to his denial of Christ and of his repentance. It is also a symbol of watchfulness. Cock fighting, a very popular sport in olden days, is occasionally depicted.

Heron To the Jews, the heron was an 'unclean food' and this is stated in the dietary laws of Leviticus and Deuteronomy. Yet it is said to be wise and discreet, more so than any other bird. 'This bird signifies the souls of the elect, who, fearing tempests of persecution's instigated by the devil, fly above all frightening temporary events, to the serenity of heaven, where it may forever behold the countenance of God'

Hoopoe According to bestiary stories the young of the hoopoe restore their parents' youth by plucking out the old feathers. Thus the hoopoe became a symbol of filial piety and duty.
See also Stork.

House Martin No symbolic significance.

Ibis Said to feed in shallow water on carrion and snakes because it cannot swim out to clean food, the ibis is equated with man who will not abandon his sins. Because the ibis was afraid to enter deep water to obtain clean food, it was like the sinner who dare not leave his sinful life to obtain divine grace. The ibis of the bestiary is said to walk near the sea shore looking for the dead fish and bodies on which it liked to feed. It was also said to feed its young on serpents or their eggs. The ibis may be confused with the spoonbill as both species live in the same habitat and flock together.

Jackdaw The jackdaw may feature in windows illustrating the parable of the Sower and the Seed, and in one church it may depict the Jackdaw of Rheims (North Hinksey, Oxon.).

Jay No symbolic significance.

Kingfisher In folklore throughout the world, the kingfisher is associated with the Flood. One story tells how the survivors were without fire and it was the kingfisher's job to steal a burning brand from God. In the process the bird's chest was scorched bright orange and because of the heat the bird dropped the burning brand in the Creator's lap, who, in His anger, threw the brand after the fleeing bird burning its rump to match its chest. Another story says that the kingfisher was originally a drab little bird with a large beak, this showed that it was full of courage. As the Flood was subsiding, Noah released a dove to search for dry land. However, Noah was not a patient man and could not wait for the dove's return, so he sent out the kingfisher. As it left the ark a storm blew up and to avoid it the bird flew high above the clouds, but it was struck by lightning, and this accounts for the blue down its back. Once above the clouds the bird felt the sun's warmth but flying too close to it, scorched its chest. Turning too quickly it then scorched its rump. By the time it managed to return to earth the waters had receded and the ark had been dismantled. That is why to this day the kingfisher flies up and down rivers looking and calling for its master. In both these stories the colour of the bird's rump is incorrect. The blue extends all the way to the tail.

Lark No symbolic significance.

Linnet Like the goldfinch and swallow the linnet is symbolic of the resurrection. Traditionally, the linnet used a leaf to clear the sight of its offspring, passing the knowledge on to man who named the herb eyebright in honour of the bird.

Magpie The magpie is an ancient symbol of death, and rhymes of fortune and disaster are associated with the bird. For example, 'One for sorrow, two for joy, three for a letter' etc., the rhyme varying depending on which part of the country it originated.

Nightingale According to an Italian legend, when God was giving all the birds their colours, the nightingale arrived too late to be coloured. In compensation God gave the bird its perfect song.

Osprey No symbolic significance.

Ostrich This bird is indicative of a disregard of earthly things (Job 39:13-18). The bestiary states that it has feet like those of a camel to indicate speed. When hunted it was believed to run for some distance then bury its head in the sand thinking that because it could not see, then it could not be seen. Because it eats stones and other hard objects to aid its digestion it was said to digest iron, hence the saying to have a 'digestion like that of an ostrich'. Since the mid-16th century three ostrich feathers have been the personal badge of the Prince of Wales. Originally they were the badge of the king of Bohemia who died on the field at Crecy. Edward, the Black Prince, then acquired the device, dying before succeeding to the throne.

Owl The bird is sacred to Minerva, goddess of wisdom and the Arts and Crafts. Owls far from being the wise birds of ancient and modern times, were, in the Middle Ages, associated with witchcraft and doom, and were seen as omens of death. Tawny Owls were birds to fear as they hunt at night and into the small hours when people are more likely to die. The owl was thought to shun the light, its sight being weakened by the rising sun. Symbolically it shunned the light of the Gospel. Owls shown being mobbed by smaller birds represent the Jews, who preferred the 'darkness of unbelief to the light of Christian revelation'. The owl was the Jew and the smaller birds were the Gentiles. It could also depict the fate of the sinner hounded by the righteous when the sin was discovered. The owl was an attribute of Satan and the devils that preyed upon human souls. It is a symbol of the morally blind and stupid.

Oystercatcher No symbolic significance.

Parakeet This bird signifies reverence.

Parrot It was once thought that the only way a parrot could learn was to hit it with an iron bar. In India the bird is an erotic symbol.

Partridge These birds were symbolic of the devil because of their lustful nature and the belief that they stole the eggs and hatched the young of other birds. However, when the young were grown, they recognised their real parents and flew to them leaving their foster parents alone. The Christian Church likened the birds to the devil, 'who sought the children of men, but when they grew in wisdom they forsook the devil and flew to their natural mother - the Church', thus symbolising the triumph of truth. The scientific name is *Perdix perdix* and classically, the nephew of Daedalus was called Perdix. He invented the saw, and his uncle being jealous threw him off the Acropolis. Athene caught him in mid-air and changed him into a partridge. To this day the bird makes a noise like the sharpening of a saw. The 'Partridge in a pear tree' from *The Twelve Days of Christmas,* was a reference to Jesus Christ

Peacock Sacred to and an attribute of Juno, a pair of peacocks drew her chariot. The eyes in the tail were obtained from Argon (Argos) who possessed one thousand eyes and was killed by Mercury. In Argon's memory, Juno took his eyes and set them in the tail of the peacock. Like man who is afraid of falling from a state of grace, the peacock would cry in terror during the night at the thought of losing his great beauty - his tail. The eyes in the tail were likened to man's foresight which he loses as the peacock loses its tail whilst moulting. From an ancient belief that its flesh never decayed, the bird became a symbol of immortality and of Christ's resurrection. It was also a symbol of pride for it was reputed to be ashamed of its ugly feet. This was interpreted as man living in splendour suddenly becoming aware of his own sins.

Pelican The pelican-in-its-piety became a common attribute of Charity in the early 16th century. The earlier bestiary story is that the hen bird smothers her young by an excess of love, but the male bird restores them to life by piercing his side and shedding his blood over them. A later bestiary states that the pelicans are devoted parents but kill their young because, as they grow they flap their wings in the faces of their parents. After three days, the female pierces her breast allowing her blood to flow over the corpses, thus reviving them. The pelican is likened to God and the chicks to ungrateful men who strike God in the face by devoting themselves to creation rather than the Creator. The blood is the redeeming blood of Christ saving man from spiritual death and sin, or it is the Fall and Redemption of mankind through the Passion of Christ (Revelations 5:9). It is a symbol of divine self-sacrificial love. The medieval carvers would probably never have seen a pelican, so the mythical pelican-in-its-piety usually looks nothing like the real bird, having an anatomically incorrect bill and feet like those of an eagle. The hen lines her nest with breast feathers and the resulting rawness probably led people to believe that she fed her young with her own blood. The bird has a crimson spot at the tip of its bill and this gave rise to the belief that the bird whilst really preening, was feeding blood to the young. The three day interval between the death and revival of the young birds is possibly a derivation from the three days between Our Lord's death and resurrection.

Penguin No symbolic significance.

Petrel As the birds fly, their legs dangle down, and this led to them being referred to as Saint Peter's birds because the saint is usually featured with two keys.

Pheasant No symbolic significance.

Plover No symbolic significance.

Raven In the Old Testament, the raven is Noah's messenger (Genesis 8:7), an 'unclean' bird (Leviticus 11:13) and a symbol of desolation (Isaiah 34:11). The belief that ravens and other Corvidae peck out the eyes of victims is mentioned in the Book of Proverbs (30:17). When a raven finds a carcass it first eats the eyes. The religious truth interpreted from this, is that, 'confession and penance are the ravens which pull out the eyes of covetousness from the soul dead in trespasses and sin'. In a series of legends inspired by the Bible, ravens are said to have succoured various saints. However, the ravens which fed Elijah were not birds but desert Arabs, ravens in this context being a derogatory term for scavenging Arabs. There is a present day superstition in this country that the prosperity of the realm is indicated by the well-being of the ravens in the Tower of London. In Wales it was thought that if blind people were kind to ravens their sight would be restored. The Greeks regard ravens as birds of Apollo and could foretell the future by the way the birds flew and croaked. Ravens croak, rooks caw and jackdaws chatter.

Robin The robin is said to have plucked a thorn from Christ's brow whilst He was carrying the Cross. The Sacred blood tinged the bird's feathers and it has worn the mark ever since. Another story says that the robin brings a drop of water each day to cool the tongues of those in hell that are parched with thirst. In carrying out this act of mercy the robin's chest becomes singed in the scorching fires, hence the red breast. Saint Kentigern had a tame robin which was restored to life. In Hereford a folk rhyme says 'The robin and the wren are God Almighty's cock and hen'. In Lancashire the rhyme is 'The robin and the wren are God's cock and hen, him that harries their nest, never shall his soul have rest'.

Skylark When God created the birds He forgot to colour them and they were all a uniform dull grey. All the birds were asked to assemble for thirty minutes for further creation. The macaw was given green wings, a blue tail and red on its head. The blackbird received a black suit and yellow bill, whilst a gold, green and blue tail fell to the peacock. Finally they all flew away, but then a small grey bird landed on God's hand. It had been at the other side of the world and had flown all night in order to be given its colouring. Unfortunately, God told the little bird, all the paint had gone except for a gold spot on the finest brush. The little bird opened its beak and the gold was painted at the back of its throat. The bird now sings beautifully.

Sparrow Sparrows, geese and partridge were sacred to Aphrodite. Saint Ambrose explained the two sparrows of the Gospels as signifying the Body and Soul, 'for both are lifted up to God by spiritual wings'. A rhyme from Lancashire states that the spink and the sparrow are the devil's bow and arrow. Spink is the colloquial name for the chaffinch.

Spoonbill This bird does not appear in the bestiaries so it may have been carved from real life. Some confusion may exist between the spoonbill and the ibis as both species like a similar habitat and they may flock together.

Stone Curlew No symbolic significance.

Stork There was a belief by classical writers which was repeated in medieval bestiaries, that the stork fed its parents when they were no longer able to look after themselves and so, like the hoopoe, it became a symbol of filial piety.

Swallow One of the legends associated with the swallow is that whilst Christ was praying in the garden of Gethsemane the swallows did their best to divert the soldiers' attention from Christ by darting hither and thither. The red patch on their throats, according to Spanish legend, was caused by the birds trying to pick out the thorns from Christ's crown. According to a Hereford rhyme, the swallow and the swift are God Almighty's gifts. It is an example of maternal care and content even in poverty. In common with the goldfinch and linnet, the swallow symbolises the resurrection, whilst with the crossbill and robin, it represents compassion for Our Lord on the Cross. It also heralds spring.

Swan The swan is said to be a virtuous bird which sings before it dies at the prospect of happiness to come. The Cambridge bestiary states that the swan sings so beautifully because the bird 'has a long curved neck, and the rich music goes round and round through the lengthy bend'. The trachea of the Whooper Swan is convoluted, and it is the expiration of air from the lungs that creates the flute-like notes. A helmet decorated with a swan is worn by Humility. The goddess Freya was goose or swan-footed and Eros drove a swan chariot. In Ireland it was thought that the souls of virgins lived in swans. The Whooper Swan is an attribute of Saint Hugh of Lincoln who had a pet swan which followed him about. Swans in general are symbolic of martyrdom and Christian resignation. The first of the Lancashire kings was Henry of Bolinbroke - Henry 1V. He married Mary de Bohun whose family badge was a swan. Henry V1 may also have used a swan emblem. A swan with outspread wings is the badge of Warwick. The seven gifts of the Holy Spirit:- contribution, exhortation, leadership, mercy, prophesy, serving and teaching are represented by 'Seven swans a-swimming' in the popular Christmas carol *The Twelve Days of Christmas*.

Thrush No symbolic significance.

Turkey A turkey lectern in a Yorkshire church commemorates the introduction of the bird into this country by the then Lord of the Manor.

Vulture See Eagle.

Wagtail No symbolic significance.

Woodpecker Once God had created the earth he asked the birds to dig out hollows where there are now lakes, rivers and seas. All but the woodpecker did as God had requested. For his punishment God made the woodpecker peck wood forever and it could never drink from lakes and rivers. These were sacred birds in Italy and their drumming was thought to be prophetic. They were credited with rain-making capabilities because of the drumming.

Wren In association with the robin, the wren figures as God's hen in rhymes from Hereford and Lancashire. Saint Malo's cloak housed a wren. Traditionally, the wren was held responsible for the death of Saint Stephen. It alerted the guards to his attempted escape from jail which led ultimately to his death. For this reason between Christmas and New Year the bird was hunted. From once being of sacred significance it was reduced to a children's pastime. A branch of either holly or gorse was decorated with ribbons and coloured paper and carried by men and boys who begged for money to " bring the wren" which is supposed to be lying in the bush being carried.

"The wren, the wren, the king of all birds,
St. Stephens's day he was caught in the furze
Although he be little his family's great
I pray you good lady give us a treat".

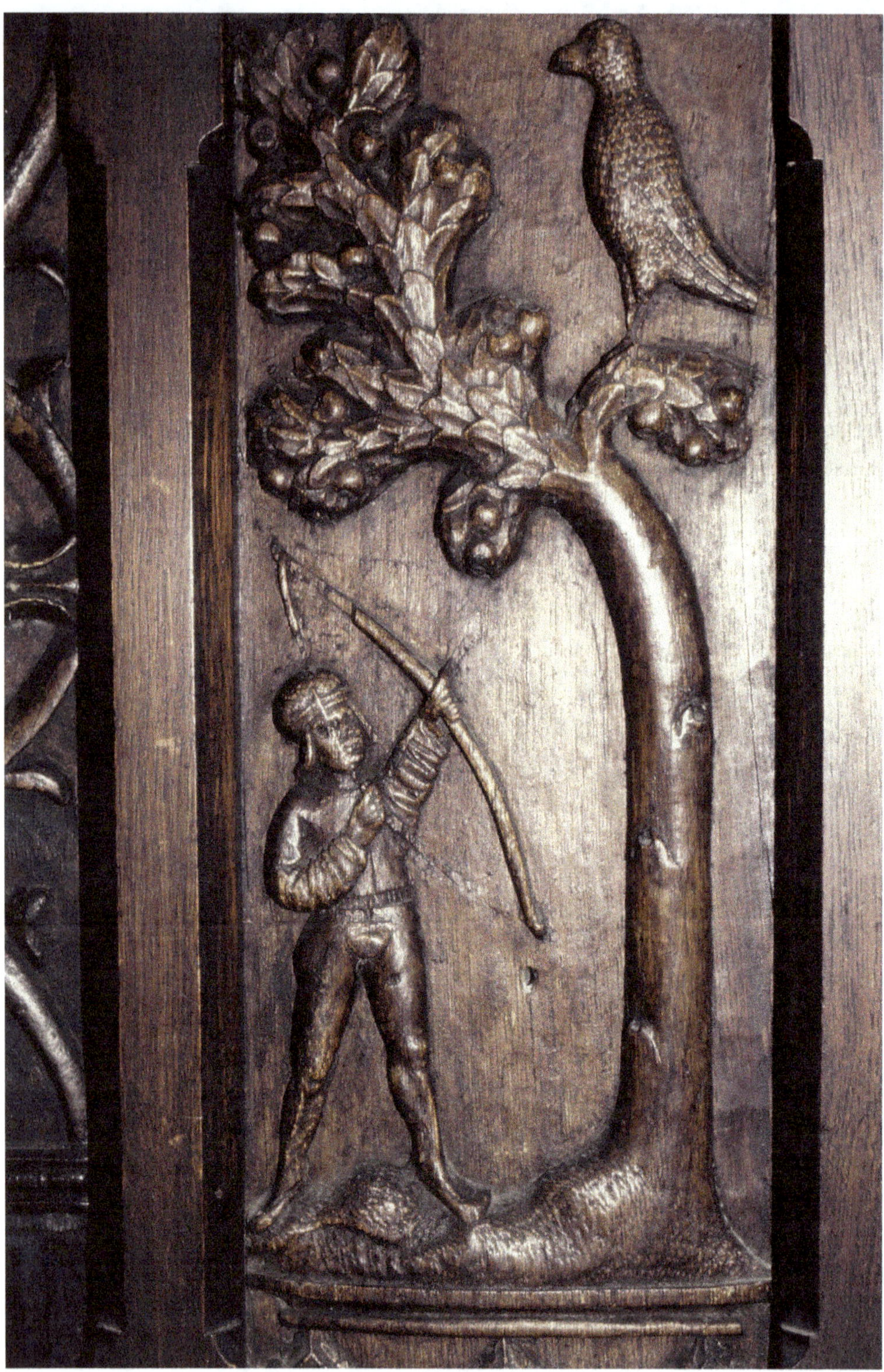

Archer aiming at a bird. Screen, 16th century. Kirkby Wharfe.

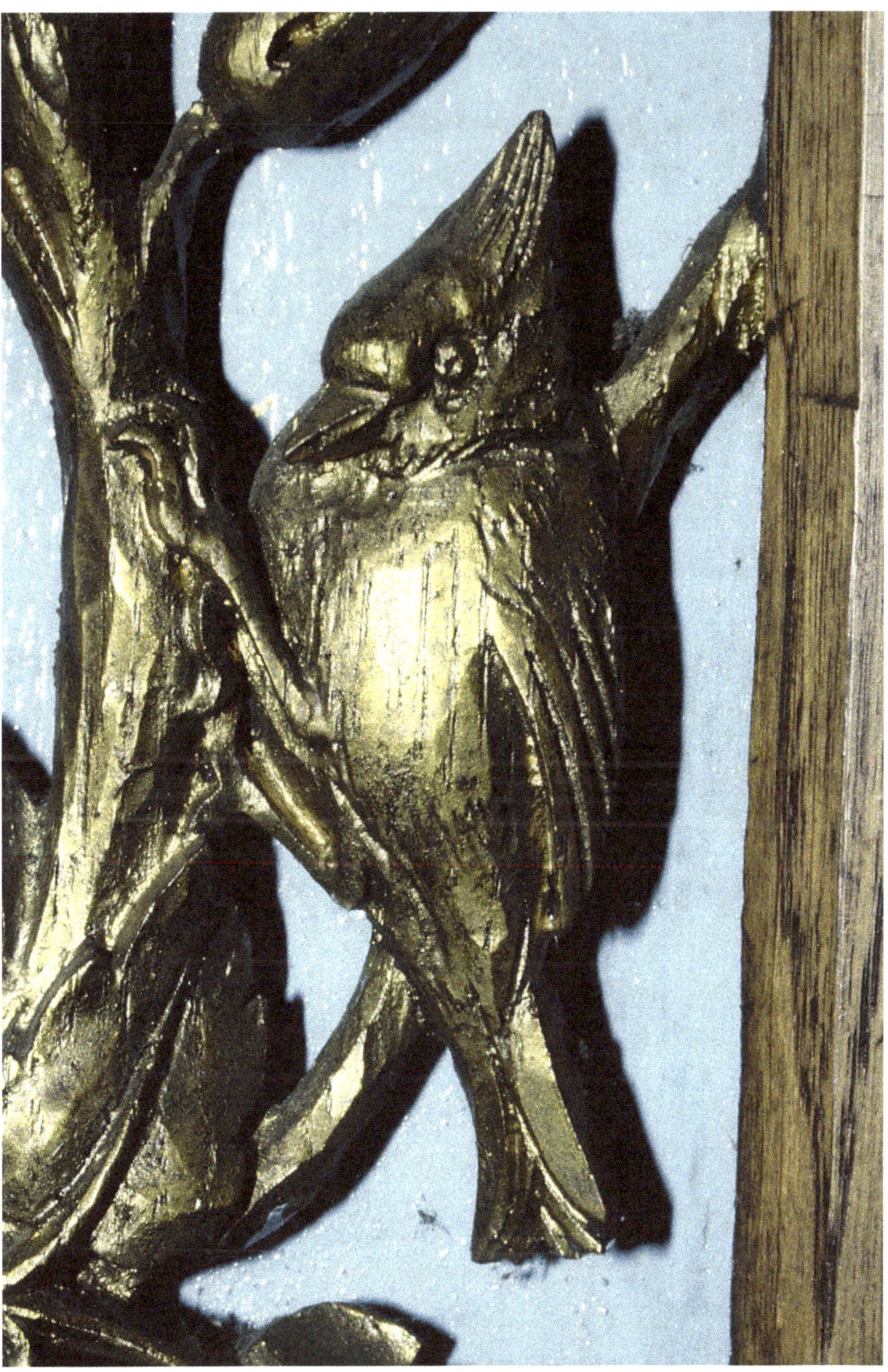

Crested Tit. Reredos, 1928. West Tanfield.

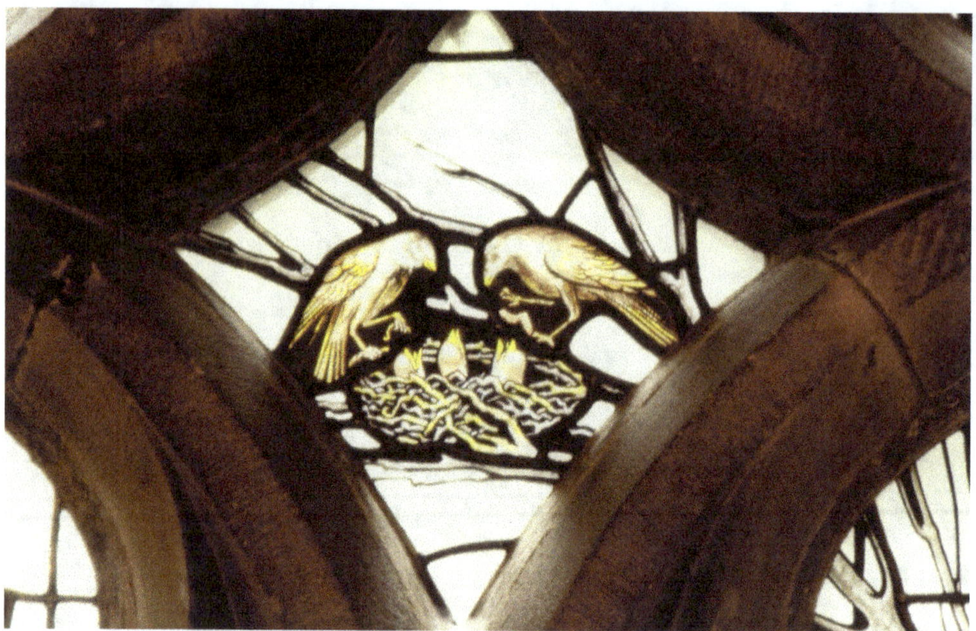

Crows feeding their young in a nest. Quarry. Greenfield.

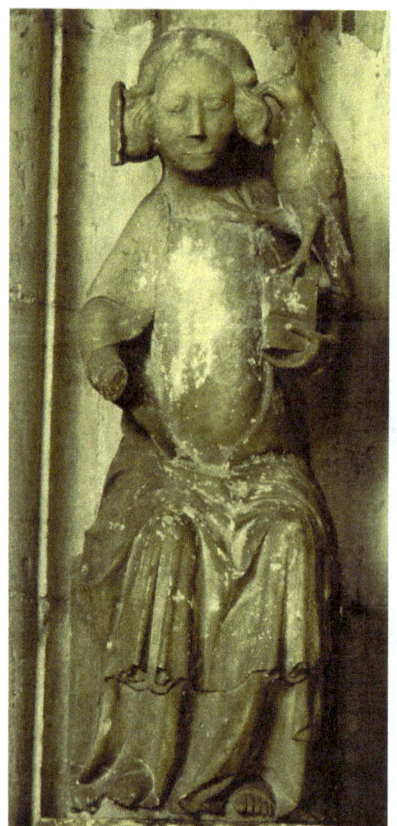

The Virgin Mary with a dove near her ear. Statue, early 14th century. Howden.

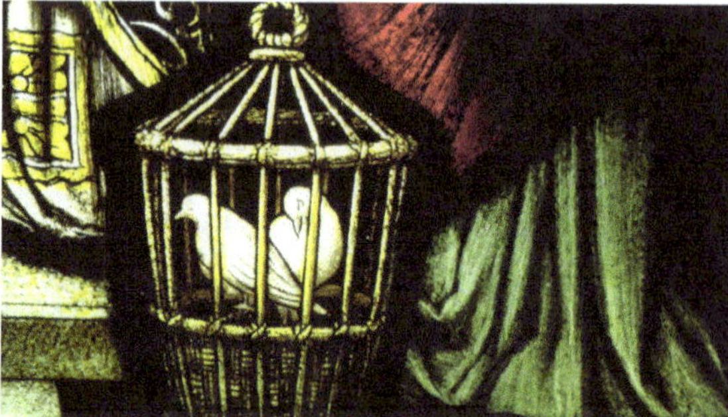

Two doves in a wicker basket. Window. Woodhouse.

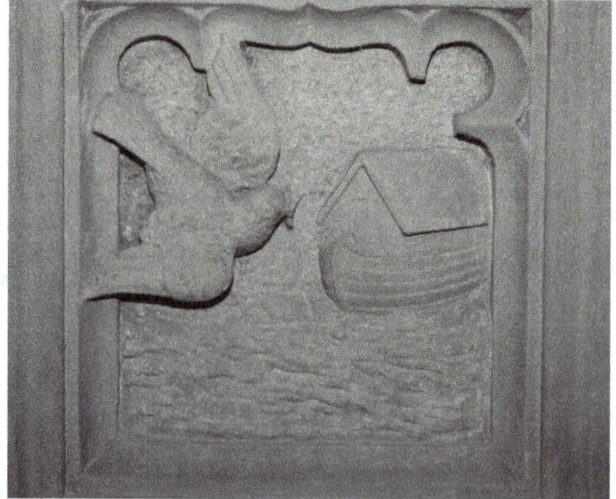

Dove with twig in its beak returning to the ark. Font. circa 1824. Woodhouse.

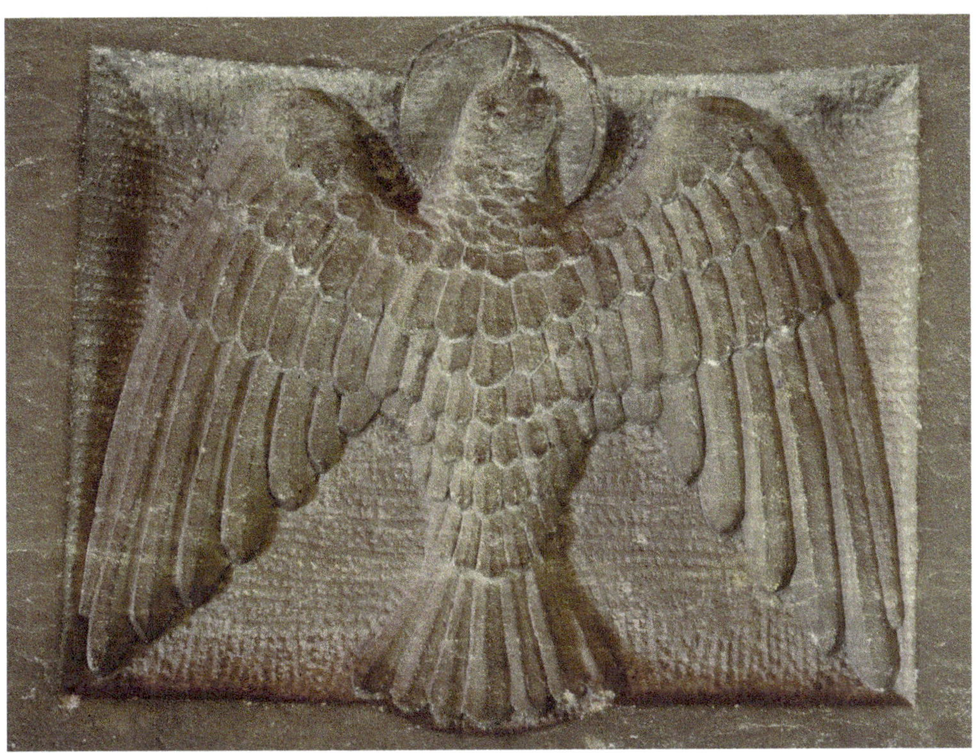

Dove with halo. Font. circa 1824. Woodhouse.

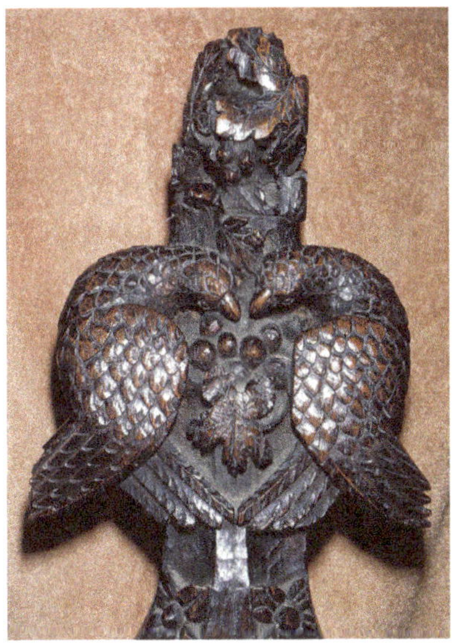

Doves pecking grapes. Poppyhead, 1858. Rothwell.

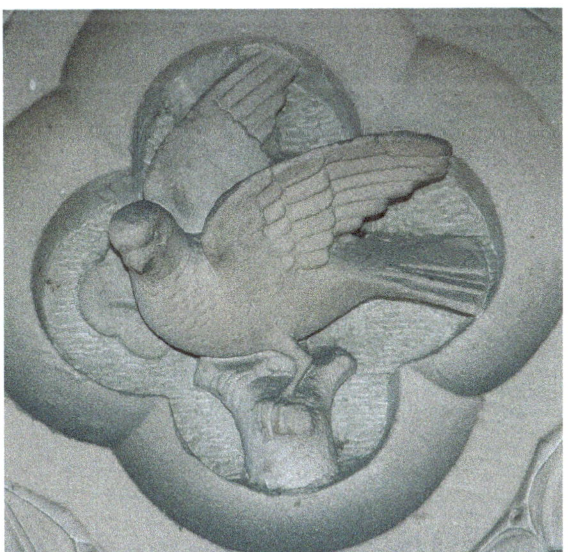

Dove. Quatrefoil, 1872-78. Studley Royal.

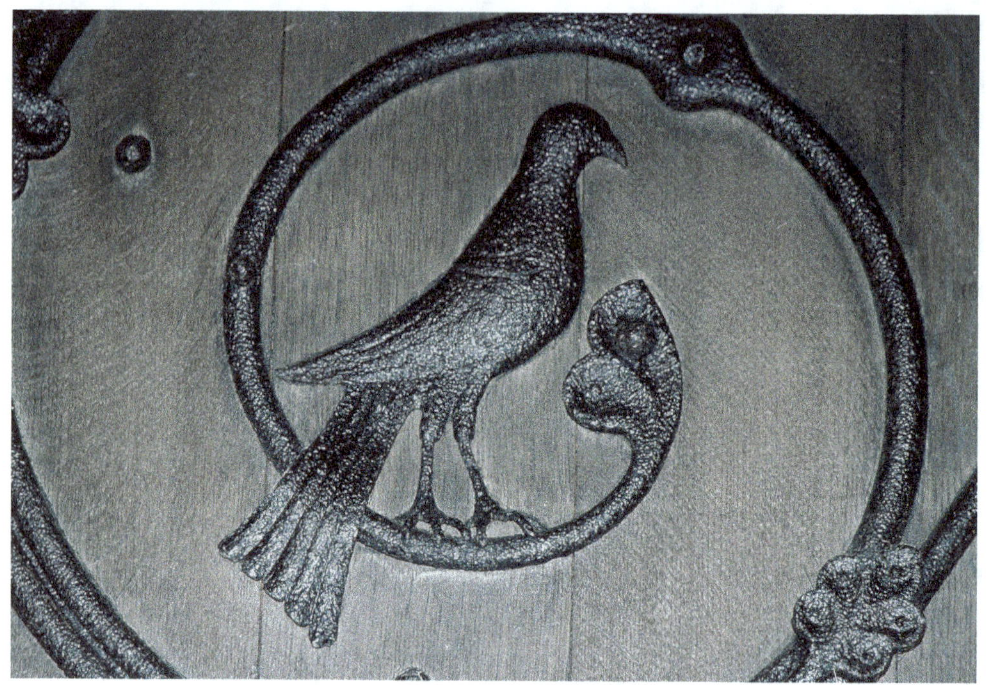

Ironwork on door. Dove. 1872-78.Studely Royal.

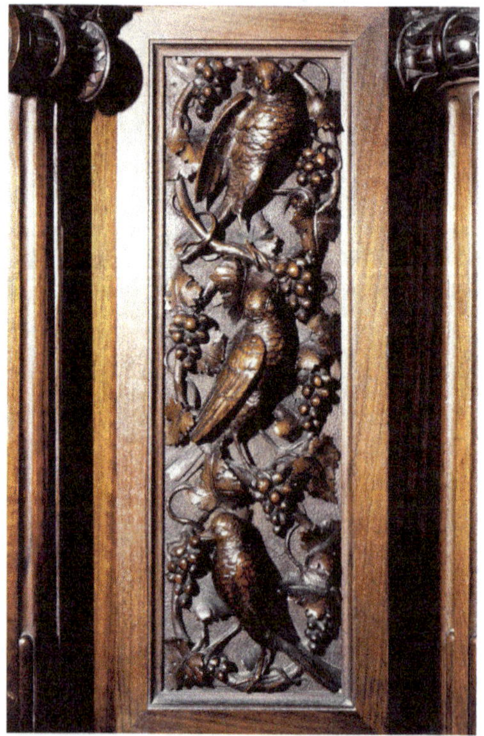

Three Doves on grapes. Lectern, 1877-80.
Harthill.

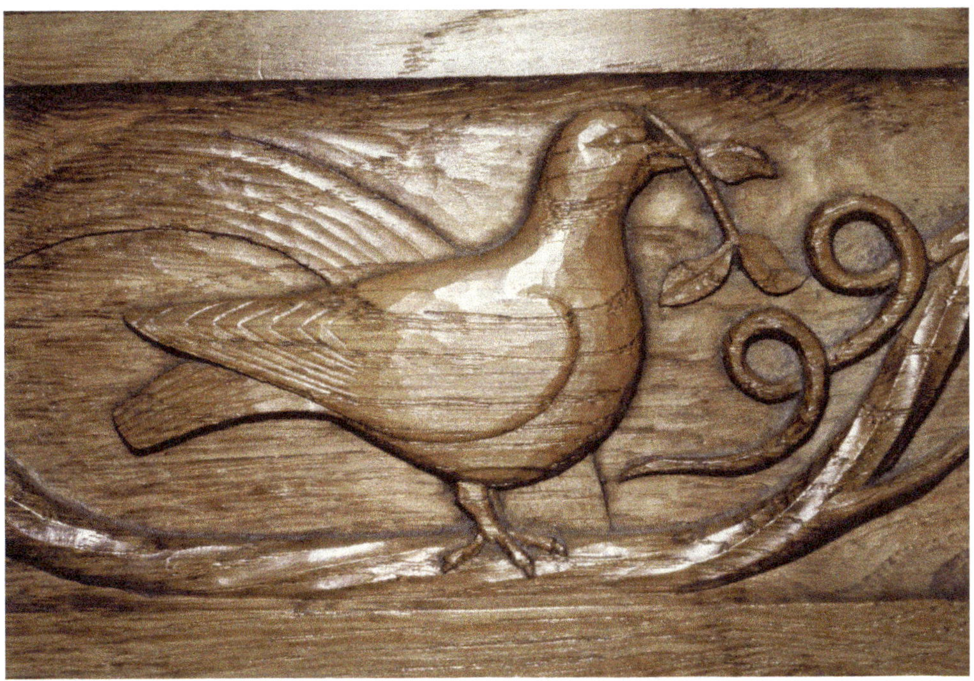

Dove with an olive branch. Communion Rail, circa 1930. West Tanfield.

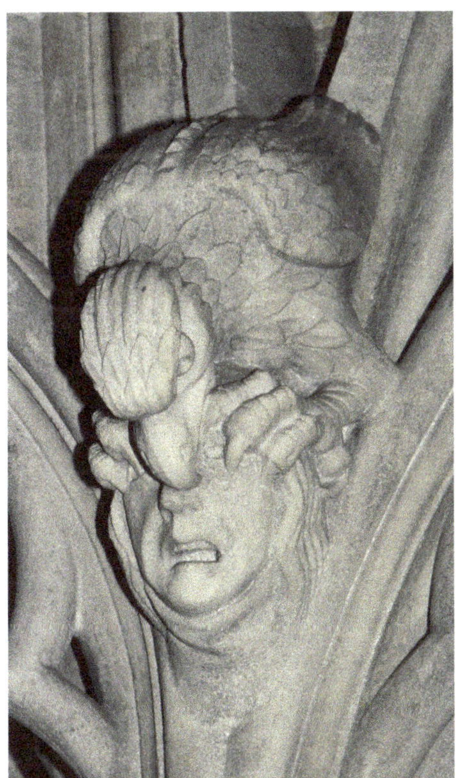

An eagle standing on a man's head whilst pecking his eye. Capital, 1260-85. York Minster..

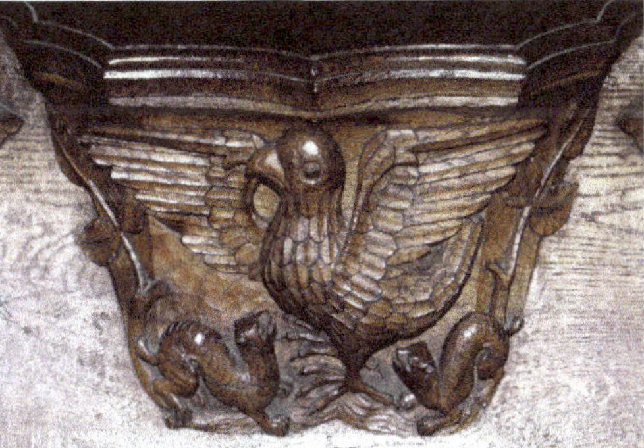

Eagle with stoat or weasel either side. Misericord, 1445. Beverley St Mary.

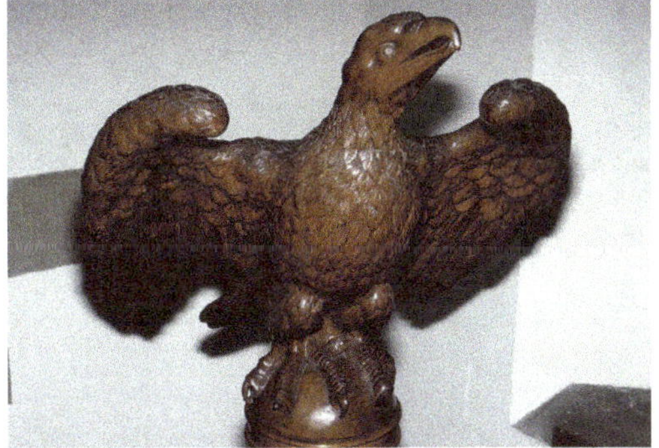

Eagle lectern, circa 1910. Cumberworth

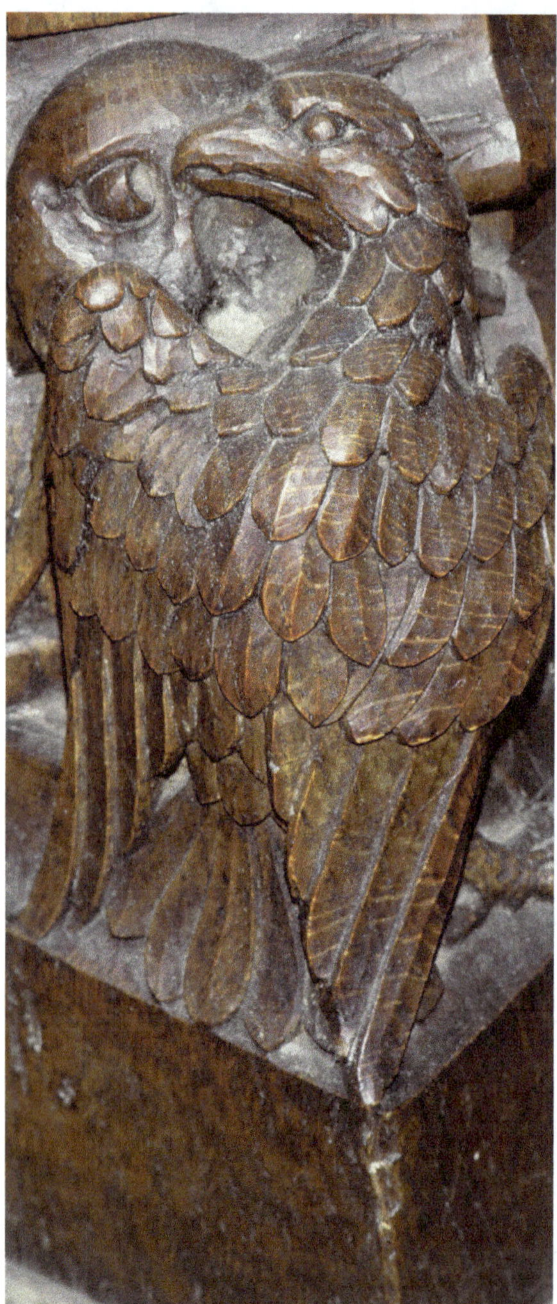
Eagle pecking the eye of a human face. Pulpit. Headingly.

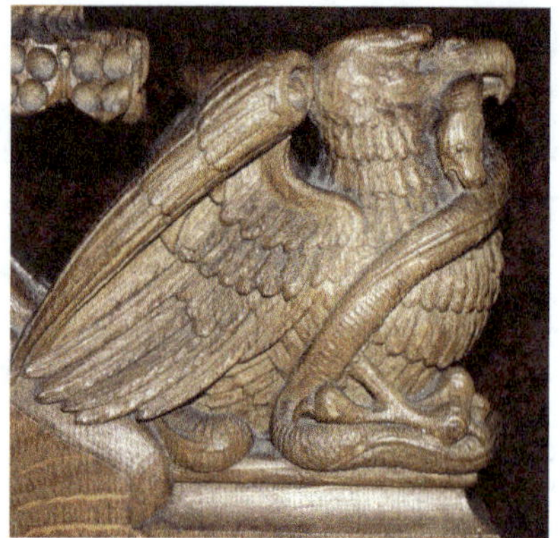
Eagle with a snake. Elbow. Sherburn.

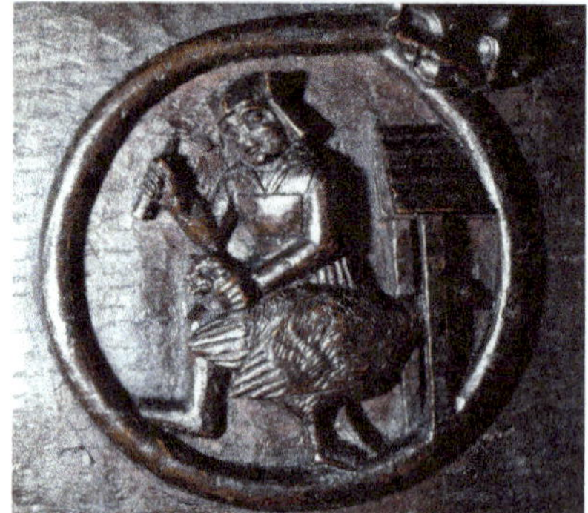
Man shoeing a goose indicating either Folly, wasting time or telling someone to mind their own business. Supporter, 1520. Beverley Minster.

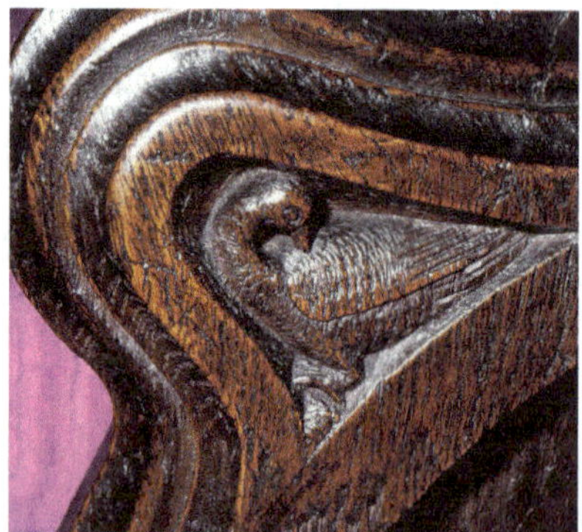
Charming small goose. Elbow, 1520. Beverley Minster.

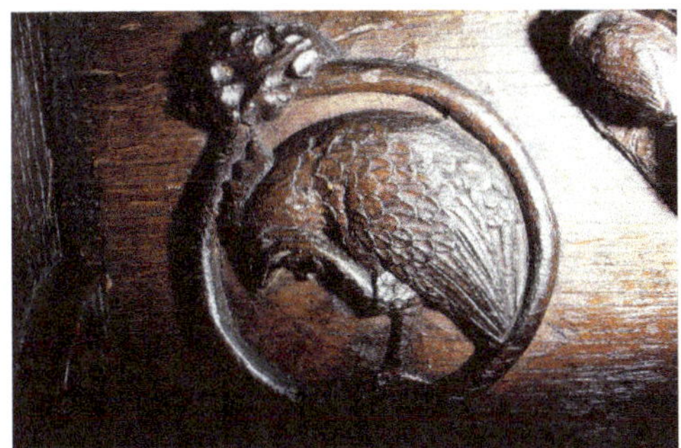

Hen scratching itself. Supporter, 1520. Beverley Minster.

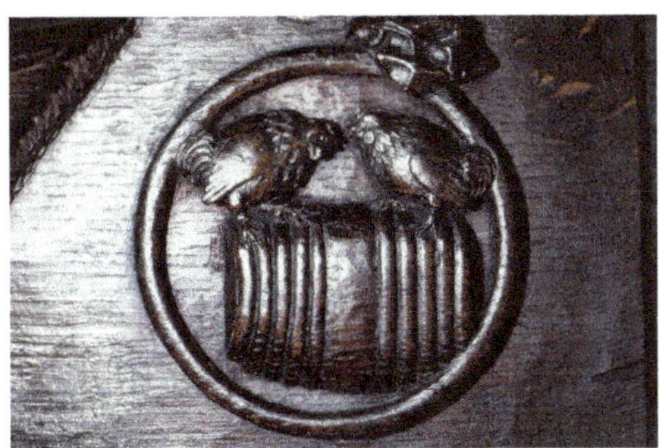

Bantams on a barrel. Supporter, 1520. Beverley Minster.

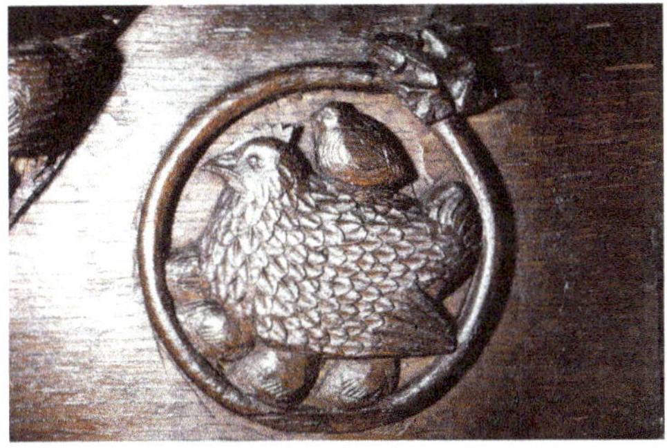

Hen with chick on her back and four beneath her. Suporter, 1520. Beverley Minster.

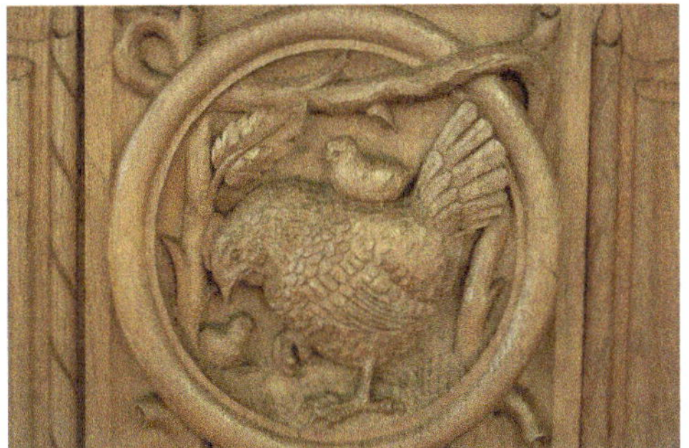

Hen with chick on her back and two at her feet. (Matt. 23:37). Choir stall, circa 1930. West Tanfield.

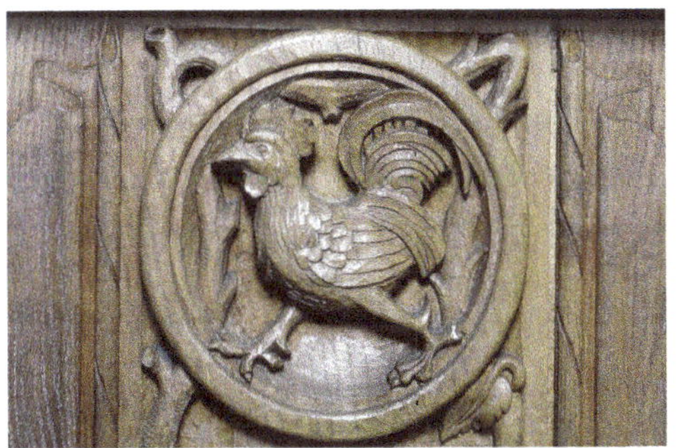

Handsome strutting cock. Choir stall, circa 1930. West Tanfield.

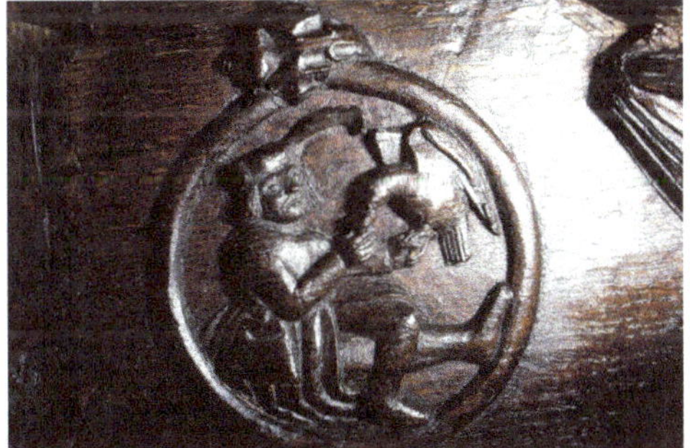

Falconer feeding a hawk. Supporter, 1520. Beverley Minster.

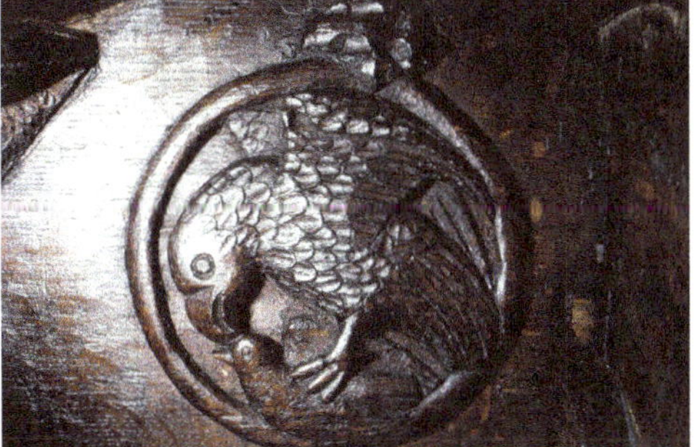

Hawk preying on a partridge. Supporter, 1520. Beverley Minster.

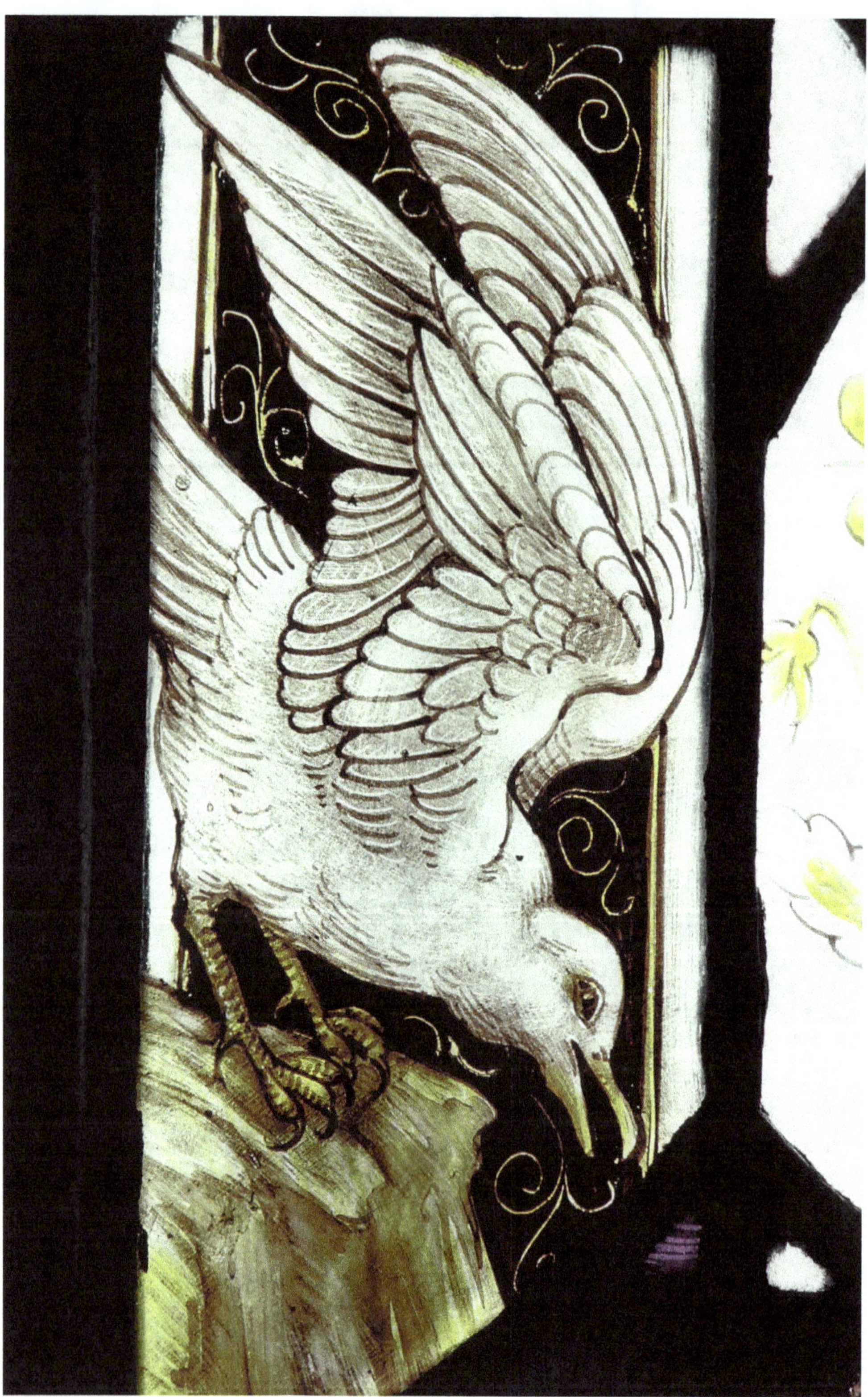

Gull with clawed feet. Window border, 1905. Bolton on Swale.

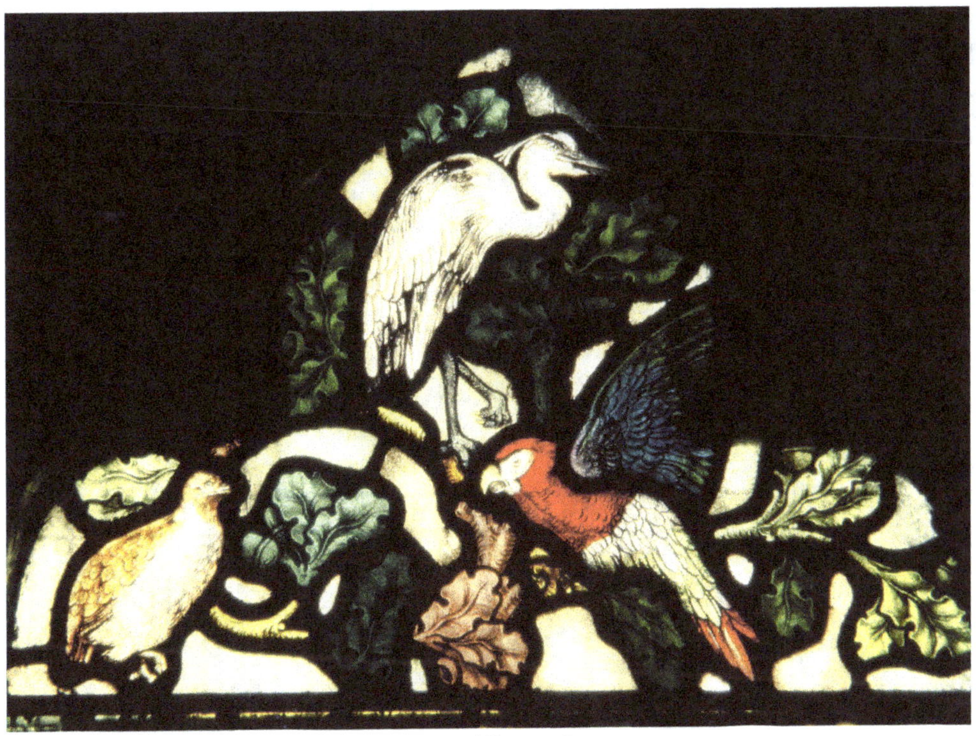

Heron, parrot and partridge. Window, 1905. Aldborough.

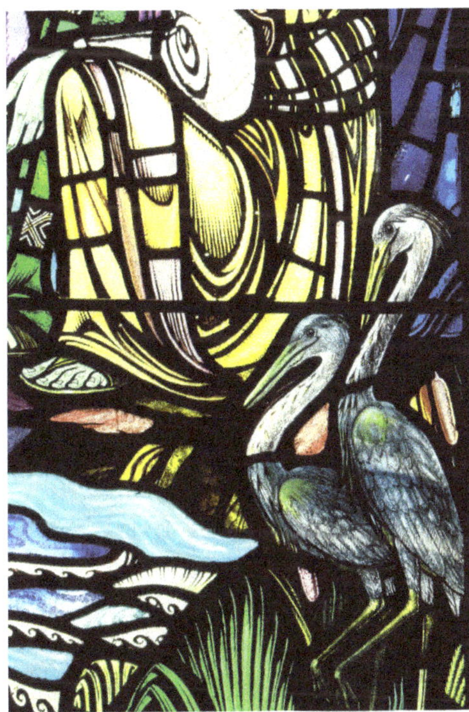

Two herons. Window, 1951. Penistone.

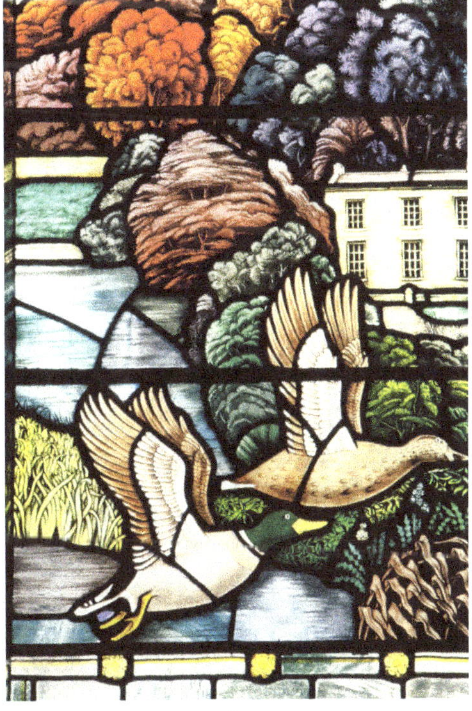

Mallard in flight. Window, 1907. Brompton by Sawdon

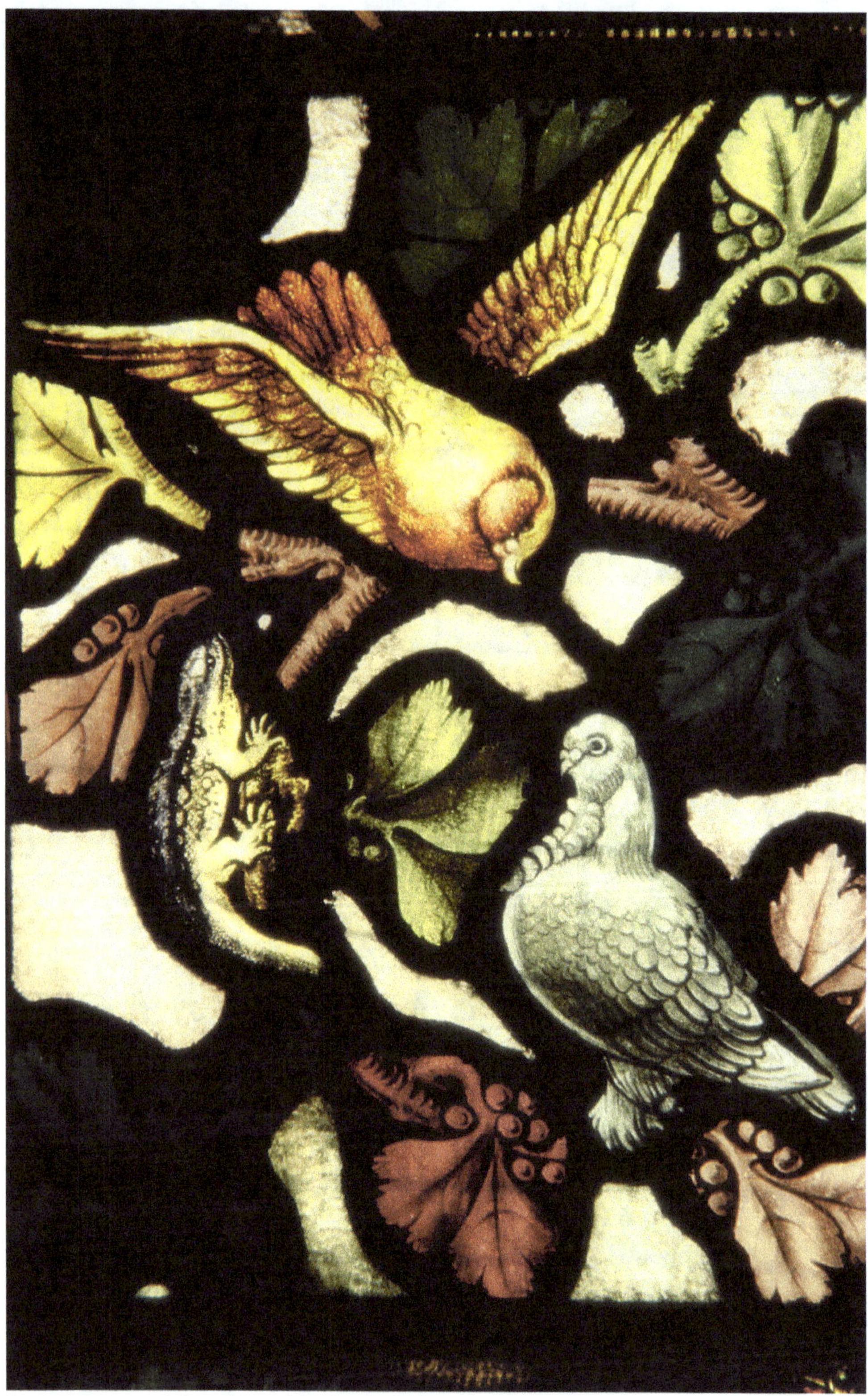

Pouter Pigeon with lizard. Window detail, 1905. Aldborough.

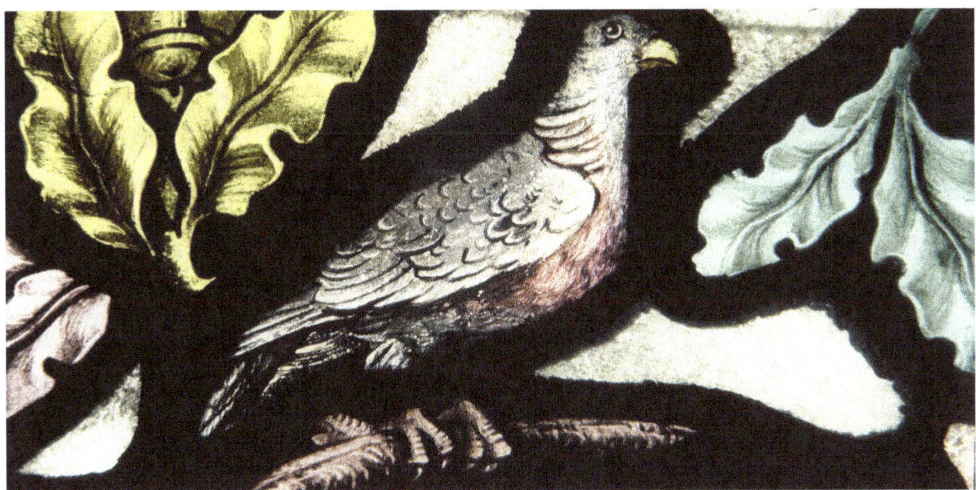

Wood Pigeon. Window, 1905. Aldborough.

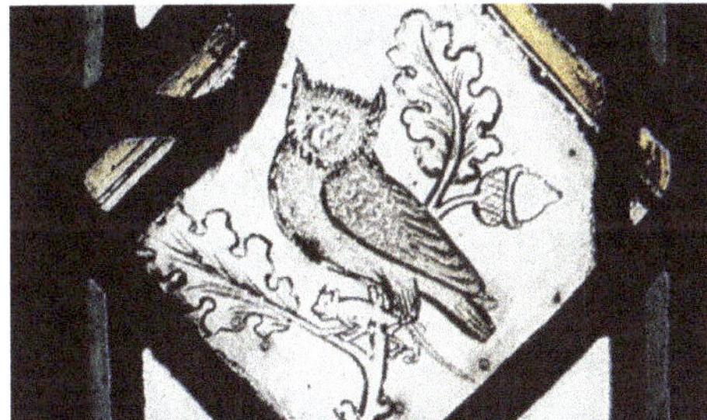

Detail of owl and mouse quarry. $14^{th}/15^{th}$ century. Zouche Chapel, York

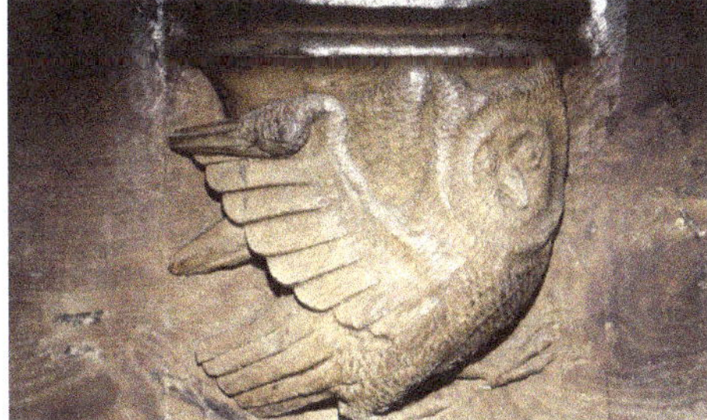

Barn Owl with curious facial disc. Misericord, late 15th/early 16th centuries. Old Malton.

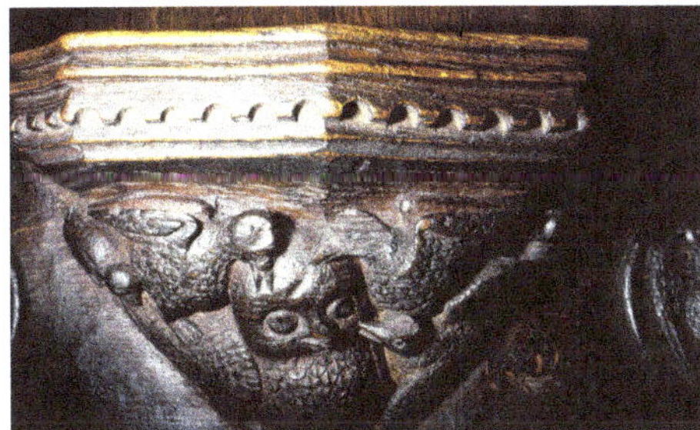

Owl mobbed by smaller birds. Misericord, 1520. Beverley Minster.

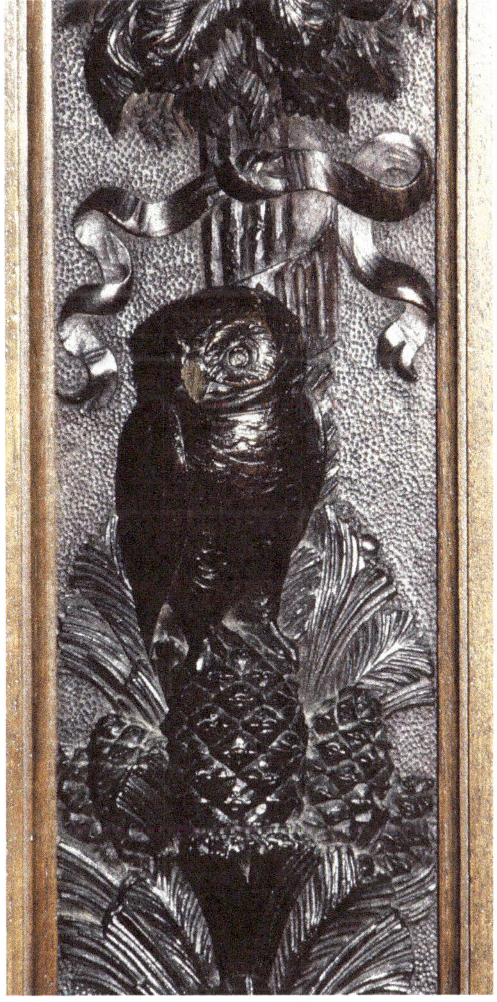

Possibly a Little Owl on conifer. Pulpit, 1877-80. Harthill.

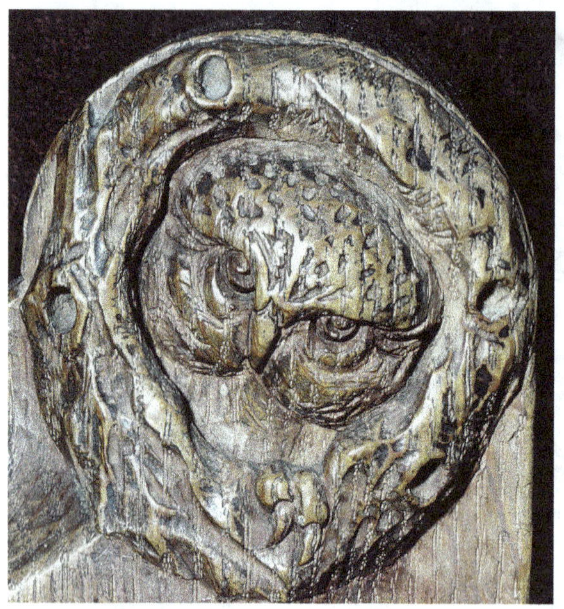
Possibly a Little Owl's face. Elbow, circa 1930. West Tanfield.

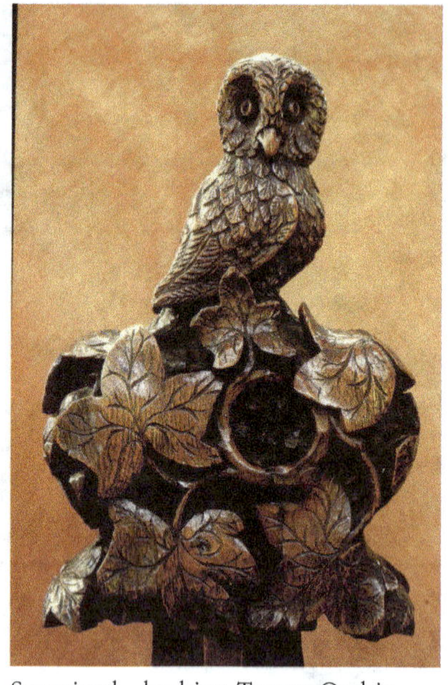
Surprised - looking Tawny Owl in ivy. Poppyhead, 1858. Rothwell.

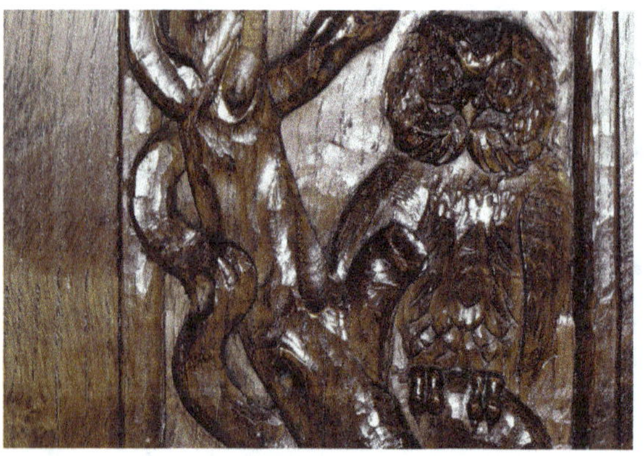
Tawny Owl. Screen. Marsden.

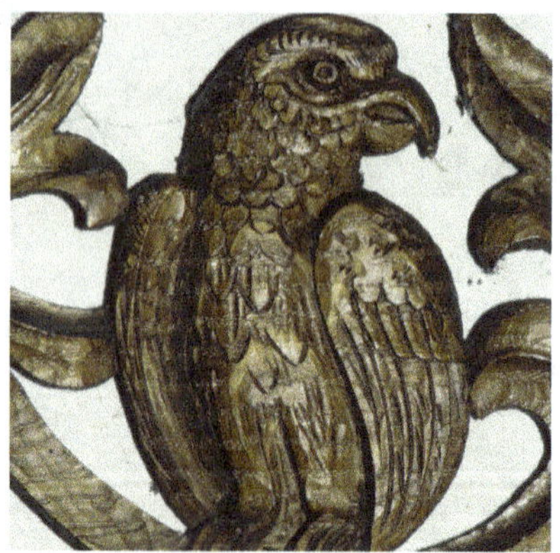
Parrot. Reredos, circa 1930. West Tanfield.

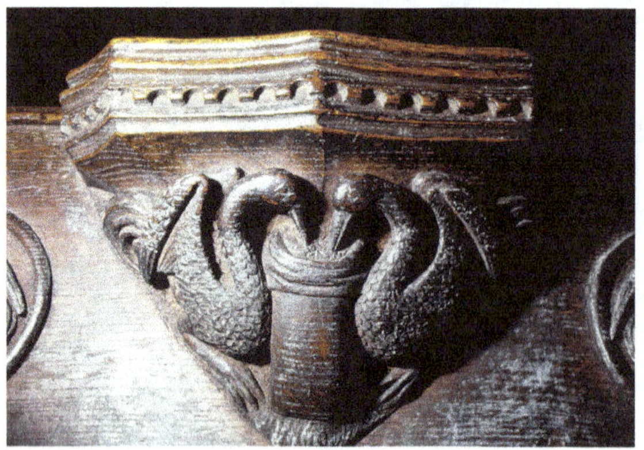
Two storks or cranes eating corn from a sack. Misericord, 1520. Beverley Minster.

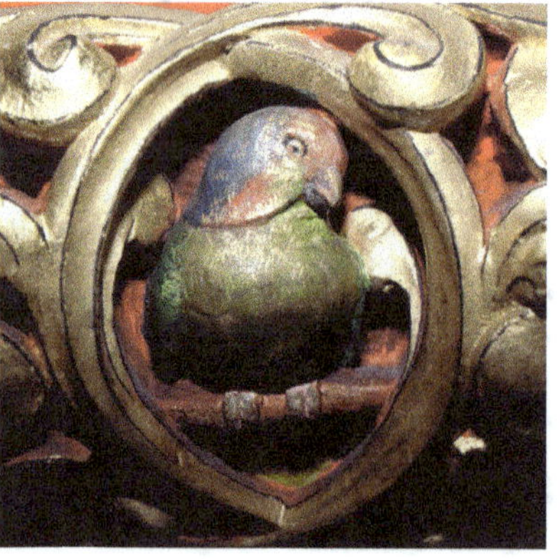
Painted parrot. Choir stall screen, 1872-76. Studley Royal.

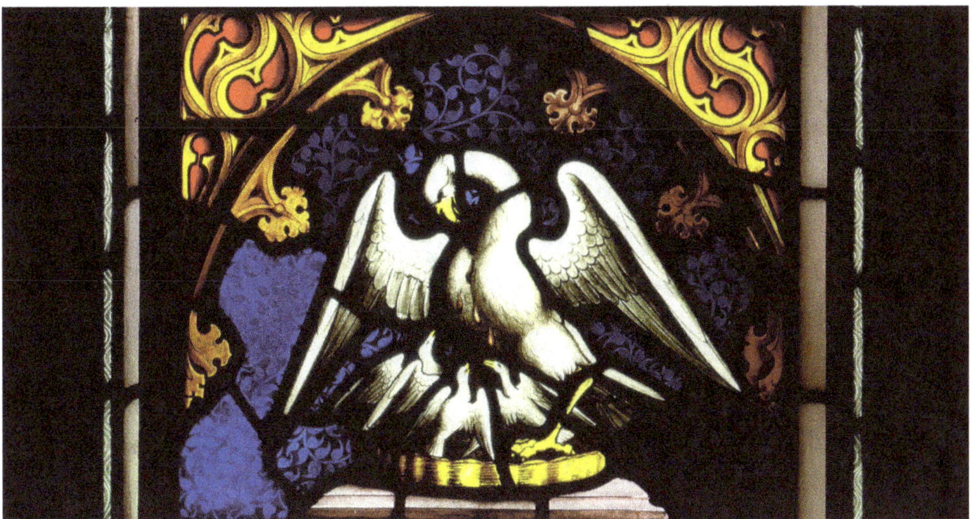

Pelican feeding three chicks with three drops of blood. Window, circa 1860. Gargrave.

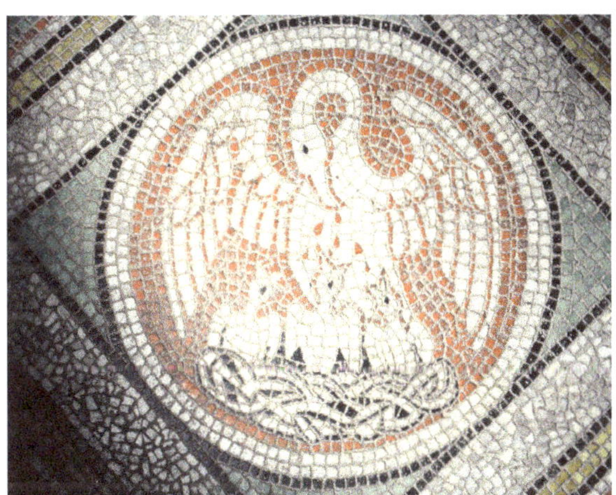

Red and white pelican and chicks.
Floor mosaic, 1874. Heslington.

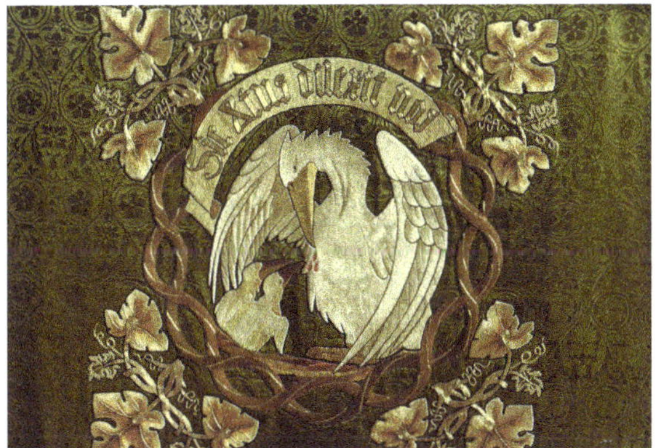

Pelican feeding two chicks with three drops of blood.
Altar frontal. Emley.

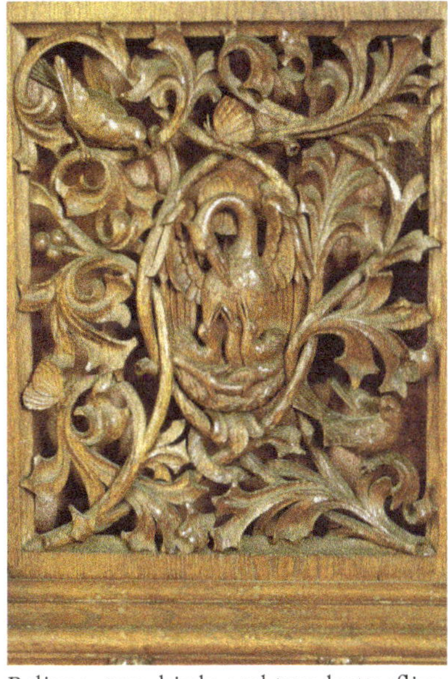

Pelican, two birds and two butterflies.
Communion rail, circa 1930.
West Tanfield.

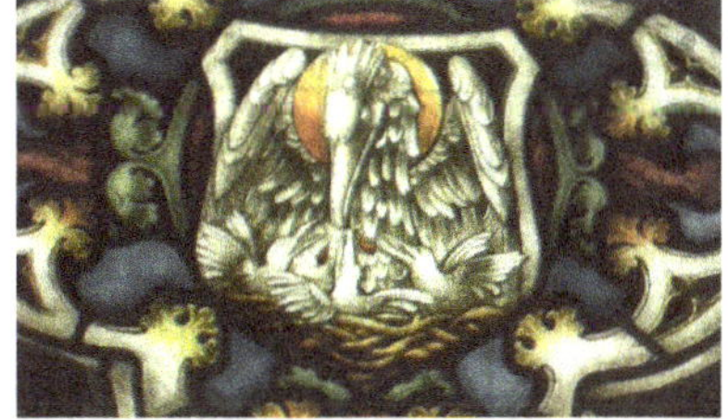

Pelican. Window. Micklefield.
Heather Walker

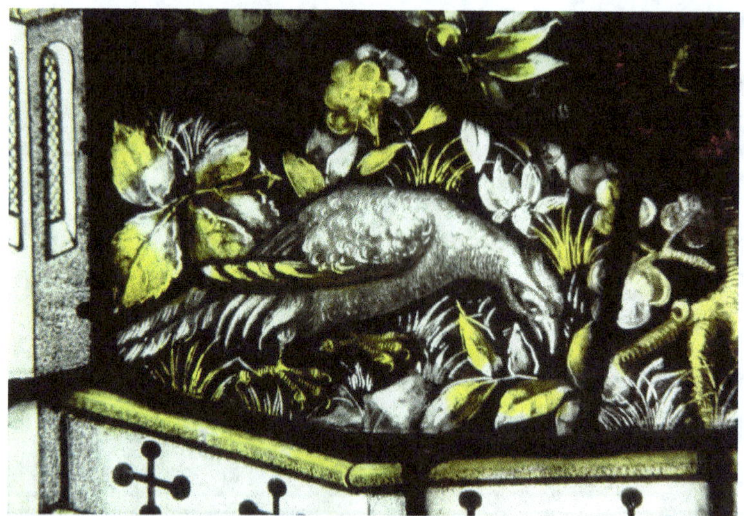

Pheasant. Window, circa 1870. Wakefield.

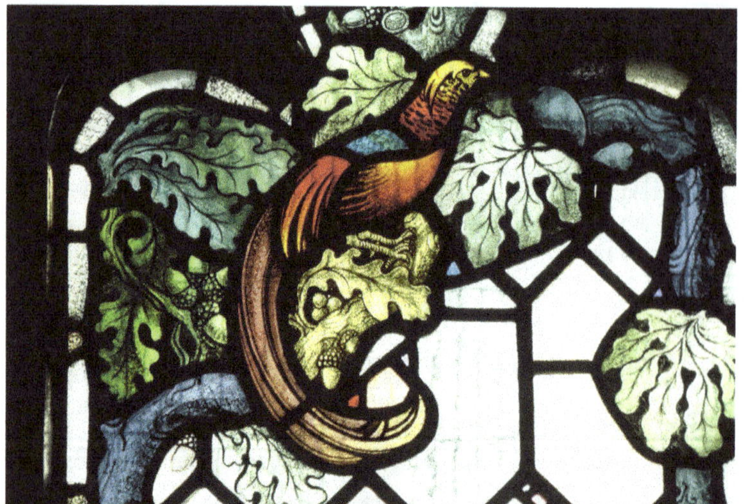

Highly coloured pheasant among oak leaves. Window, 1930. Baildon.

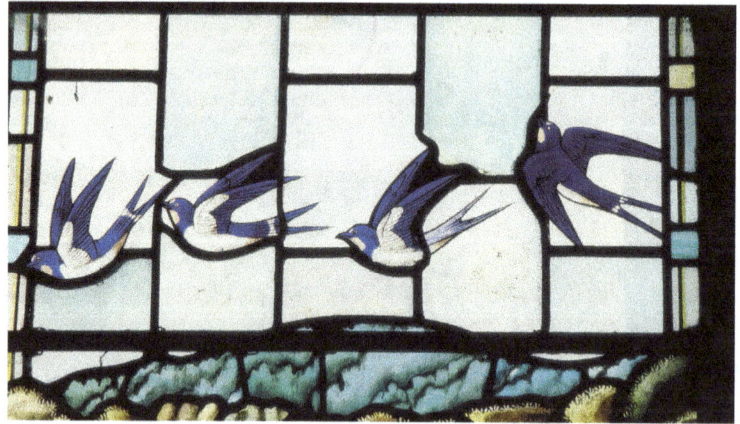

Swallows in flight. Window, 1907. Brompton by Sawdon.

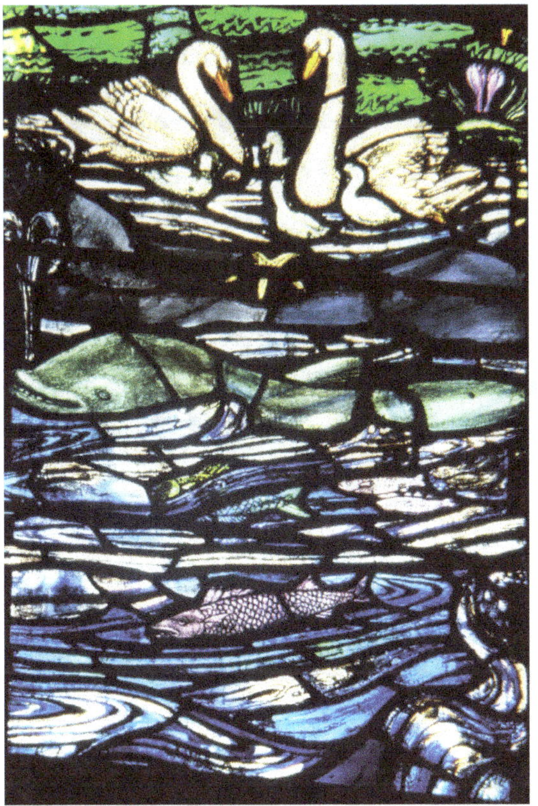

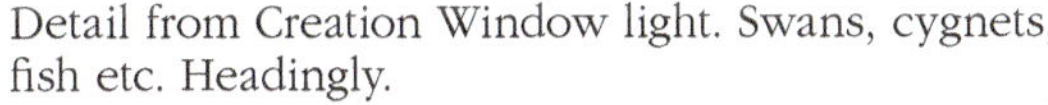
Detail from Creation Window light. Swans, cygnets, fish etc. Headingly.

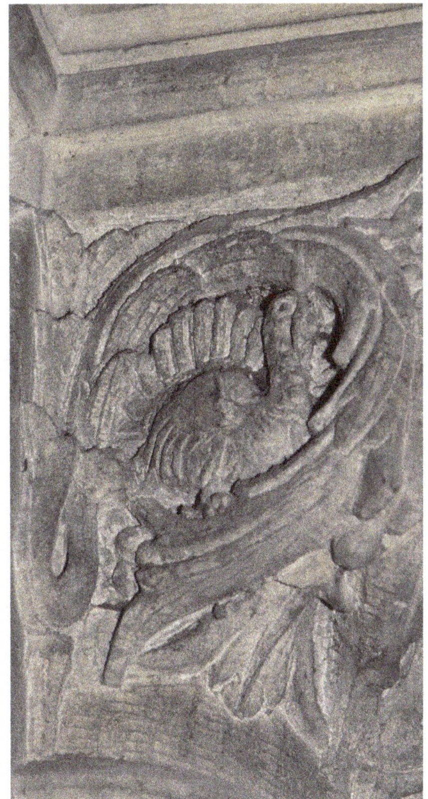
Turkey capital, 1922-61. Ampleforth

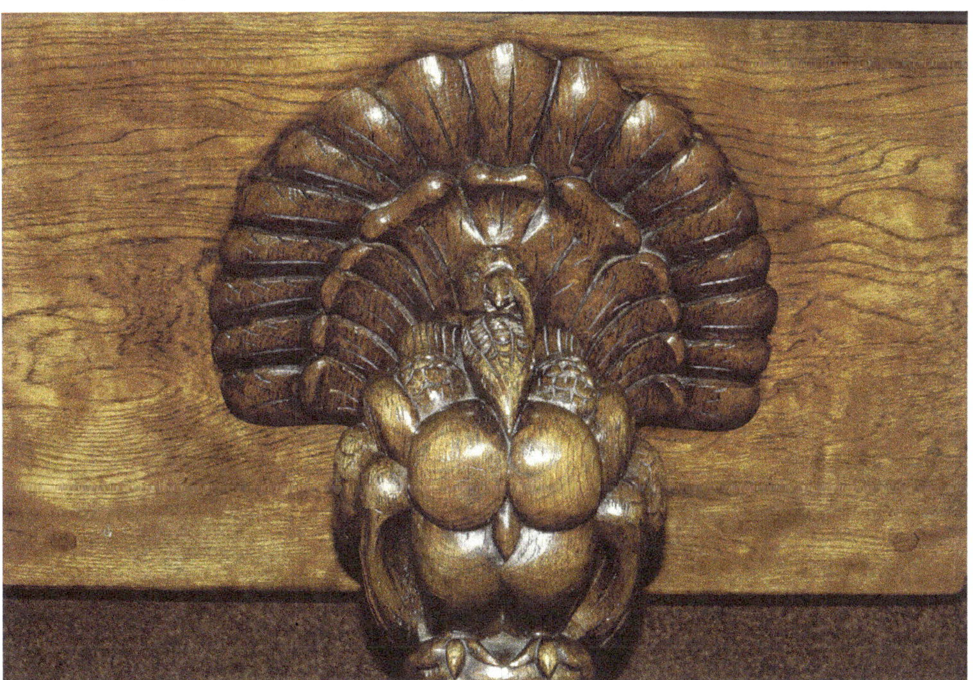
The only turkey lectern as far as is known. Boynton.

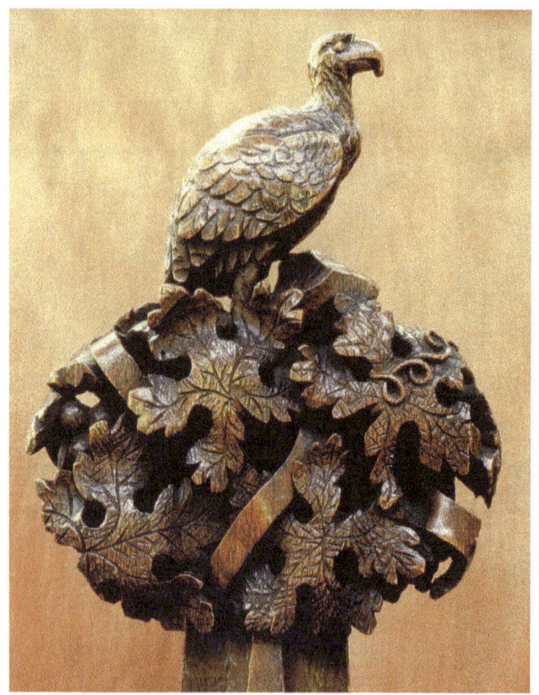
Vulture. Poppyhead, 1858. Rothwell.

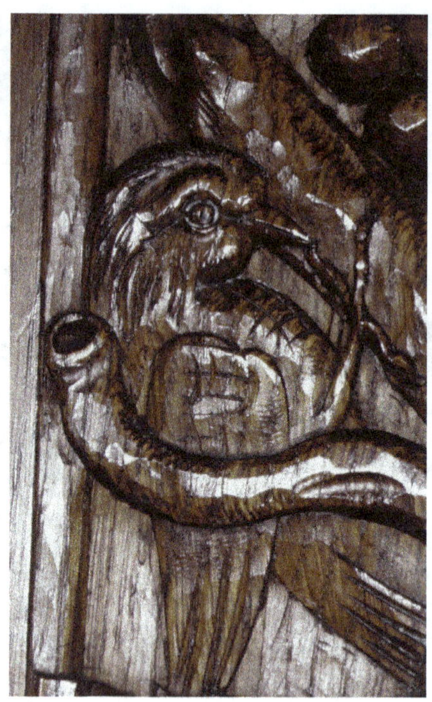
Woodpecker. Screen. Marsden.

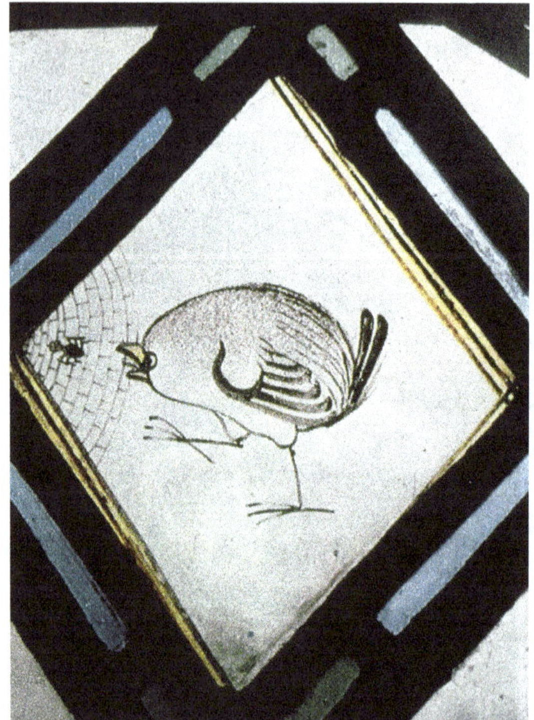
Wren and spider quarry. $14^{th}/15^{th}$ century. Zouche Chapel, York Minster

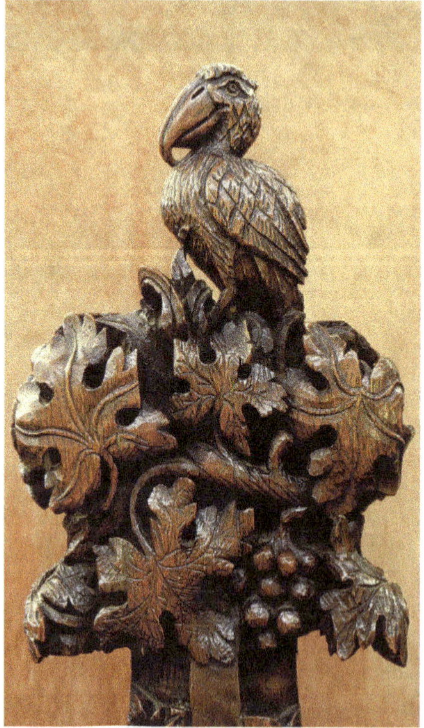
Bird, species unknown, could be a Hornbill. Poppyhead, 1858. Rothwell.

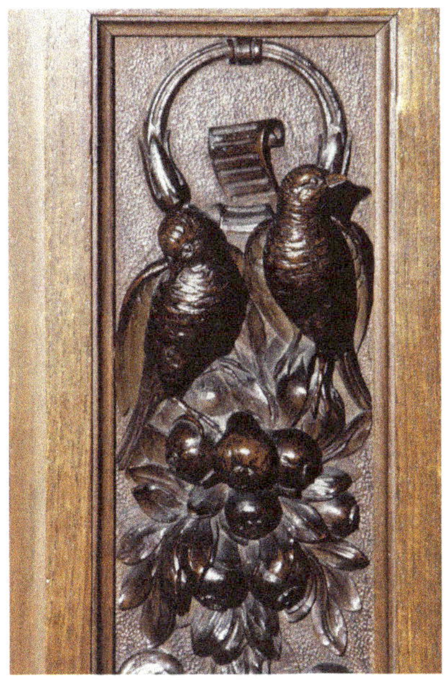
Birds on figs. Pulpit, 1877-90. Harthill.

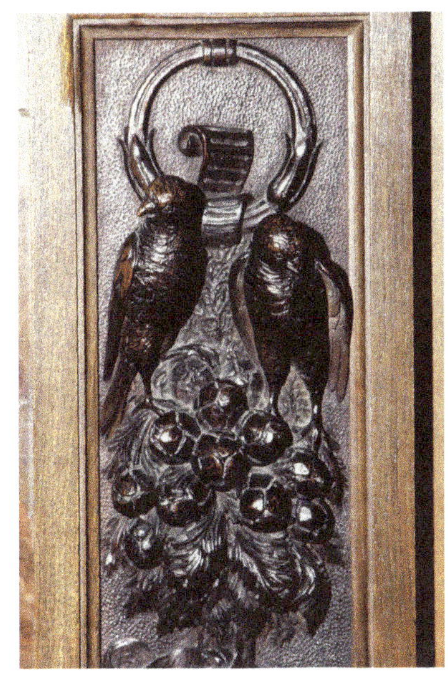
Birds on Juniper. Pulpit, 1877-90. Harthill.

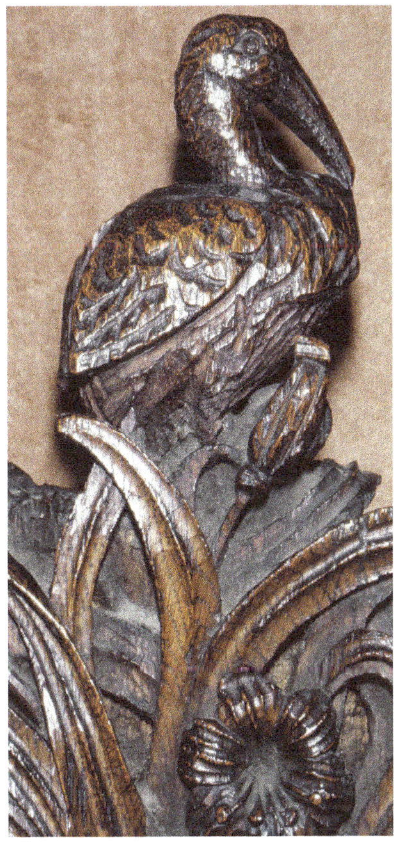
Pelican or spoonbill. Poppyhead, 1858. Rothwell.

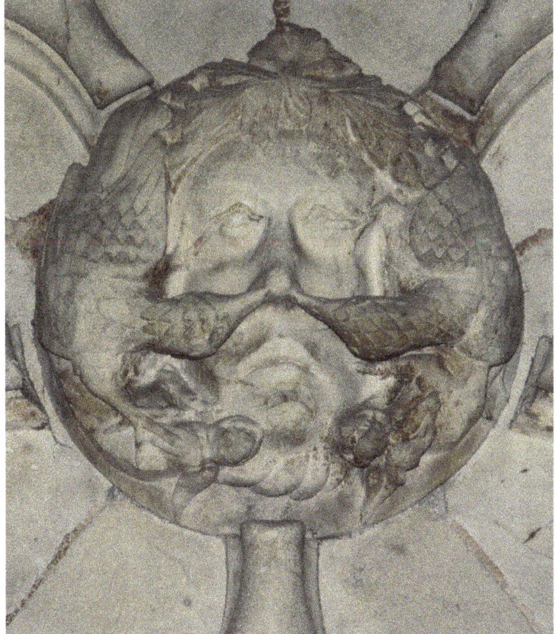
Birds pecking up a man's nose. Roof boss, 1260-80. York Minster.

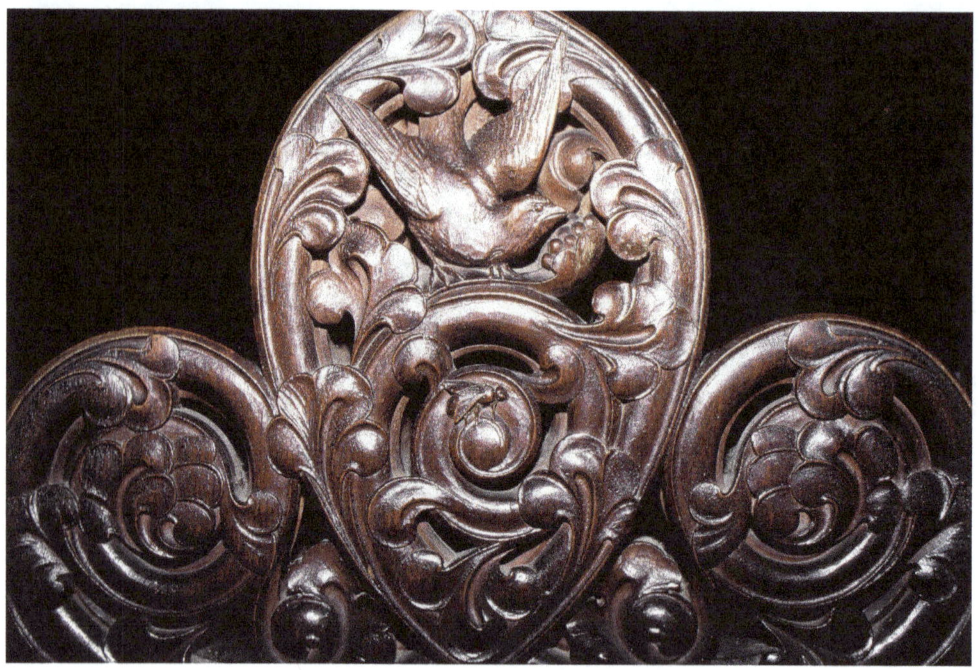

Bird and fly in stylised foliage. Poppyhead, 1872-78. Studley Royal.

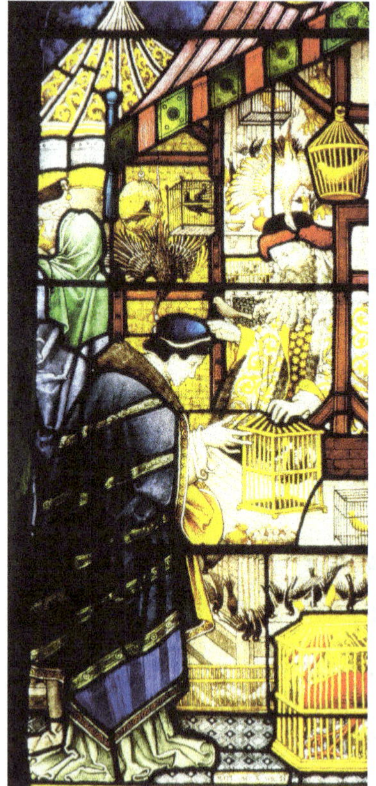

Dead birds and birds in a variety of cages. Window, 19th century. Ecclesfield.

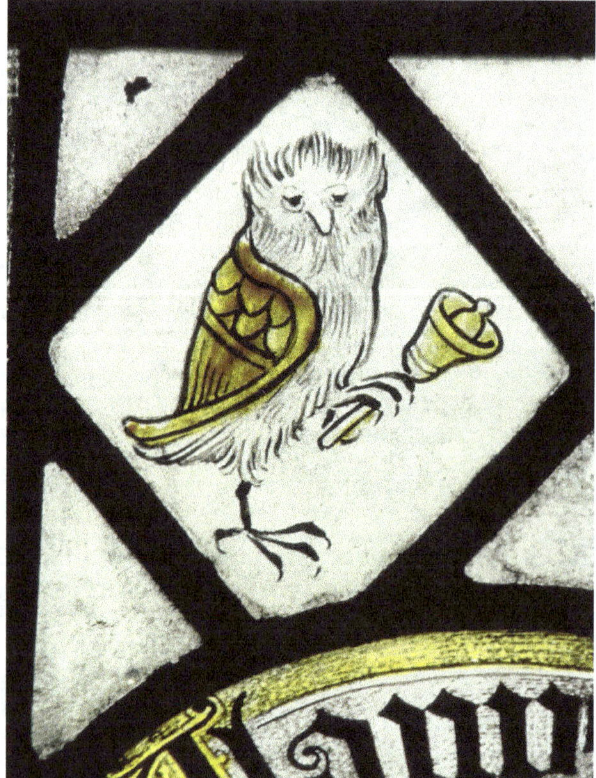

Owl bellman. Window, circa 1933. Adel.

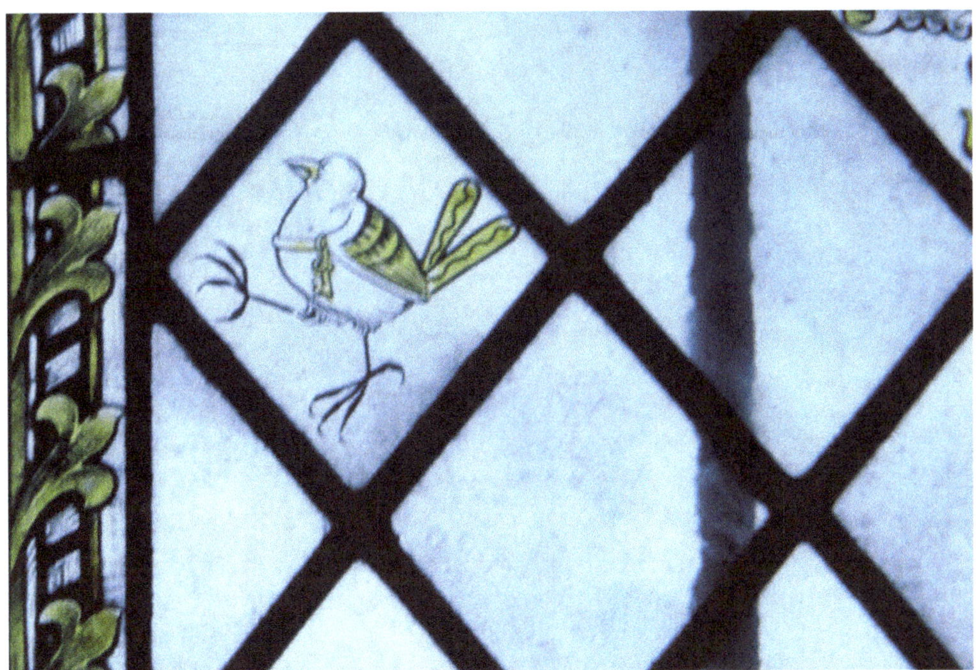

Cellarer bird minus the dish. Quarry. Marsden.

Unidentified birds in circa 1880 mosaic floor. Bishop Wilton.

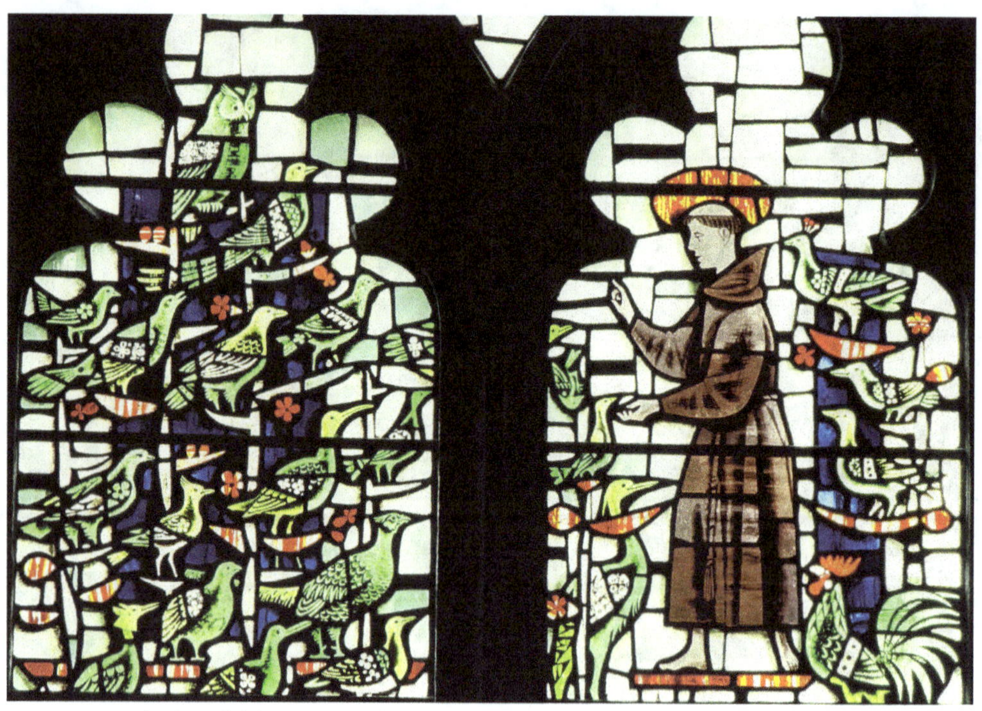

St Francis with identifiable green birds. Window, modern. Masham.

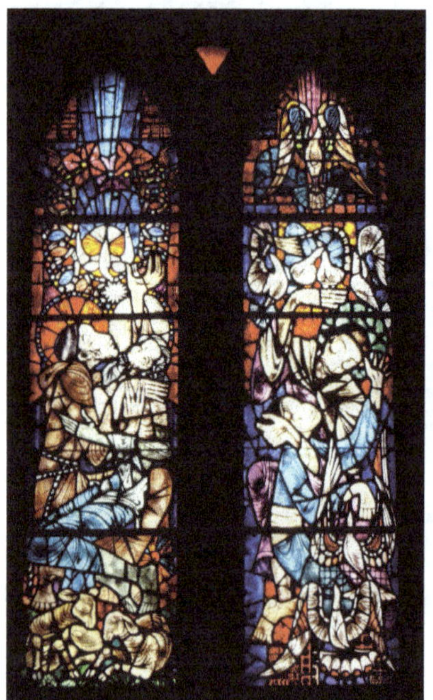

St Francis with birds and healing a leper. Window, 1944. York Minster.

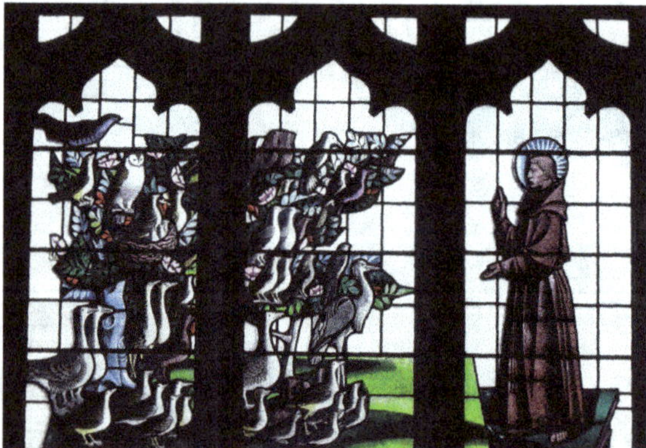

St Francis preaching to a mass of identifiable birds. Window, 1950. Stocksbridge.

MAMMALS in YORKSHIRE CHURCHES

Antelope	Giraffe	Rabbit
Ape	Goat	Rhinoceros
Ass	Hare	Seal
Bat	Hedgehog	Sheep
Bear	Horse	Shrew
Beaver	Hyena	Sloth
Camel, Bactrian	Kangaroo	Squirrel, Grey
Dromedary	Leopard	Red
Cat	Lion	Stoat
Cattle, Cow, Ox	Marten	Swine
Deer, Fallow	Mole	Tiger
Reindeer	Monkey	Walrus
Dog, Dachshund	Moose	Weasel
Greyhound	Mouse	Whale
Donkey	Otter	Wolf
Elephant	Polar Bear	Zebra
Fox	Porcupine	

The variety of mammals to be found in churches ranges from jungle beasts like the lion, tiger and elephant to a tiny mouse eating cheese seen in a window. The number of species identified so far is fifty seven and of these forty nine can be found in Yorkshire with the fox and the lion being the most common.

Some of the mammals were very well known but in spite of this, errors in the anatomy of the animals sometimes creep in, for example, bats are rarely correctly carved until the late 19th century, before this date they are usually found minus feet or standing on their own wings. Elephants (understandably, as they were not seen in this country until 1255) not only have their tusks in the wrong jaw (they should be in the upper jaw sweeping down), but also have a trumpet-ended trunk and the feet and flowing tail like those of a cart-horse. A three-toed fox and a club-footed cat, cow and fox have been seen (Fawsley, Northants.). Three toes indicate a bestiary source, i.e. a book of beasts usually with a moral attached to the descriptions. Mammals behaving naturally include a bat catching a moth, a bear scratching its head and another bear being stung by bees, a cow chewing the cud, dogs gnawing bones, dogs with their heads in stew pots and one dog with its foot caught in a trap. Dogs also feature in stag hunting and hare coursing scenes. There are mice in cornfields, mice on their nests and mice as a maker's mark. Otters catch fish, pigs suckle their young and rabbits feed near their warrens.

The wild boar hunt, bear-baiting, stag hunting and hare coursing are all illustrated. Apes and monkeys play the lute, trumpet, drum and bagpipes. Bagpipes are also played by the fox, bear and pig; a bear dances to bagpipes; and a cat, dog or fox having their tails bitten and their chests squeezed, is a satirical reference to the bagpipes. Other musical mammals are cats blowing Pan's pipes, playing the viol and the fiddle; a donkey shaking a tambourine; monkeys clashing symbols; pigs plucking harps and blowing pipes; a rabbit blowing a pipe and a sheep playing the fiddle.

The fox appears in a number of situations, some reflecting reality and some fable. He is depicted as the robber of the farmyard, making off with geese, ducks and hens and being chased by the farmer's wife who carries a distaff. He appears in clerical garb preaching to a congregation of unwary poultry and often accompanied by an ape. He is figured in scenes illustrating Aesop's Fables, the epic story of Reynard the Fox and the Shifts of Reynardine, his son.

There are doctor apes and monkeys, elephants with howdahs, elephants lifting logs and elephants killing snakes (perhaps a reference to the bestiary dragon). Lions and tigers may illustrate bestiary stories and the lion can be a sign of the zodiac.

Antelope The antelope had the reputation of being so untameable and so fierce that no hunter could get near it. The horns were serrated like the teeth of a saw and with these it felled trees. The symbolism was in the horns which were likened to the Old and the New Testaments. They could be used to saw off the vices of the flesh, i.e. adultery, avarice, envy, fornication, lust, murder, pride and slander but the same horns could also deliver man to the devil as they could become entangled in bushes, as man, though armed with the two testaments, is caught by his own sins and falls into the devil's power when indulging himself. The horns could also represent the two virtues of abstinence and obedience. Heraldically, the antelope has tusks like those of a wild boar and often a collar and chain, the latter not always visible, around its neck. Gorged and chained it was the personal badge of Henry 1V. The bestiary antelope does not have tusks. A fine example can be seen in Ripon Cathedral.

Ape In the early middle ages, the ape was a symbol of heresy and paganism. Man recognised a baser, distorted image of himself and thus the animal became associated with vice in general, but particularly bestiality, lust, fraud, deceit and the devil. In the 17th century the ape was depicted as a parody of man, playing musical instruments, dancing etc.. An ape holding, looking at or using a urine flask, was a satirical reference to quack physicians who were held in low regard by the general public. Apes riding on goats, hounds or pigs are symbols of lechery, sin and sexual licence. When depicted as a hunter the ape was the devil snaring souls. If accompanied by an owl, the bird was used as a lure to catch small birds which symbolised human souls. A fettered ape or monkey was a symbol of the world in pre-Christian times. A 13th century stone carving in the Chapter House of York Minster features an adult ape driving a youngster in front of it.

Ass The Biblical ass is thought to have been domesticated in Neolithic times. They average about thirty kilometres a day and were important to the poor nomadic people. Abraham used asses as transport when going from Mesopotamia to Egypt. On peaceable occasions, royalty rode on asses, whilst horses were associated with war. In medieval homilies, the ass was a symbol of sloth and could also signify the Jews who were foolish in that they never believed until forced to do so. It was a beast of burden, carrying a heavy load of idolatry. Today the animal is a symbol of stupidity. In Buddhism the ass is used as a pattern of humility and patience. Its reputation for stupidity probably originated in Western Europe as the jester's cap has ass's ears. According to Physiologus (a natural philosopher from Greece) if an ass begets a colt, the father will bite off his son's testicles so that it produces no seed. The wicked God of Darkness, Seth, (one of the Egyptian deities) represented as an ass, was castrated during a battle with his brother Osiris, God of the Underworld and Judge of the Dead whom he murdered. The equinox was announced by an ass braying twelve times. The Onager is probably the animal referred to in the above examples. See Donkey.

Bat Bats are creatures of darkness and symbolic of evil. Because they shun the light of day they are associated with night and the devil. However, they roost in communities so they also represent the cohesive power of common affection. They are a forbidden food in the dietary laws.

Bear According to the bestiaries bear cubs were born formless and were literally 'licked into shape' by the mother. The medieval church made this act into a symbol of the heathen converting to Christianity. A bear can also symbolise gluttony and sloth because it feeds on others' labours, i.e. it steals honey from the hives of the bees that make it. It can also represent lust and typifies the devil and Satan. It can be found dancing or playing musical instruments. Bear baiting along with cock fighting, was a very popular sport in the Middle Ages. A heraldic bear with a ragged staff is the badge of Robert Dudley, Earl of Leicester, and of the Warwick's.

Beaver Considered by the bestiaries to be the most gentle of animals the beaver was pursued for its testicles which were believed to have medicinal properties. When hunted the animal would bite them off and throw them to the hunters to escape being killed. If chased a second time, it would lift itself up and show the hunters that the organs were not there. The moral was that those wishing to follow God's ways must cut themselves off from vice and cast such things to the devil which would then leave them alone.

Camel It is stated by the bestiaries that the female camel kneels in adoration, in humility and in pleas for copulation. Symbolically, when kneeling to take up a load, this is Christ's humility in taking on the sins of the world (John 1:29). The camel is a metaphor for Israel (Jeremiah 2:23), and a symbol of temperance.

Cat The cat and monkey are symbols of heresy, and the bestial, lustful part of man's nature was portrayed by these animals, but the cat may also be a symbol of watchfulness against heresy from its ability to see in the dark. A cat illustrated with mice is 'evil lying in wait' or the devil catching souls. A domestic cat may also be encountered. A cat and mouse appear as a domestic subject in the Chapter House in York Minster. Unusually the animals are found in foliage with the cat peering out at the mouse. Another cat and mouse are in Beverley.

Cattle The ox typifies patience and gentleness. In primitive religions, the bull was an object of worship for its strength and fertilising power. The winged ox is the symbol of Saint Luke the Evangelist.

Deer Deer signify piety and religious aspirations, whilst the hart is a symbol of good in both pagan and Christian beliefs. A hart or a stag with a serpent symbolises Christ waging war on the devil. A hart or stag on its own represents a soul thirsting after salvation: 'As the hart panteth after water brooks so panteth my soul after thee O God.' (Psalm 42:1). Stags, when they were ill, were credited with an appetite for serpents, which they were said to suck out from their holes and, after eating them, were restored to health. This is indicative of a bestiary source as deer would not favour such a diet. It was also believed that the stag was the dragon's enemy 'which, on being sighted, fled into a crevice, whereupon the stag drank from a stream and squirted water into the crack thus drawing out the dragon'. It was then stamped upon and killed. A hart at rest is the badge of Richard 11. A stag with a crown around its neck is an emblem of the French Royal house from the reign of Charles V11 (1403-61). A stag with a crucifix between its antlers is the attribute of Hubert or Eustace. Saint Giles befriended a hind which was later shot with an arrow. Stag hunting scenes are not uncommon.

Dog When used as a footrest to recumbent effigies, dogs are a symbol of fidelity and watchfulness, but they are symbols of vice and gluttony when depicted as hounds chasing a hare.

Donkey It is surprising that the word 'donkey' was not used until the late 18th century. It is perhaps a word referring to the dun colour of animal's coat. According to tradition Christ rode in triumph to Jerusalem on the back of an ass and the animal has worn the cross ever since. See Ass above.

Elephant

Early carvings depict the tusks in the lower jaw projecting upwards instead of in the upper jaw pointing downwards. The elephant was a gentle animal whose lifespan was said to be between two and three hundred years. It bred only once during its lifetime. Wanting a baby, the female gave a mandrake to her mate. Eating this caused the formerly platonic couple to mate. The animals travelled as far east as possible to copulate and when the calf was due, the cow immersed herself up to her abdomen in water and gave birth whilst the bull stood guard in case a dragon attacked. Elephants were supposed to possess the virtue of modesty and for this reason the genitalia were put on backwards, so whilst copulating, they could look in opposite directions. In fact the testicles are internal and descend prior to copulation. Before he ate the forbidden fruit which she gave him, Adam was believed to have no carnal knowledge of Eve. The mandrake represents the fruit of the Tree of Knowledge. The ability of the mandrake to aid fertility is mentioned in the Bible (Genesis 30:14-24). Rachel's barren womb is made fertile by God after she accepted the mandrakes which Reuben offered to her. Elephants never quarrelled with their mates nor committed adultery. They took care of and looked after tired and wounded members of the herd. Man could learn from and apply these virtues to his own life. The elephant could also stand for the Fall of Man. Since it was believed to have no joints in its legs it could rest only by leaning against a tree and when the tree against which it rested was sawn through by a hunter, it fell and could not get up. Other elephants (prophets) would try unsuccessfully to raise it and then a young elephant (Christ) would put his trunk beneath the fallen animal and lift it up. The elephant which came to this country in 1255 was a gift from King Louis to King Henry111 and was kept in the Tower of London. This beast was drawn more or less accurately by Mathew Paris, a monk. Previously, carvers and others would have had to rely on traveller's descriptions of the animal as they would not have seen one for themselves. In the Middle Ages it was thought that Indians and Persians would fight from the howdah on the creature's back. The howdahs became wooden castles and were frequently carved with soldiers inside them, hence the fairly common inn signs of the Elephant and Castle. Examples of elephants bearing howdahs can be found in Beverley Minster and St Mary's. In Ripon the castle contains what is believed to be eleven of the twelve disciples with the twelfth, Judas, being held in the animal's trunk. 1Maccabees Chapter 4:34-39 describes the elephant as a fighting animal. The wooden turret became the indestructible church supported by Mary - the elephant - or alternatively, it could represent the warrior animal fighting the dragon of evil. See Dragon under Fabulous/Mythical Beasts.

Fox Representations of foxes are many and varied. They can symbolise the cunning and the guile of the devil; vice and gluttony when carrying a hare, goose or other bird and they can be a satirical reference to the mendicant orders when found preaching. Reynard is the wicked hero of epic poems and fables; the personification of hypocrisy, deceit and evil "Beware of false prophets --- in sheep's clothing" (Matthew 7:15) is represented as a fox in vestments preaching to a congregation of farmyard birds. The fox will suddenly pounce on one of the audience, thus signifying the devil as a sly thief and murderer capturing the souls of the unwary. The same theme could also indicate unworthy priests who were more likely to fleece than to feed their flock, or tyrannical landowners who stole the livelihood of the poor.

Giraffe One of the animals depicted as part of creation.

Goat The goat is an ambivalent symbol representing both good and evil. The good goat of the bestiary had keen eyesight and was found on high mountains. It could tell whether men were travellers or hunters coming to kill it. This represented Christ the far-seeing Son of God who foresaw His own betrayal by Judas. It also signified the Christian browsing on the bush of truth. The evil goat stands for the damned at the Last Judgement, (Matthew 25: 32-33, 41). The wild goats of the Bible are Nubian Ibex. Symbolically, when the ibex falls over a cliff, it is protected by its horns. This is interpreted as learned men cushioned by the Old and New Testaments. In antiquity it was a symbol of lust.

Hare Timidity and cowardice were portrayed in medieval days as a knight pursued by a hare. A hare riding a hound is an example of the topsy turvey theme where the correct order of things was turned upside down. Saint Martin of Tours and Saint Melangell were the protectors of hares. See Rabbit.

Hedgehog A symbol of vice, gluttony and covetousness, the hedgehog is said by the bestiaries to feed its young on grapes which it impales on its prickles and then takes back to its offspring or, alternatively, it hoards them for the winter. It thus symbolises the deceits of the devil who robs men of their souls. In fact the animal neither eats nor feeds its babies on grapes and does not store food for the winter.

Horse Both Old and New Testaments refer to horse owners as being associated with war and power. Lechery can be signified by the horse and it may also symbolise fidelity and virility.

Hyena Generally considered to be a dirty brute, it was said to live in sepulchres where it fed upon corpses. Its spine was thought to be rigid and thus the beast was unable to turn without turning its whole body. From time to time it was believed to change sex, so being neither male nor female it was likened to the Jews who were neither pagan nor faithful. The reason for this belief lies with the female. She has an appendage which is similar in looks and position but not in function to the male penis. The animal was a symbol of many evils:- avarice, hypocrisy, impurity and wantonness. It signifies the Jew who first had knowledge of the true living God, but now subsists on dry bones and dead ceremonials. The Jews were the prophets of the Messiah and foretold His advent but rejected Him when He appeared. The creature was a type of Jew of whom the prophet Jeremiah said "My heritage is made for me as the den of the hyena"; the den meaning the synagogue. When shown with a corpse it symbolises vice battening on corruption. The animal was supposed to have a stone in its eye which, when placed under a man's tongue, gave him the gift of prophecy. The bestiary hyena with its title is carved on a medallion in the doorway of Alne.

Kangaroo No religious or symbolic significance has so far been discovered

Leopard The leopard is symbolic of cruelty, evil and sin. In Jeremiah (13:23), the question is asked "Can the Ethiopian change his skin or the leopard his spots?". It was thought that the leopard was the result of the adultery of a lioness and a pard (panther).

Lion The lion may signify pride and vice, an evil to be fought, or it may signify courage, strength, vigilance and virtue. The king of beasts symbolises Christ as the king of all people. The bestiary lion when it smells a hunter erases its footprints by sweeping with its tail so the hunter cannot find and follow its tracks. This is emblematic of Christ who hides His heavenly origins in human form. It was also interpreted as the Incarnation, when God sent his Son in human flesh to cheat the devil and redeem mankind. In the Middle Ages the lion was a symbol of the resurrection because, according to the bestiary story, when lion cubs are born they lie dead for three days. Then the father brings them to life by either roaring or breathing in their faces. The bestiary also states that when a lion sleeps his eyes remain open. This belief caused images of lions to be placed at the doors of churches to act as guardians of the sanctuary. Also when sleeping with its eyes open as carved on a misericord in Ripon Cathedral, this equates with the Song of Songs "I sleep and my heart is awake". The lion represents evil when its jaws are rent by Samson or when it is found fighting Samson (Judges 14:5-6). The medieval church interpreted this as the struggle of Christ against the devil (Peter 5:8). David 'delivered' a lamb out of the lion's mouth (1Samuel 17:35). Other bestiary beliefs were that a sick lion will eat a monkey to cure itself and that lions fear cocks, especially white ones. The lioness had a reputation for infidelity because a leopard was believed to be the offspring of a lioness and a pard (panther). The lion probably occurs more frequently than any other animal.

Marten No religious or symbolic significance but the animal may occur as an attribute of Saint Martin of Tours.

Mole The habitat and poor eyesight of this animal symbolised those 'engrossed with earthly cares and vain delights', or, because it lives underground and has poor eyesight, the heretic blind to the true faith.

Monkey The physical, lustful bestial part of man's nature and vice and wickedness were represented and symbolised by the creature. One holding an owl signifies lust producing spiritual blindness. In the Middle Ages the monkey, like the ape, was usually a satirical reference particularly in attacks on physicians. Like the ass it was an announcer of the equinox, but not by using its voice as the ass does, but by urinating seven times.

Moose No religious or symbolic significance has as yet been discovered.

Mouse and Rat Mice and rats are symbols of decay and passing time, or evil destructively gnawing away substance. Saint Colman was kept awake by a mouse nibbling his ear whilst he was working in the scriptorium and a fly kept his place on the page whilst he attended services. The mouse is the maker's mark of a modern carver – Robert Thompson of Kilburn.

Otter An enemy of the crocodile the otter wallows in mud until thickly coated. When this has dried and hardened to form armour, it runs into the crocodile's jaws, down its throat and into its intestines which the otter then eats, thus killing the crocodile. The otter emerges unharmed as Our Lord rose from the grave on the third day, alive and uninjured.

Rabbit Rabbits arrived with the Normans, presumably so did some of the symbolism attached to them. They were kept by monks and nuns on islands called coney - garths. It was held that a newly born rabbit could be eaten on a

Friday (fish day) because it swam in amniotic fluid. The symbol of three rabbits or hares with three ears between them chasing each other in a circle is a motif in Christian, Buddhist and Islamic art. Dating from the late 6th/early 7th centuries it is found in Buddhist cave temples. In Cornwall a circle of three rabbits with three ears between them is a symbol of the tinners and is also known as the Tinners' Trinity. In some other counties they represent the Holy Trinity and may also represent eternity. A burrow into which a rabbit enters is representative of a sepulchre, whilst a rabbit coming out of a burrow represents resurrection. Rabbits have been a byword for fecundity in all ages and thus they are a symbol of lust. They may also represent meekness and a soul in danger. Rabbits cooking a hunter over a pot were an example of the topsy turvey theme.

Rhinoceros No religious or symbolic significance has been discovered so far.

Sheep In ancient Near Eastern religious rites the lamb was the sacrificial animal, and it was adopted by Christians as a symbol of Christ in His sacrificial role as the Lamb of God or Agnus Dei. Sometimes the Agnus Dei is metamorphosed into a ram and is a reference to the Sacrifice of Isaac when Abraham looked round and saw a ram caught in a thicket (Genesis 22:13). A ram can also typify Christ's leadership. The ram is a classical symbol of sexuality and the vice of Luxuria (lechery), which is sometimes depicted as a naked female figure riding on the back of a goat, stag or ram.

Shrew No religious or symbolic significance.

Sloth No religious or symbolic significance.

Squirrel It was believed by our forefathers that squirrels crossed water by sitting on a piece of wood and by using their tails as sails. This was later interpreted as Christians crossing the troubled seas of this life on the Cross of Christ. Squirrels are also symbols of the constant strivings of the Holy Spirit. The squirrel's habit of storing nuts for winter made it a symbol of prudence.

Stoat In winter the stoat has white fur except for a black tip to its tail. From the legend that if the whiteness was soiled the animal would die it became a symbol of purity.

Swine For hygienic reasons the Children of Israel were divinely forbidden to eat swine (Leviticus 11:7) and this ban caused the pig to be regarded by Jews as something despicable and hated. The relationship between the animal and a parasitic tape-worm harmful to man was proved in the 19th century. Christ cured the insane by expelling devils and causing them to enter the Gadarene swine. In Luke (15:15) the Prodigal Son has sunk as low as possible when feeding the swine of the Gentile. Music especially when played on wind instruments by pigs symbolised the ascendancy of animality over spirituality with bagpipes being the devil's instruments. A boar was evil personified and symbolised sensual greed but it also symbolised courage. Boar hunting scenes can be symbolic, the hunters representing priests who are trying to destroy the sins of which the boar is a symbol. In the West Country, a sow and farrow, in commemoration for marking a divinely selected site, are portrayed on roof bosses and bench ends. A pig is said to have carried stones in its mouth from an unfinished church to a new site hallowed by the blood of Saint Oswald. It is an attribute of Saint Anthony of Egypt who is a Christian saint said to be the founder of monasticism. The pig is supposed to have been his only companion during his meditations in the desert. In the 11th century, during an epidemic of what was thought to be erysipelas, many cures were claimed in the saint's name and the disease became known as St Anthony's fire. He is depicted holding a bell and accompanied by a pig. The bell sometimes hangs round the animal's neck. Lard obtained from the creature was used as a remedy for the ailment. Richard 11 had a boar as his emblem. In the 17th century the Hospital Brothers of St Anthony were allowed special grazing rights for their herds. Wild boar hunting and pig killing are often featured. In the Occupations of the Months series (a Kalender illustrating the farming year), October's occupation is knocking down acorns to feed the pigs and November's is pig killing. In heraldry the pig appears, like the lion and the leopard, on the coat of arms of Henry 111 and it was the badge of the House of York.

Tiger The tiger was believed to have been deceived by its own reflection and it is therefore a symbol of man 'taken in by unreal 'vanities'. The story is told by Pliny, of the tigress who is tremendously swift. Whilst the mother is away from the lair, a hunter steals the cubs and escapes on horseback. When pursued by the angry tigress, he throws down a cub which the tigress returns to the lair. She then continues to pursue the hunter who throws down another cub and this goes on till the hunter reaches his ship. This story was modified in the medieval bestiaries with the hunter keeping the cubs and throwing down either a mirror or a crystal ball. On seeing her own reflection the tigress mistakes it for her cub. This story illustrates a warning against decoys which enable the devil to steal men's souls. The mirror was a 'token of the pursuit of goodness interrupted by the blandishments of the world'.

Walrus No religious or symbolic significance.

Weasel It was thought that the female weasel received the male's sperm in her mouth and that the young were born through her ears. From her left ear came young females and from her right young males. Some theologians believed that the Holy Messenger speaking into the Virgin's ear caused her to conceive. See also Dove under Birds and Basilisk under Fabulous and Mythical Beasts.

Whale The Leviathan mentioned in Psalm 104:26 is believed to be a whale as is the Aspido Chelone of the bestiaries. The Aspido opens its mouth and blows out a sweet-smelling breath which attracts small fish. When the creature feels its mouth is full, it closes it and swallows the catch. This was interpreted as humans who lack faith and become addicted to pleasure and are then gobbled up by the devil.

Wolf The wolf of the bestiary could only have cubs during a thunderstorm in May. When it was hungry and no food was to be found it filled its stomach with a ball of clay. On food becoming available it disgorged the clay by putting its paw into its mouth. The wolf was said to bite its own paws to make them tread more softly when the animal was out hunting. It could make a man lose his voice if he had his mouth open when he saw a wolf. Conversely, if the man had his mouth shut when he saw the wolf, then the wolf would be unable to open its mouth again. A wolf will put a paw in its own mouth whilst hunting sheep so as to change its voice, and in this way will frighten the shepherds by the strange noises it makes. This signifies rapacity, wrath and Satan, and is the devil approaching the sheepfold of the followers of Christ (John 10:12). In the Middle Ages it was a symbol of evil because of its cunning, greed and fierceness. It was seen as typical of stiff-necked people, as it was thought not to have any joints in its neck so that it was unable to move its head from side to side. It was a symbol of evil, common to both pagan and Christian beliefs.

Zebra Windows illustrating scenes of the creation sometimes feature a zebra.

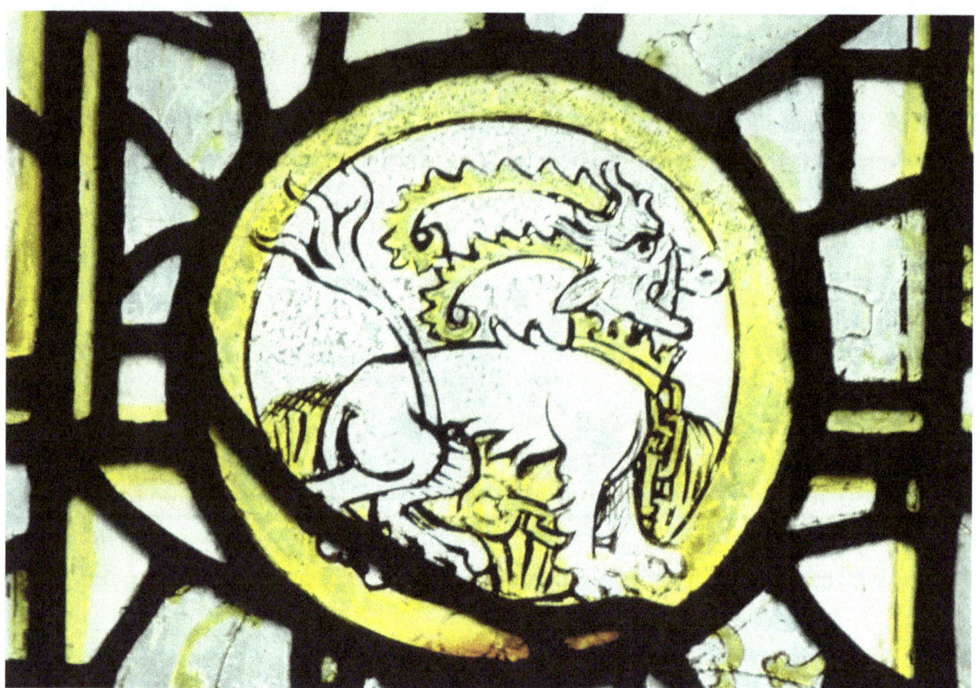

Antelope gorged and chained. The badge of Henry VI. Roundel, 1437. St Martyn le Grand, York.

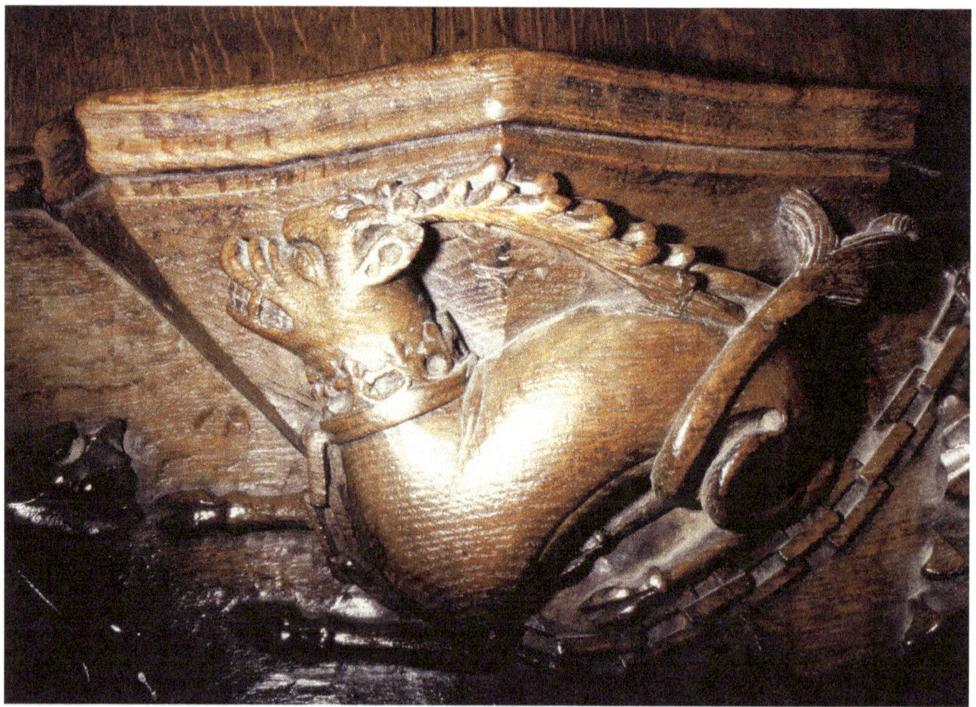

Antelope, gorged and chained. Misericord, 1489-94. Ripon Cathedral.

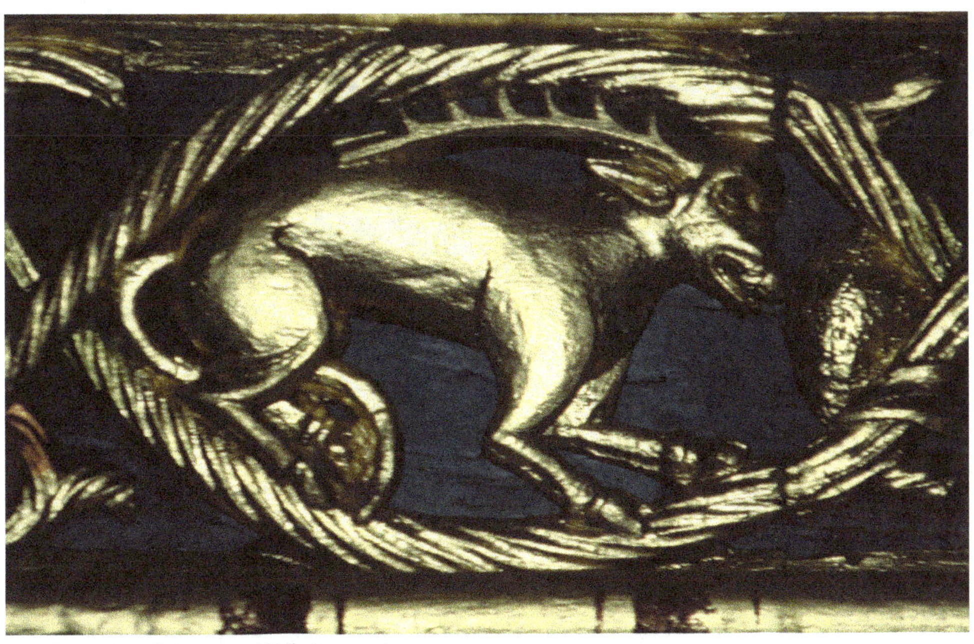

Antelope. Rood Screen, 1506. Aysgarth.

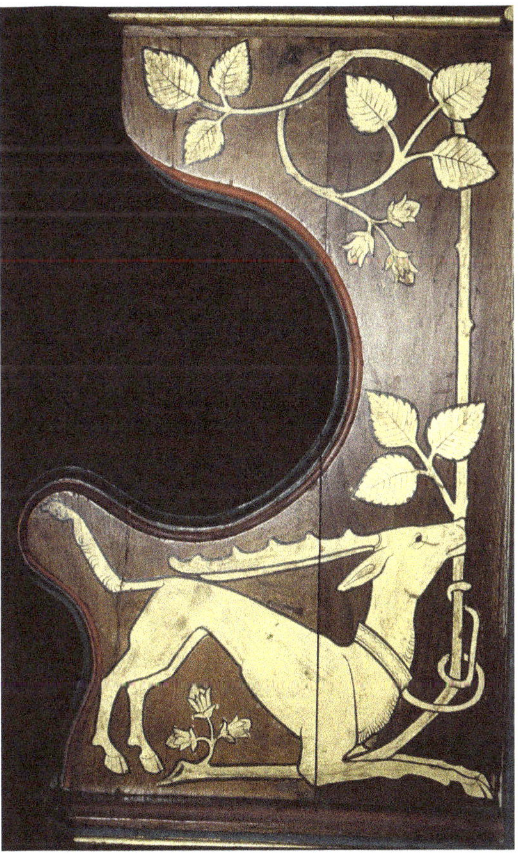

Antelope gorged and chained, twig of hazel leaves and nuts. Stall end, 1506. Aysgarth.

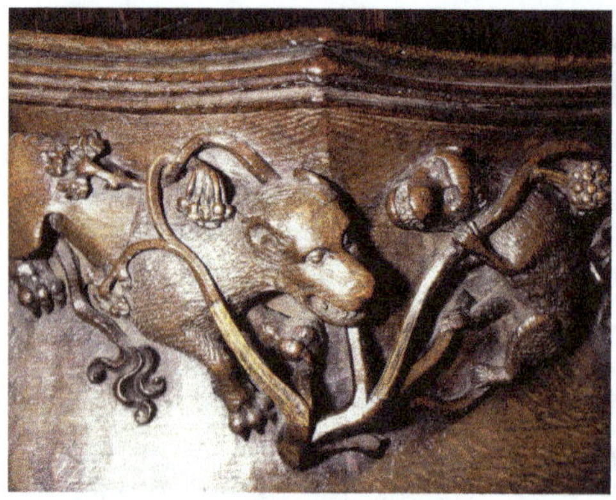
Ape attacked by lion. Misericord, 1489-94. Ripon Cathedral.

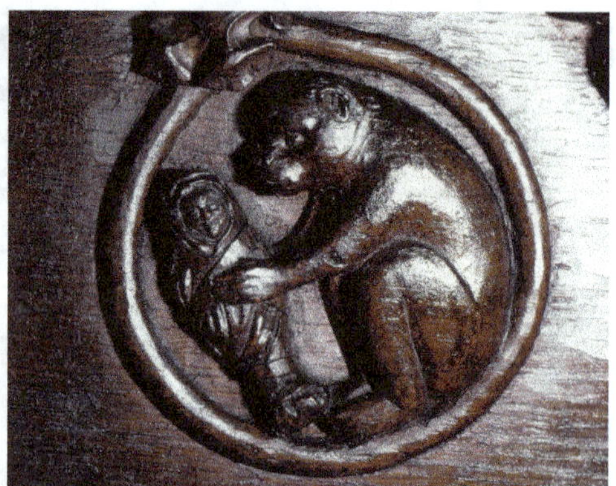
Ape holding or nursing either a child or a toy. Supporter, 1520. Beverley Minster.

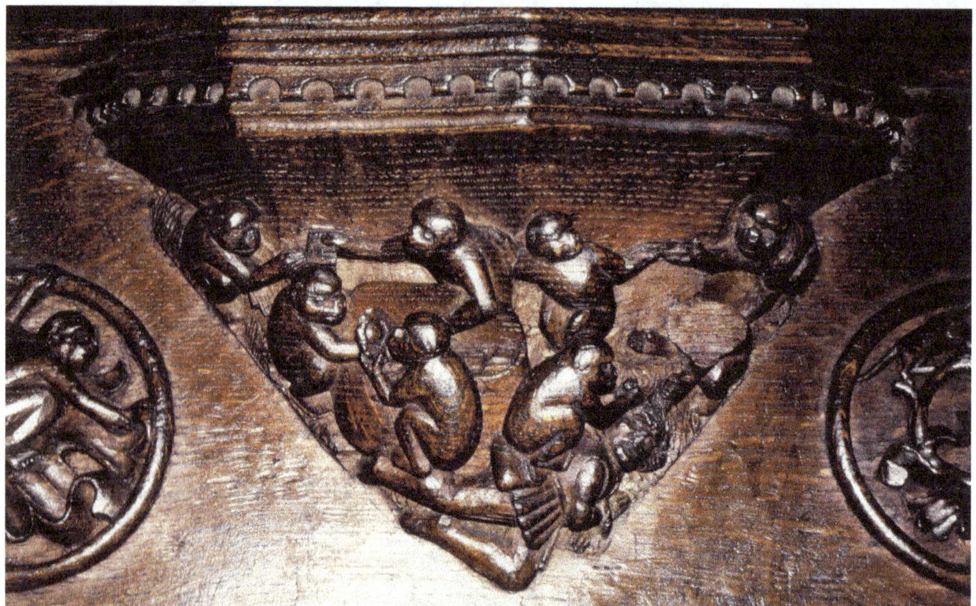
Apes, one with a mirror another with a comb, rob a peddler and pull his hair. Misericord, 1520. Beverley Minster.

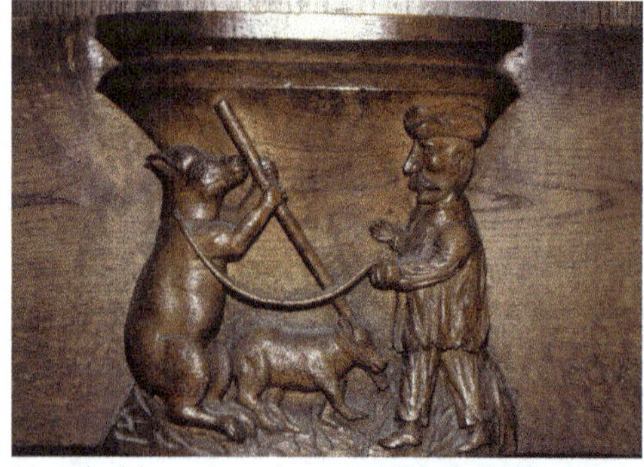
Muzzled bear carrying a staff is led by a man, between them is a bear cub also muzzled. Misericord, modern. Old Malton Priory.

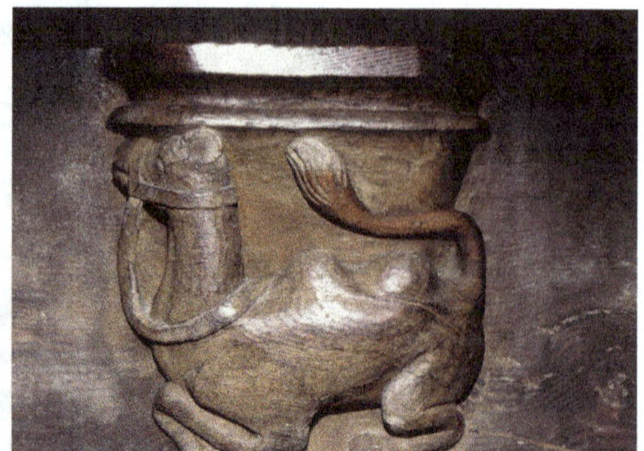
Bactrian Camel, bridled and kneeling. Misericord, late 15th/early 16th century. Old Malton Priory.

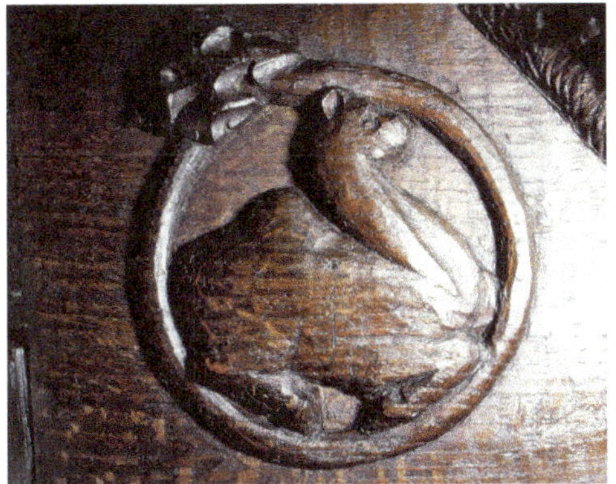

A kneeling Dromedery Camel. Supporter, 1520. Beverley Minster.

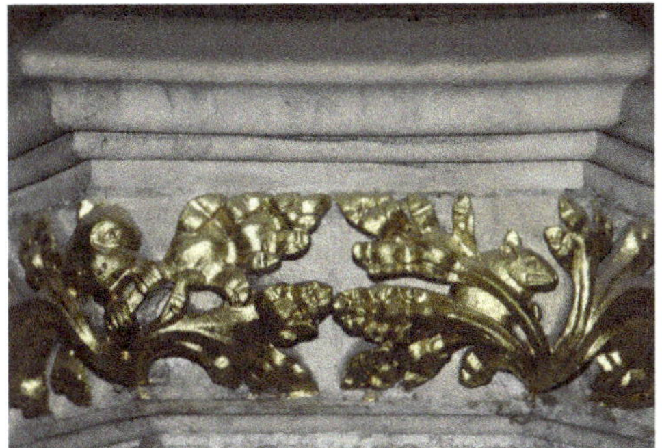

Cat and mouse painted in gold. Screen of Kings, 15th century. York Minster.

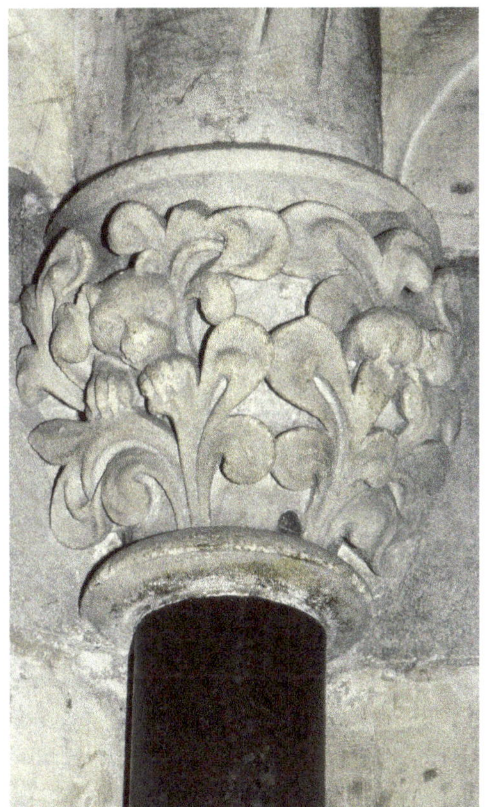

Cat's face and a mouse running away. Capital, 1260-85. York Minster.

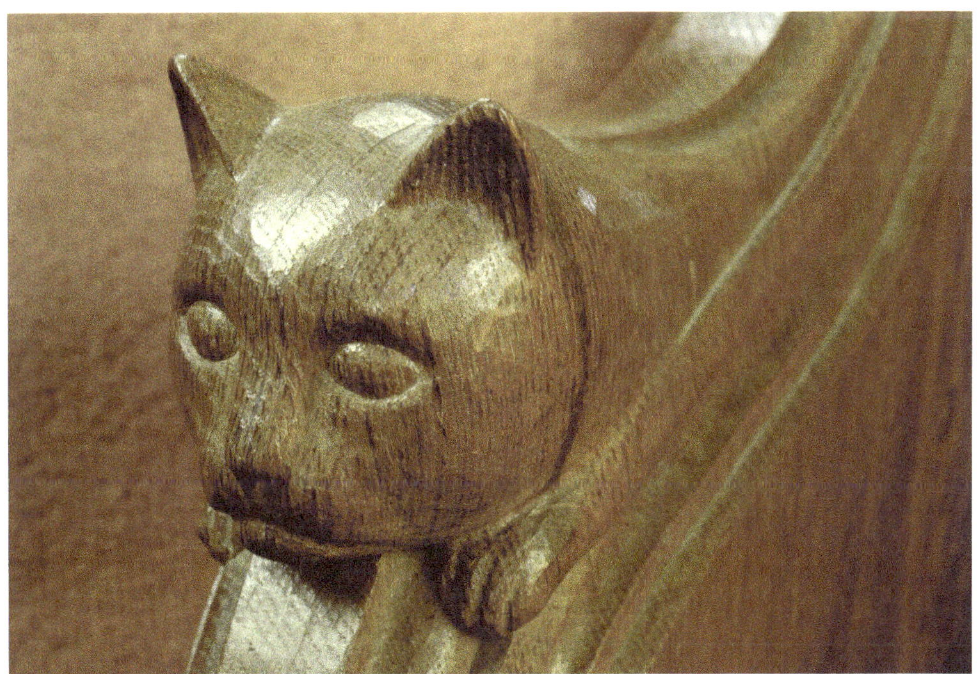

Charming cat's face. Elbow, modern. Hemingborough.

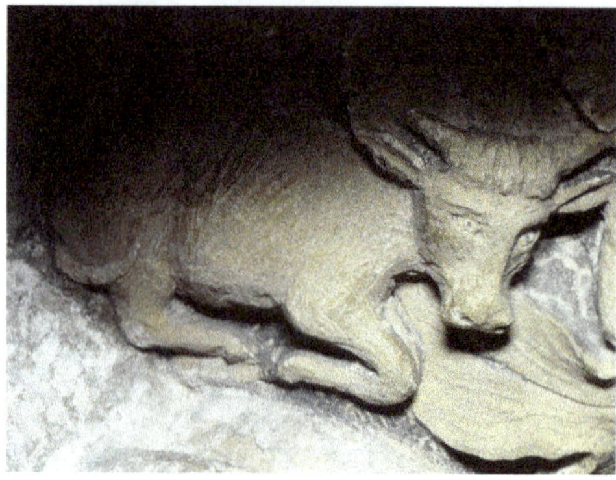

Ox or cow ruminating. Capital, circa 1320. Selby abbey.

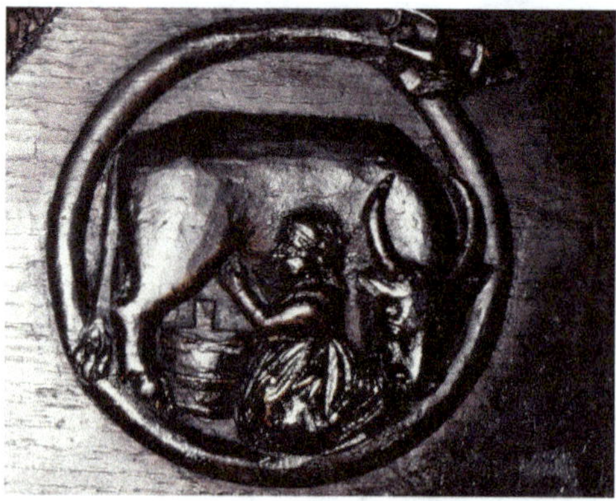

Milkmaid milking a cow. Supporter, 1520. Beverley Minster.

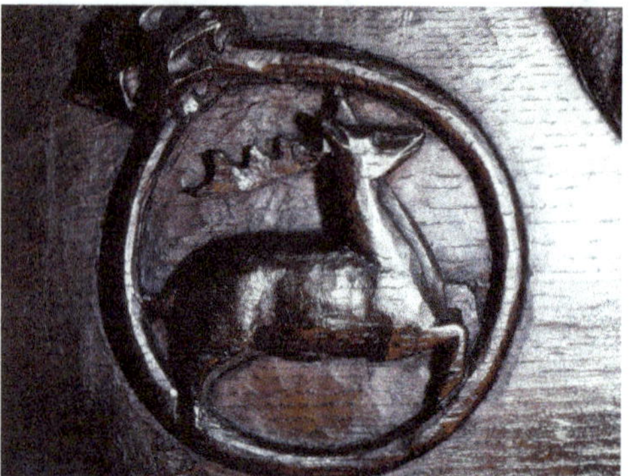

Fallow Deer buck. Supporter, 1520. Beverley Minster.

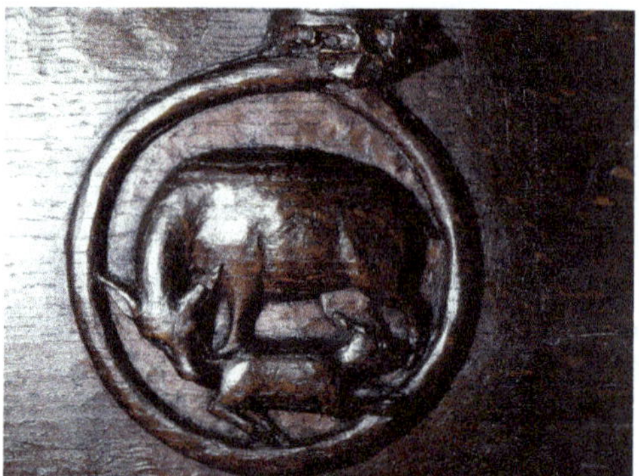

Deer with fawn. Supporter, 1520. Beverley Minster.

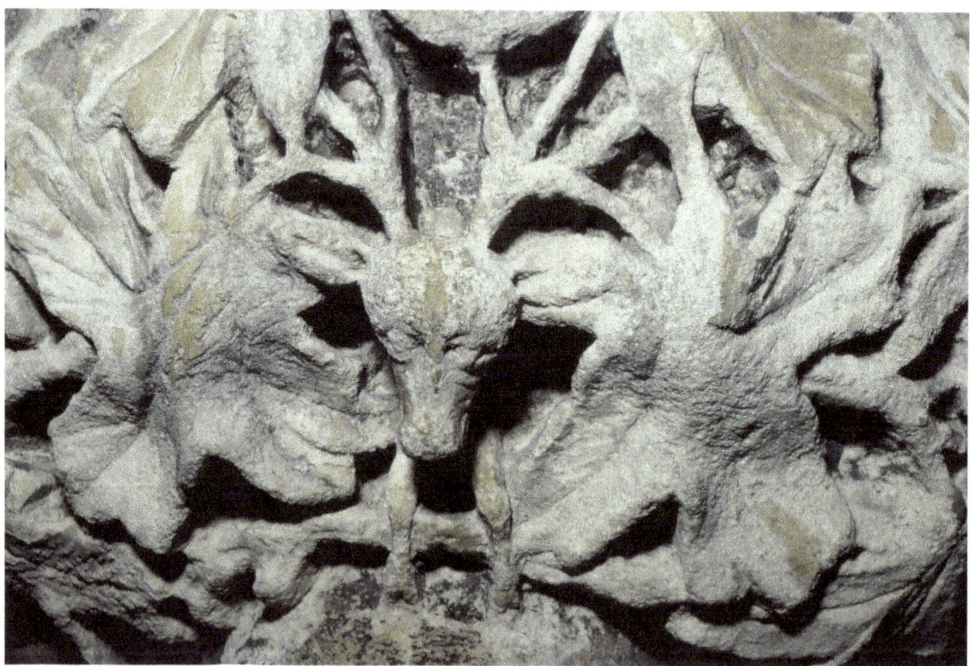

Stag with head and forelegs in foliage. Capital, circa 1250. Selby Abbey.

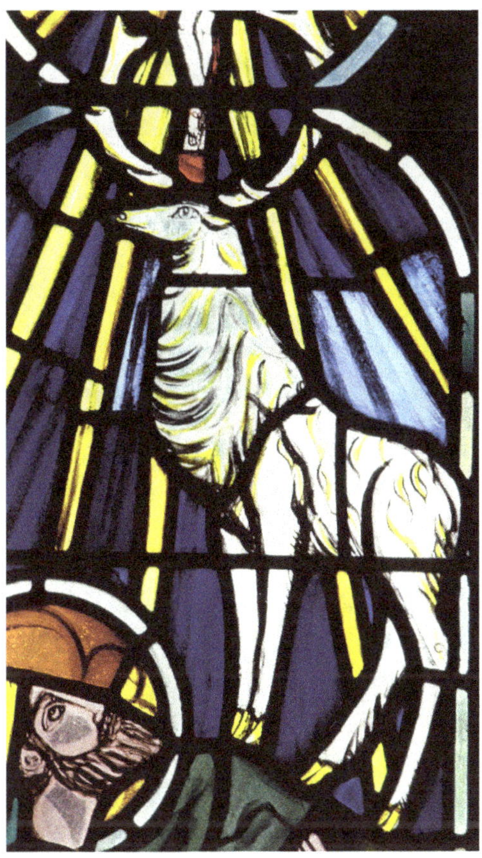

Stag with enormous antlers and looking more like a Borzoi than a deer. Window, 1958. Flockton.

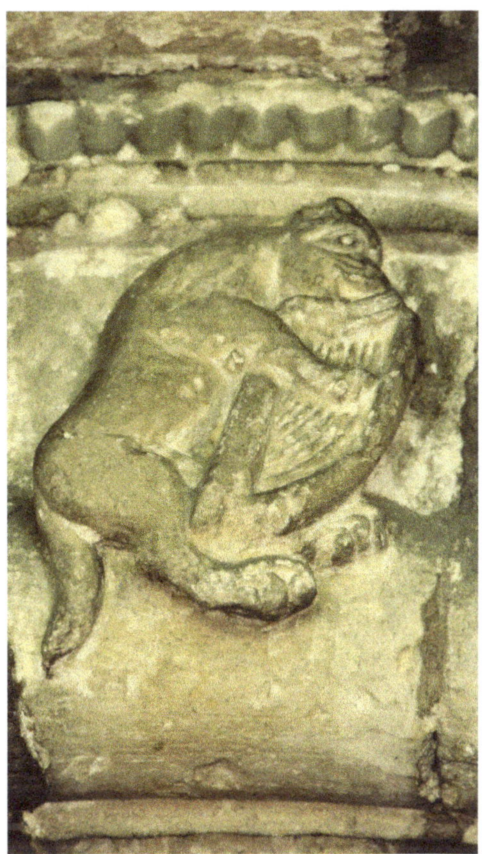

Dog plucking a harp. Doorway, circa 1160. Riccall

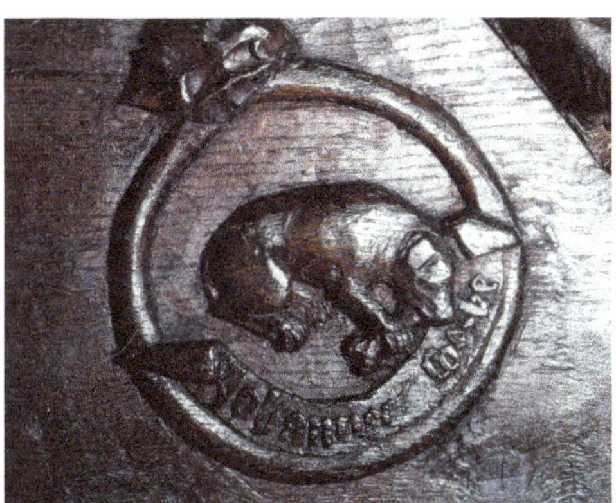

Dog gnawing a bone. Supporter, 1520. Beverley Minster.

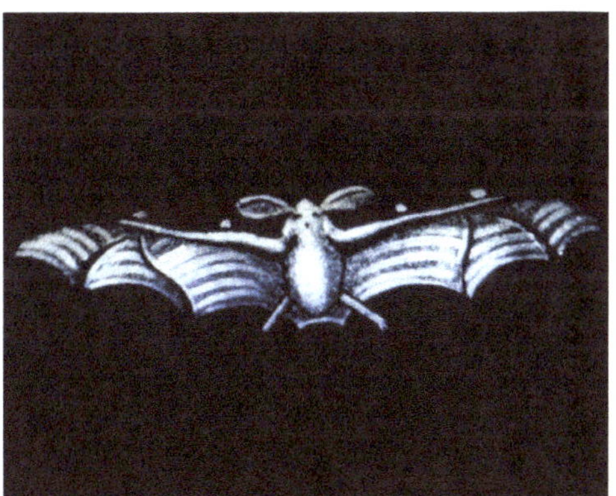

Long-eared Bat, 1930. Baildon

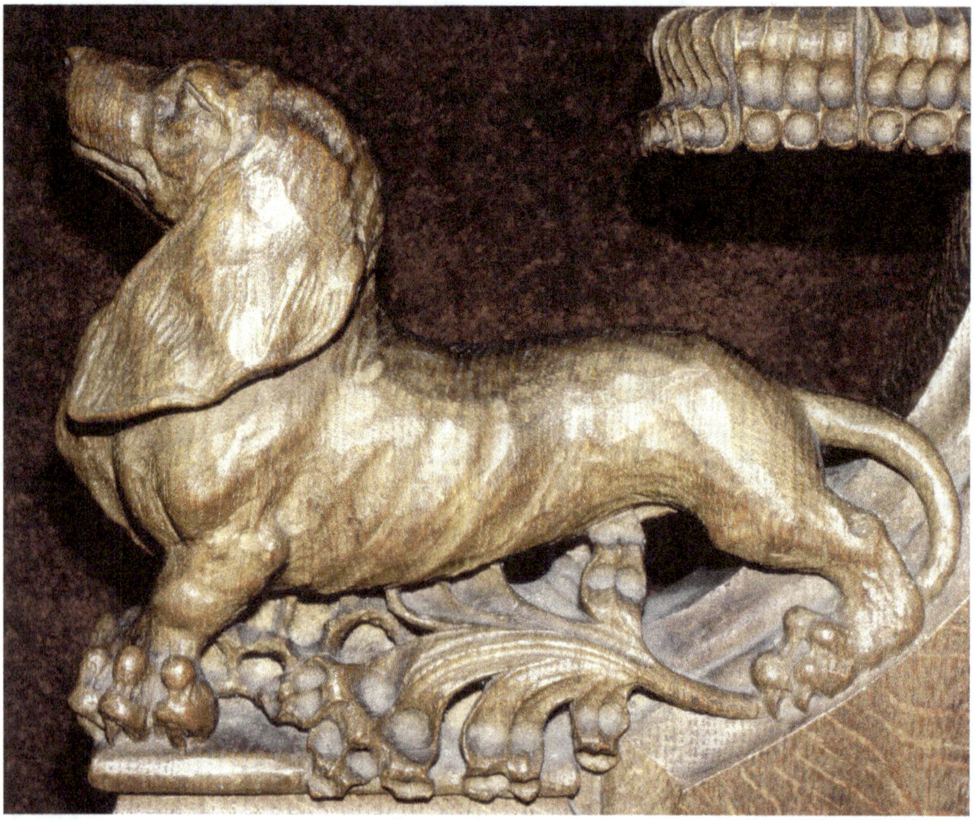

Dachshund. Elbow, modern. Sherburn.

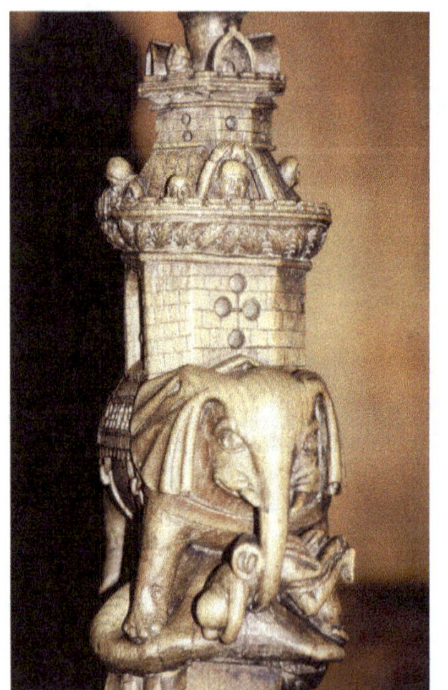

Elephant bearing a castle within which are men. Finial, 1494. Ripon Cathedral.

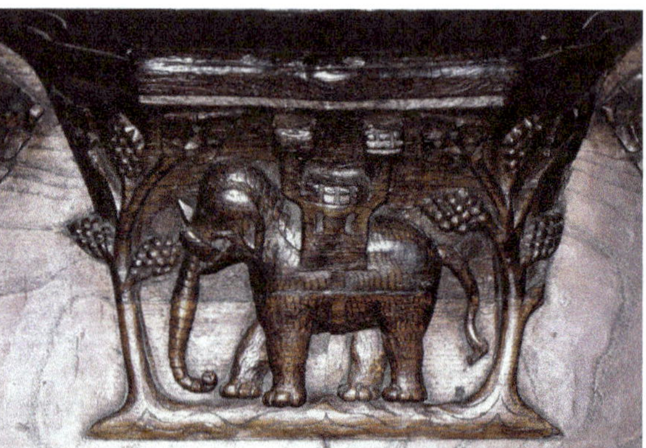

Elephant bearing a most curious howdah. Misericord, 1445. Beverley St Mary.

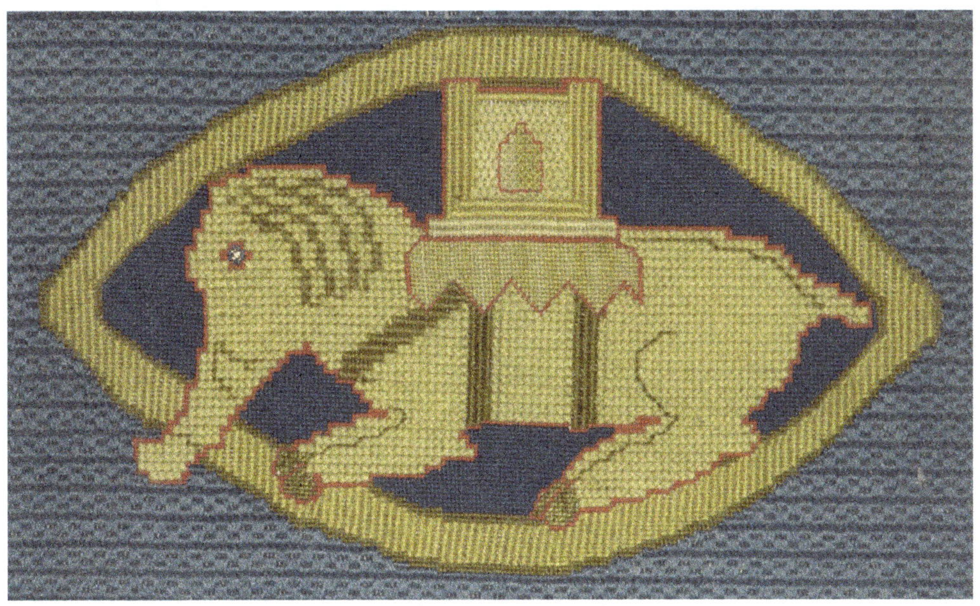

Elephant kneeler, a copy of the one on the screen. Aysgarth.

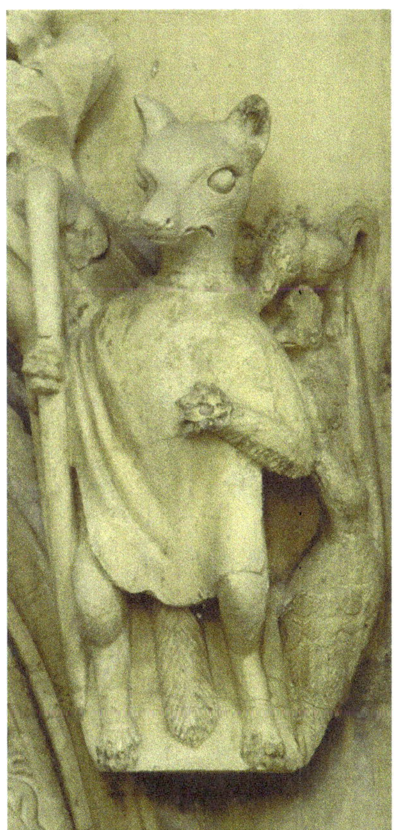

A pilgrim fox leads a cock, hen and duck. Spandrel, early 14th century. Beverley Minster.

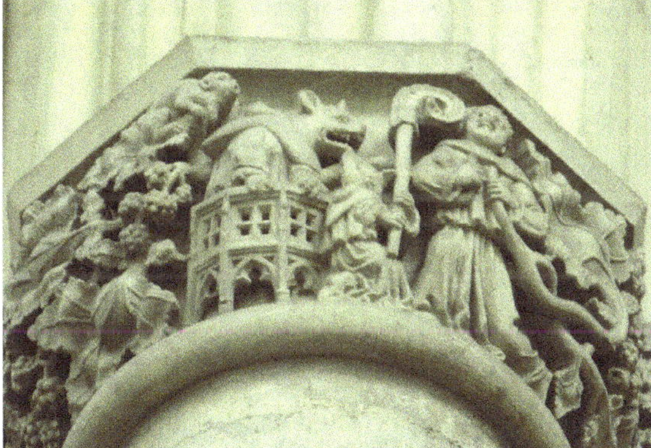

An animal preaching to a fox with a crosier whilst an ape howls in the background. Capital, circa 1400s. York Minster.

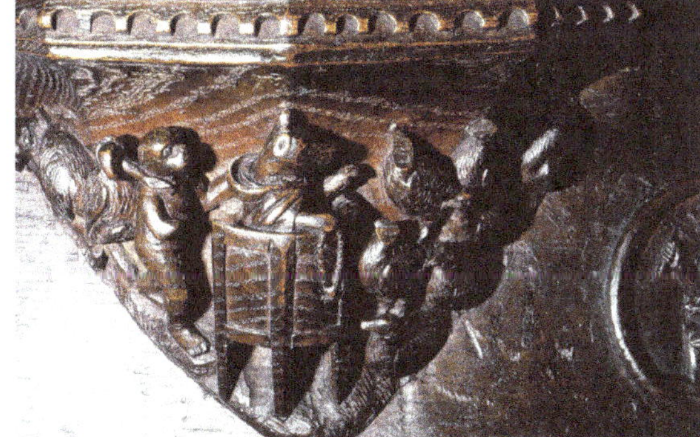

A fox with his rosary preaches to a congregation of birds, whilst behind him an ape dangles a dead goose from a stake. Misericord, 1520. Beverley Minster.

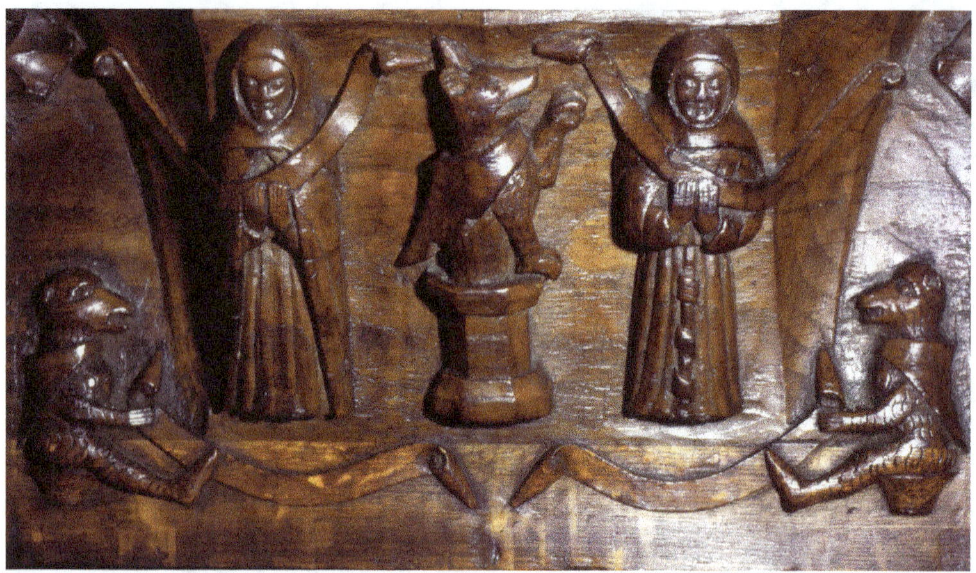

A fox preaches to a monk, nun and two seated apes all holding scrolls, possibly meant to contain the text of the fox's sermon. Misericord, 1445. Beverley St Mary.

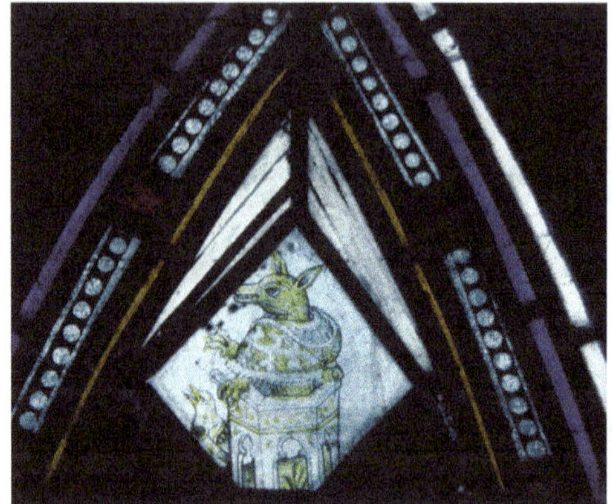

Fox in an ornate pulpit preaching to a bird. Quarry, late 16th century. Kirkby Wharfe.

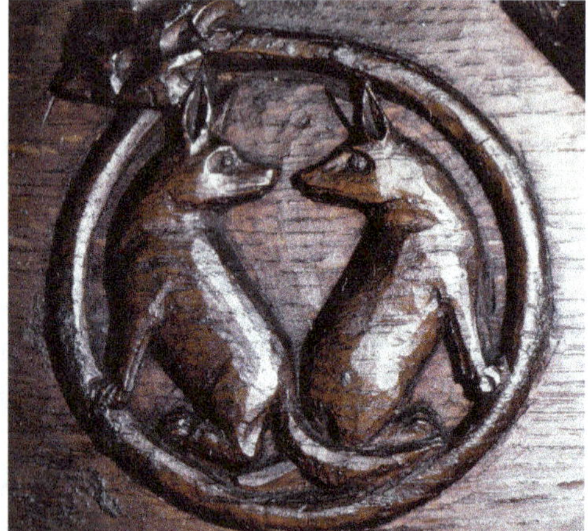

Two foxes plotting mischief. Supporter, 1520, Beverley Minster.

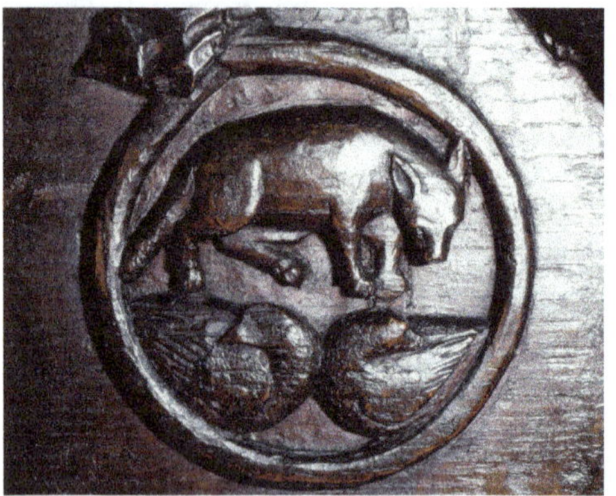

A fox watches two sleeping geese. Supporter, 1520. Beverley Minster.

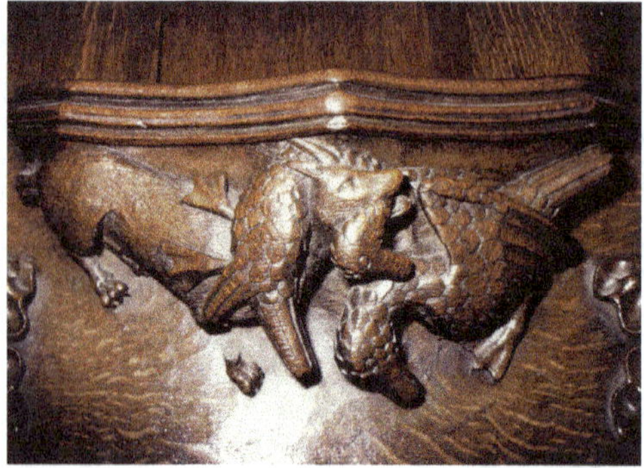

A fox with a goose in its mouth and a sleeping goose. Misericord, 1490. Ripon.

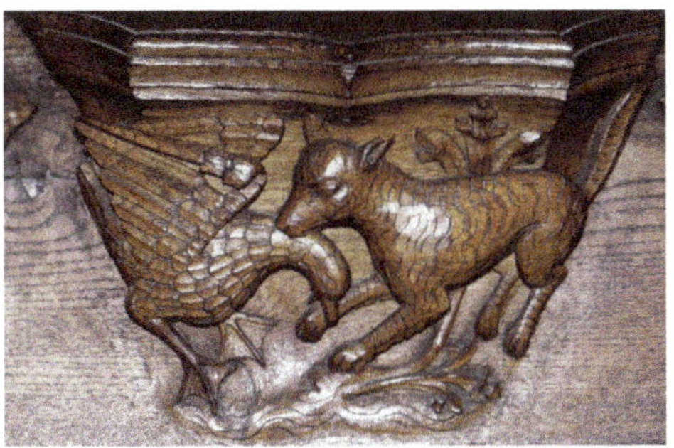
A fox and goose attack each other. Misericord, modern. Beverley St Mary.

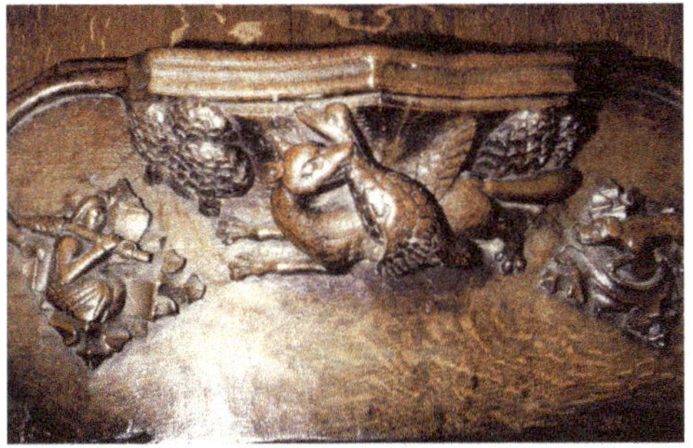
A fox making off with a goose. Supporters are the farmer's wife with her distaff, and a hound in hot pursuit. Misericord, 1490. Ripon Cathedral.

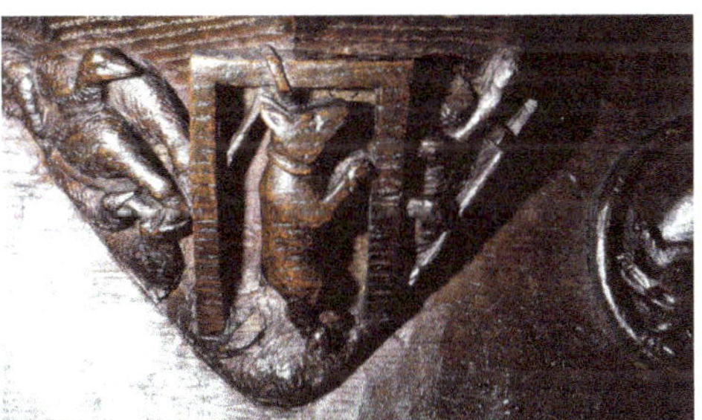
Geese hanging a fox. Misericord, 1520. Beverley Minster.

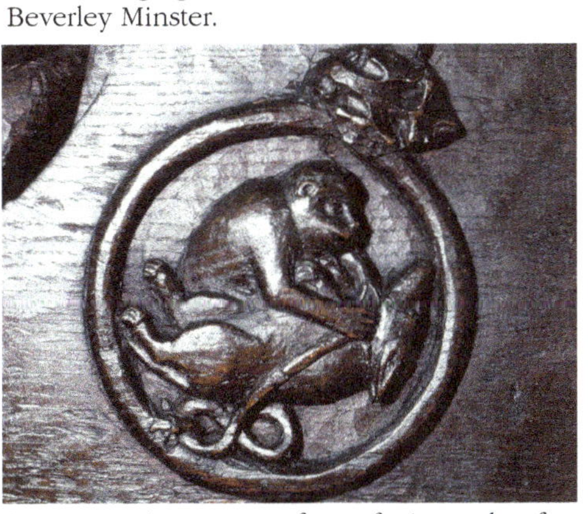
Ape removing noose from fox's neck after hanging. Supporter, 1520. Beverley Minster.

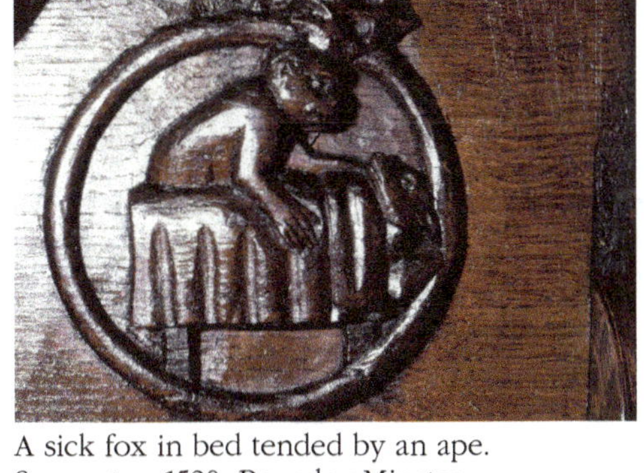
A sick fox in bed tended by an ape. Supporter, 1520. Beverley Minster.

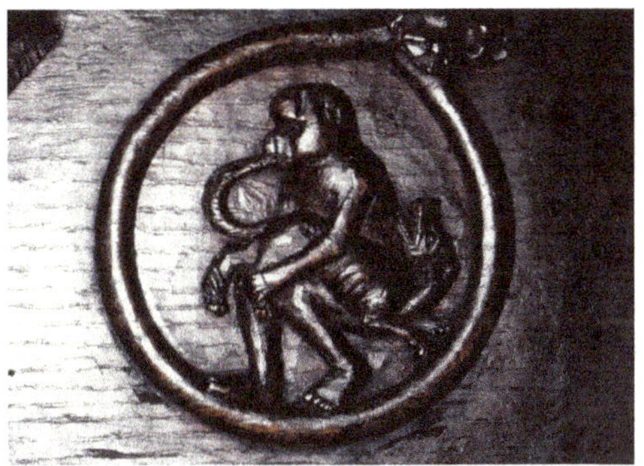
Ape using a fox as bagpipes, biting its tail whilst squeezing its chest. Supporter, 1520. Beverley Minster.

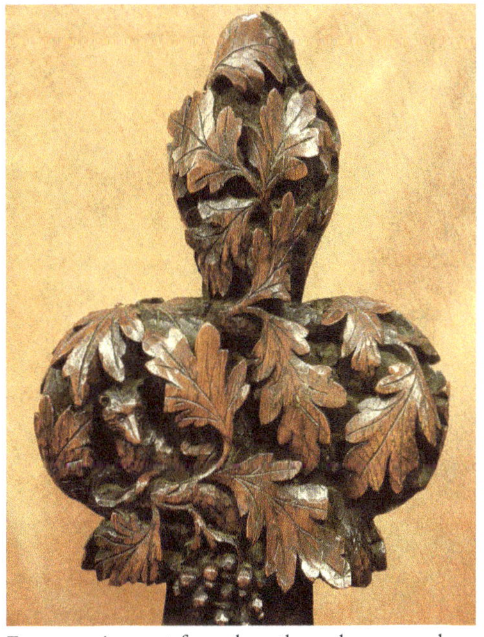
Fox peeping out from hawthorn leaves and berries. Poppyhead, 1858. Rothwell.

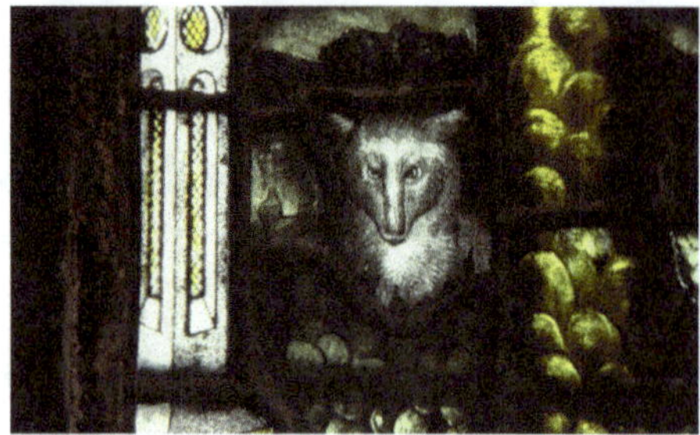

Fox's head detail. Window, 1870. Wakefield.

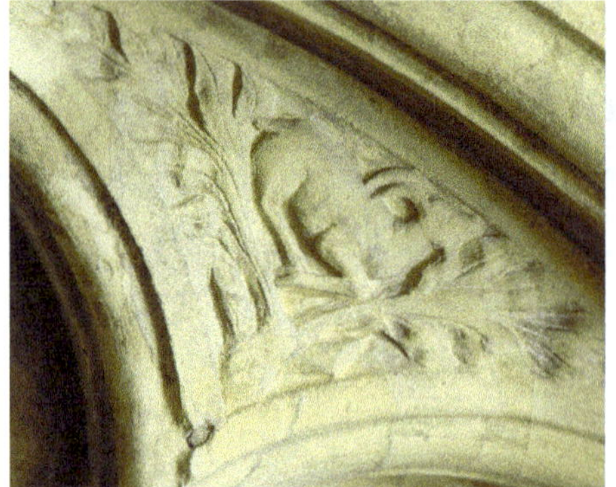

Goat browsing. Spandrel, 14th century. Beverley Minster.

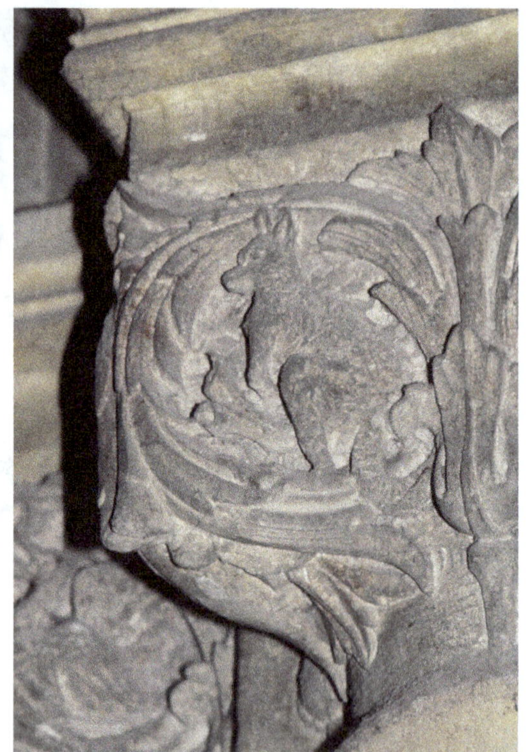

Kangaroo. Capital, 1924-61. Ampleforth.

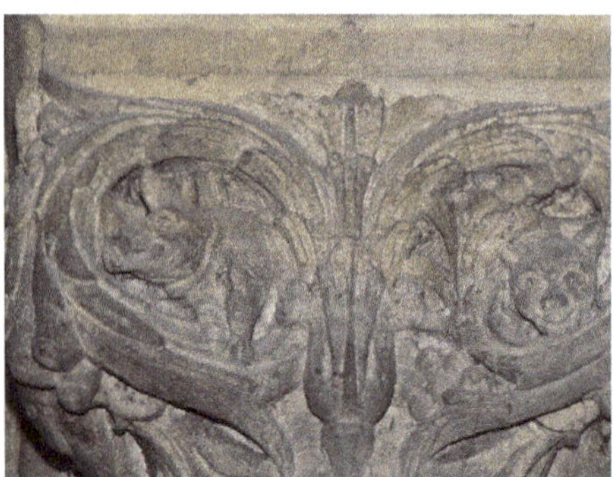

Rhinoceras. Capital, 1924-61. Ampleforth.

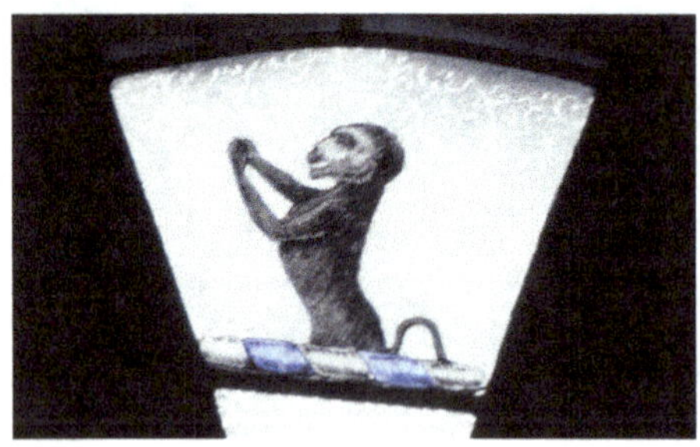

Praying monkey. 15th century. Howden

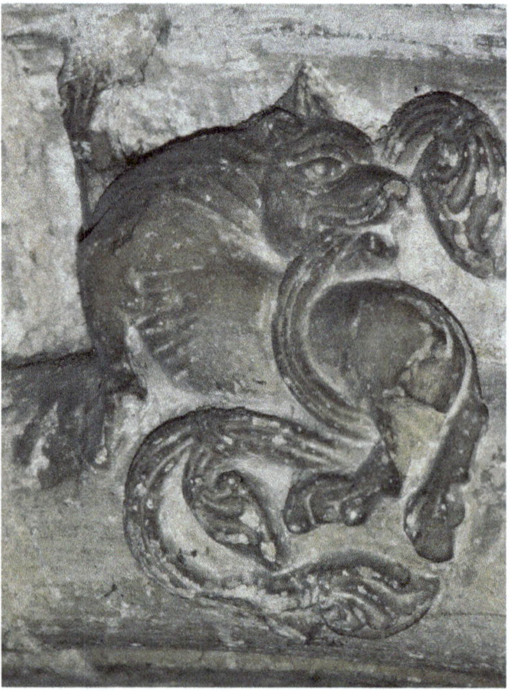

Lion sweeping with its tail in its mouth. Doorway, 1160. Riccall.

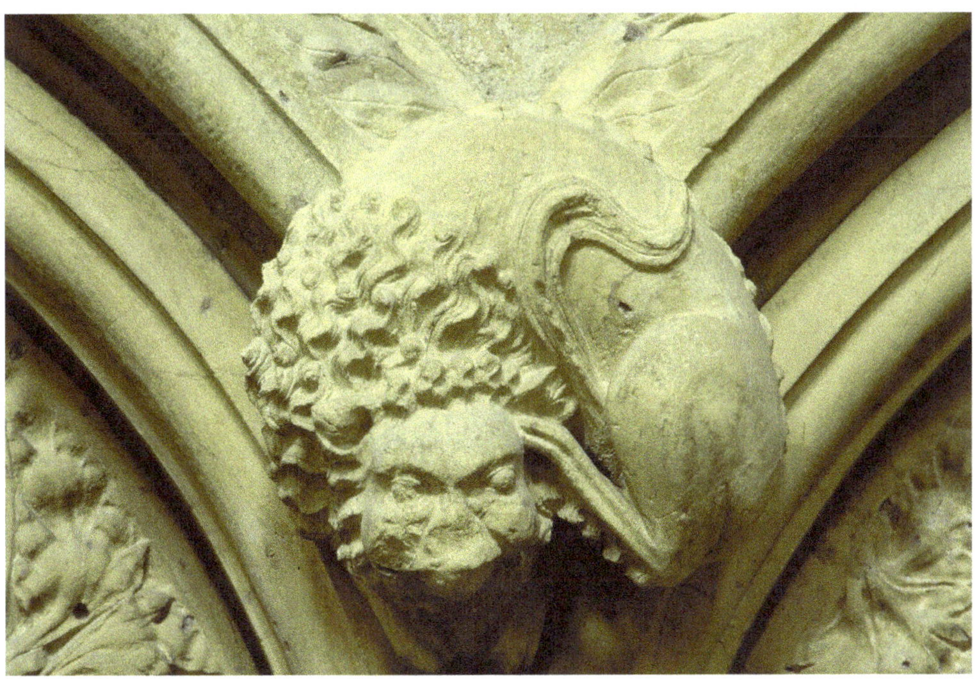

Lion sleeping or scratching its ear. Label Stop, 14th century. Beverley Minster.

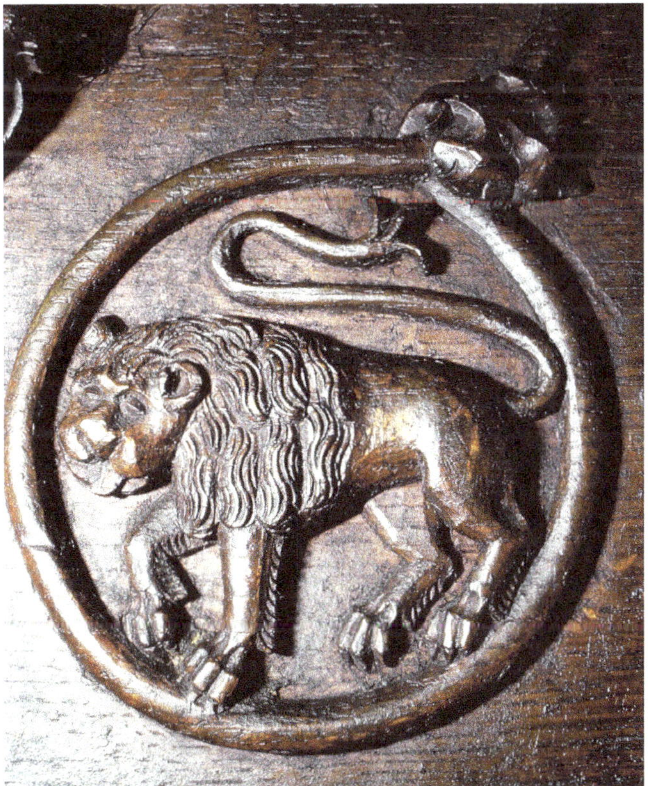

Benign-looking lion. Supporter, 1520.
Beverley Minster.

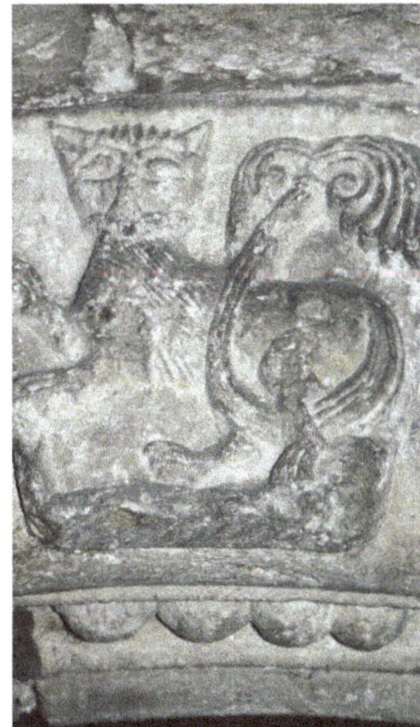

Lion guarding the entrance to the church. Voussoire, 1160. Riccal.

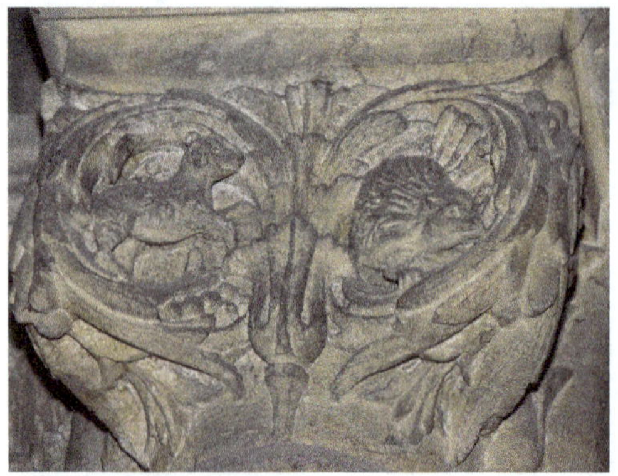
Lamb and hedgehog. Capital, 1924-61. Ampleforth.

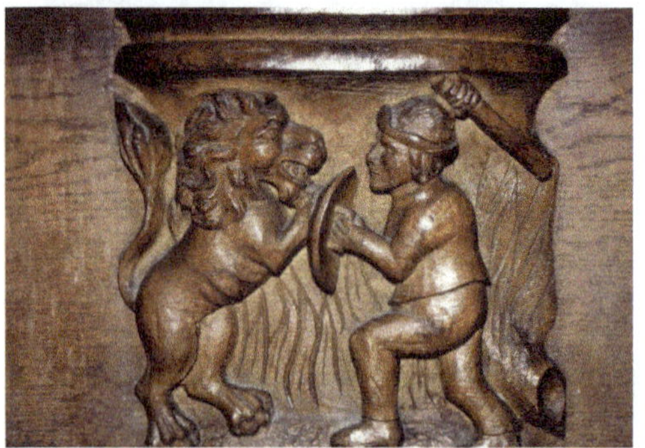
Man with stick and shield fighting a lion . Misericord, modern. Old Malton Priory.

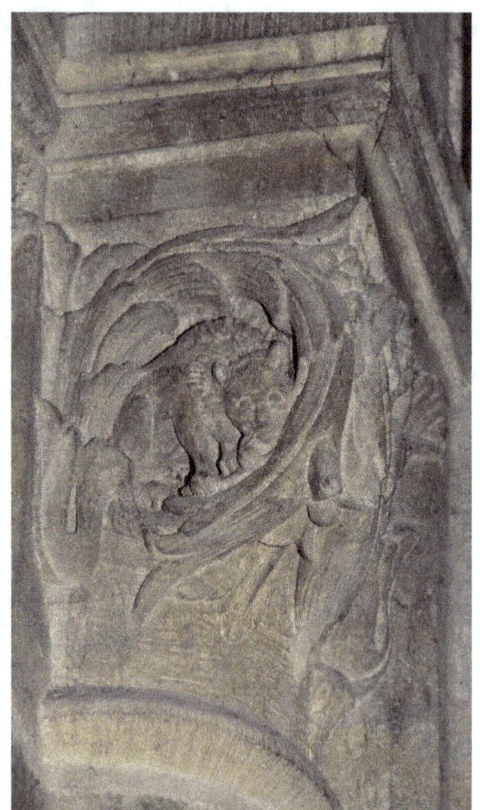
Lion on the prowl. Capital, 1924-61. Ampleforth.

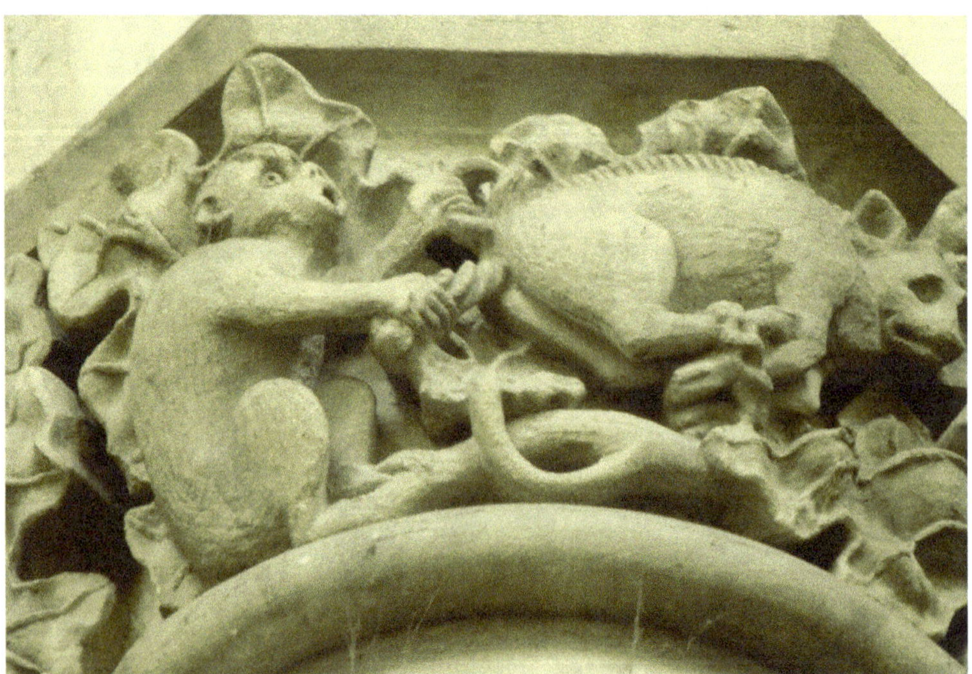
Monkey twisting pig's tail. Capital, circa 1400. York Minster.

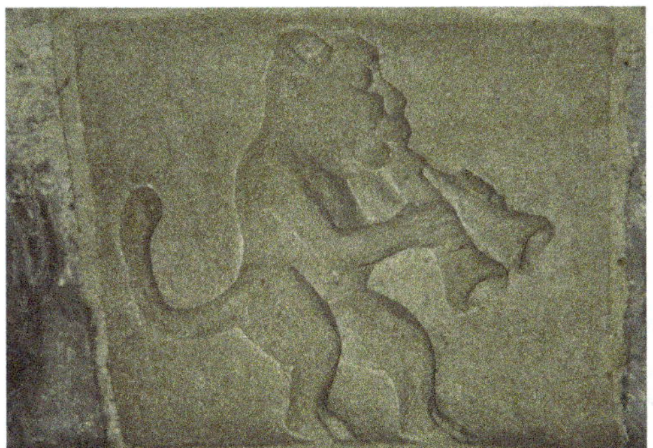

Monkey blowing double pipe.
Modern. Bishop Wilton.

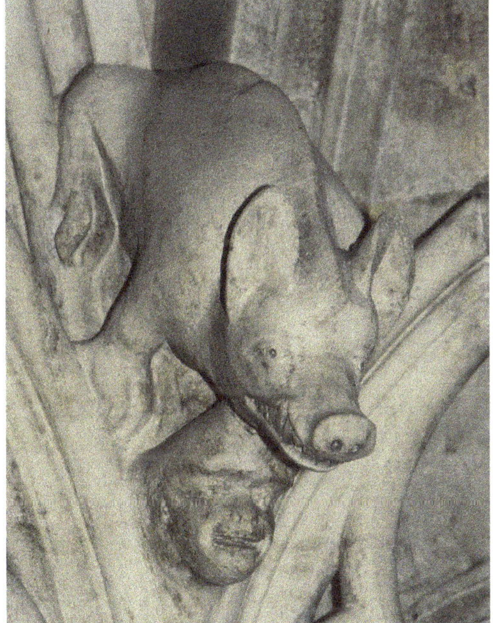

Pig above a human head. Label stop, 1260-85.
York Minster.

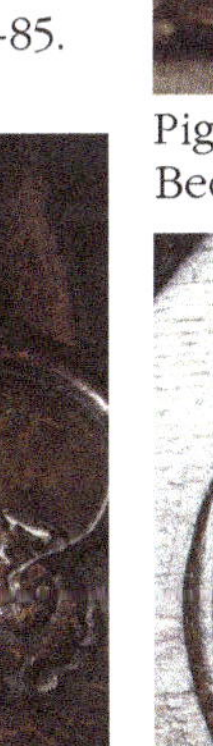

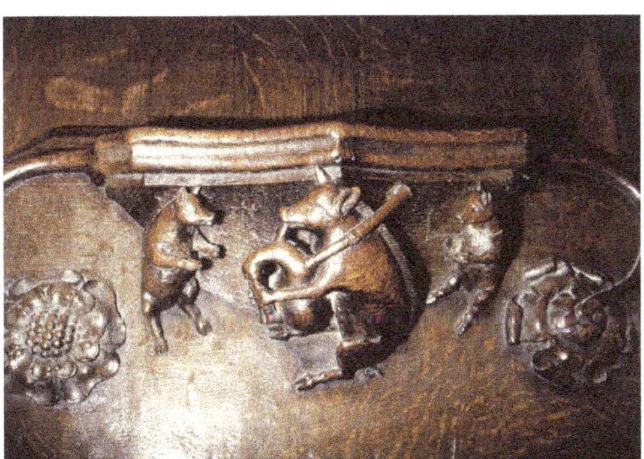

Sow playing bagpipes to two dancing piglets. Notice the front and back views of marguerites on the supporters. Misericord, 1489-94.
Ripon Cathedral.

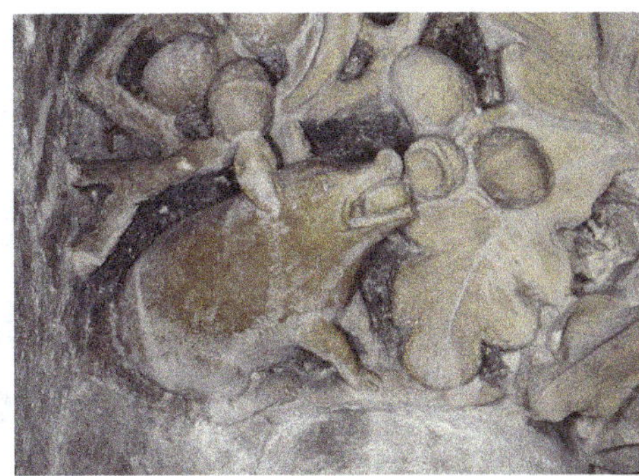

Pig eating acorns. Capital, circa 1250.
Selby Abbey.

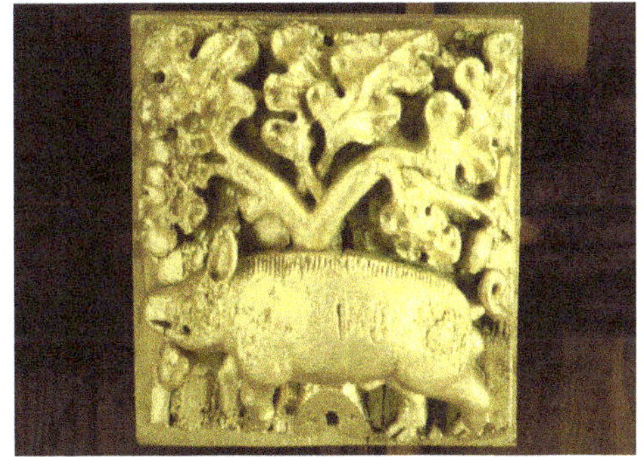

Pig amongst oak leaves. Roof Boss, circa 1300.
Selby Abbey.

Pig eating an acorn. Font, 14th century.
Bedale.

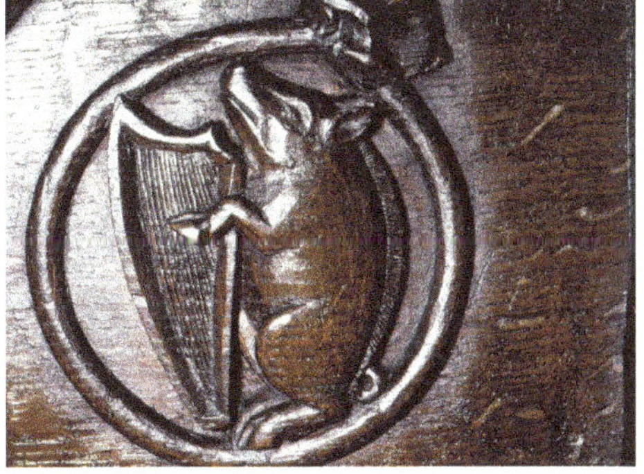

Boar plucking a harp. Supporter, 1520.
Beverley Minster.

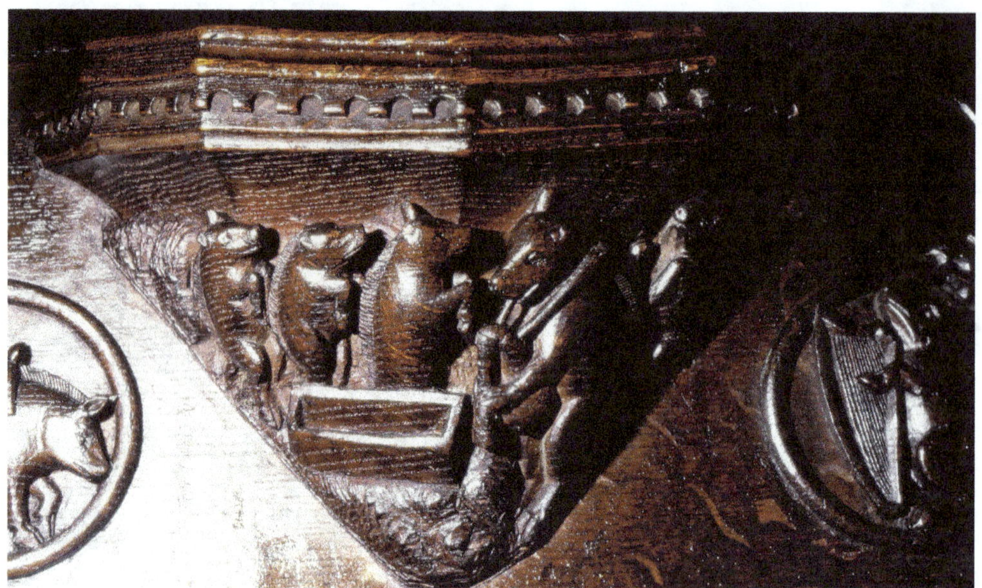

Sow blowing bagpipes to dancing piglets, notice the trough in the foreground. Misericord, 1520. Beverley Minster.

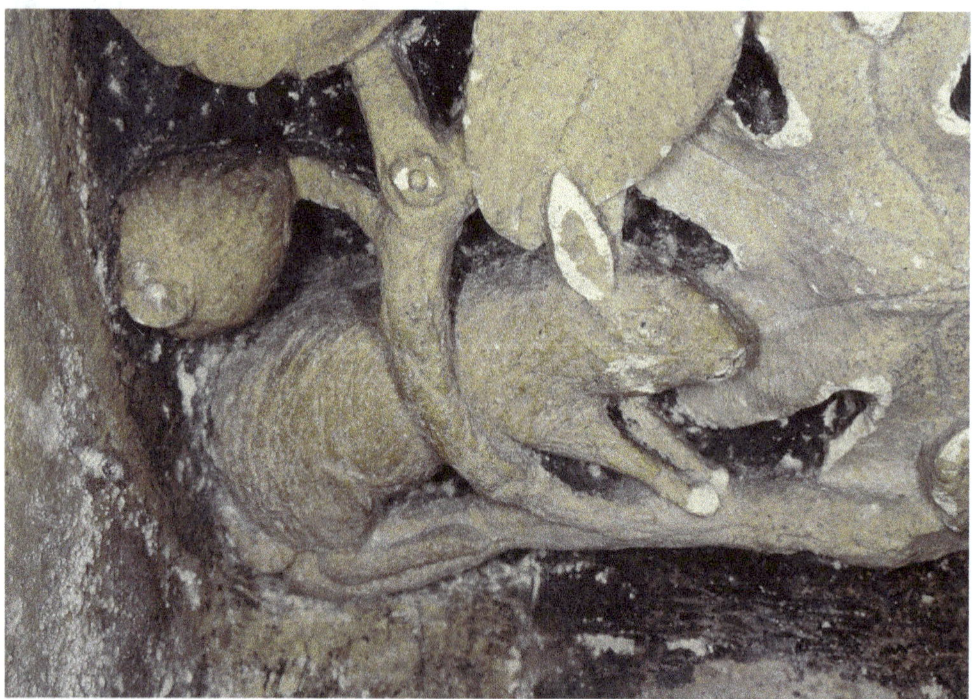

Close-up of rabbit among figs. Capital, circa 1250. Selby Abbey.

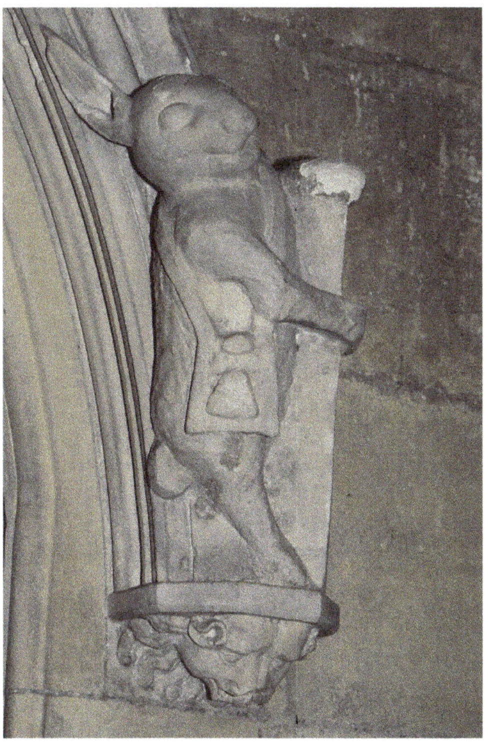

Pilgrim rabbit above a lion's head corbel. 1325. Beverley St Mary.

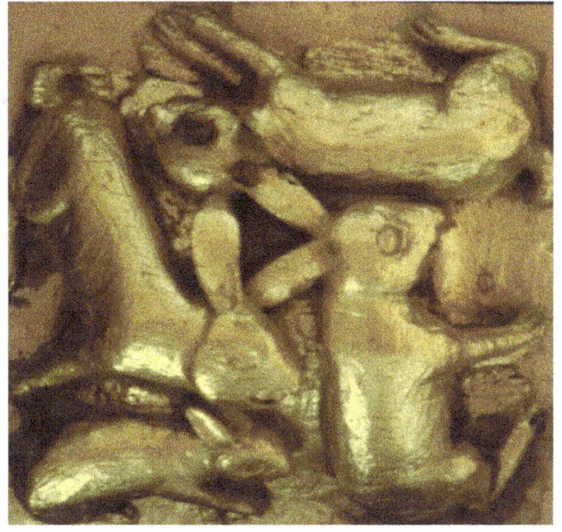

Rabbits or hares, notice the baby outside the circle. Roof Boss, circa 1300. Selby Abbey.

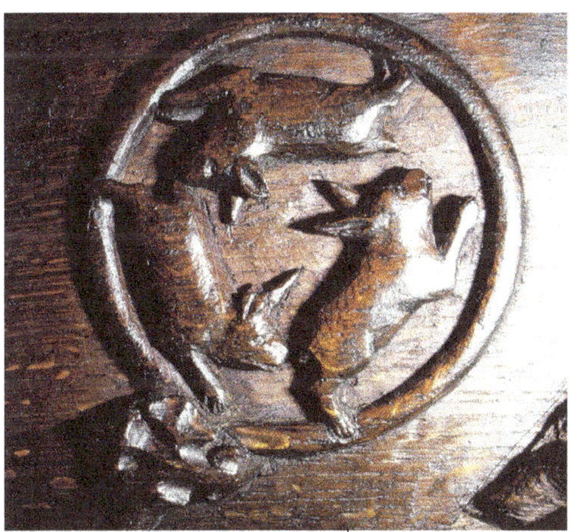

Three rabbits each with two ears. Supporter, 1520. Beverley Minster.

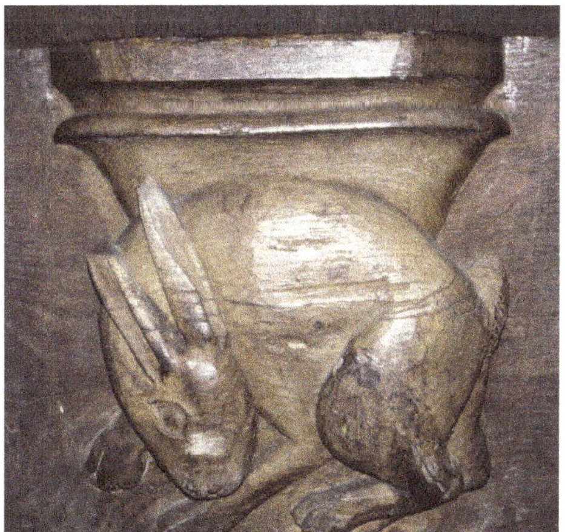

Hare. Misericord, 15th century. Old Malton.

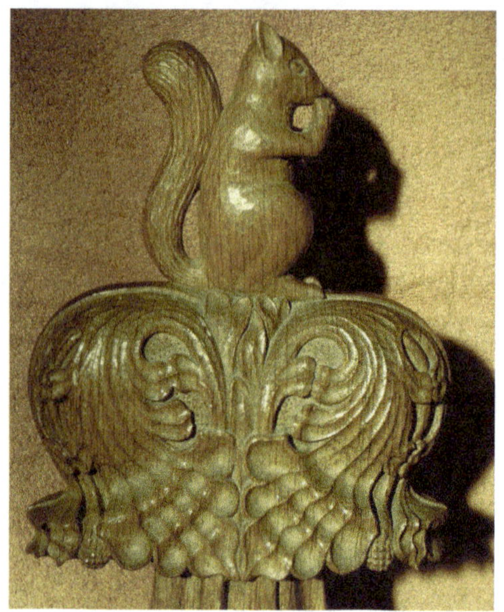

Squirrel on top of stylised leaves. Poppyhead, modern. Hemingborough.

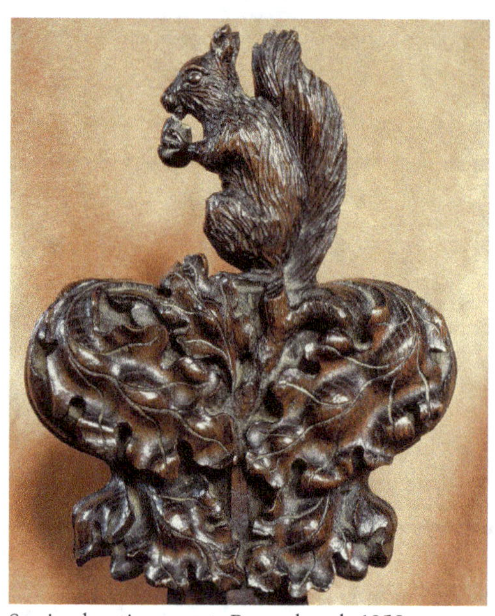

Squirrel eating a nut. Poppyhead, 1858. Rothwell.

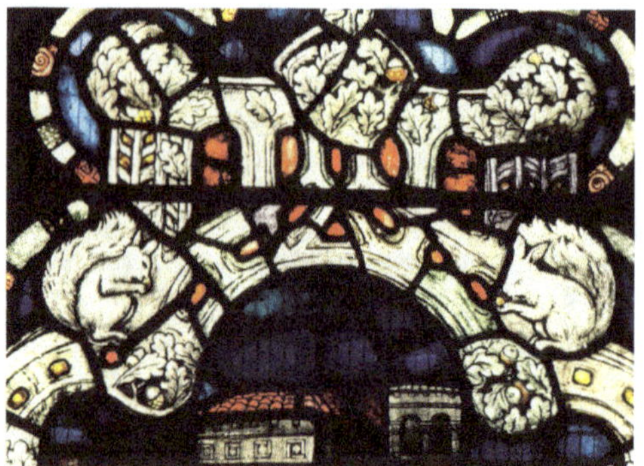

Squirrels. Window, 1905. Aysgarth.

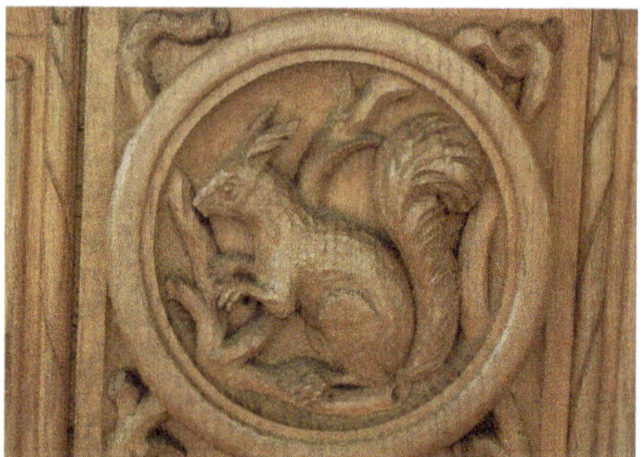

Squirrel with large bushy tail. Choir stall circa 1930. West Tanfield.

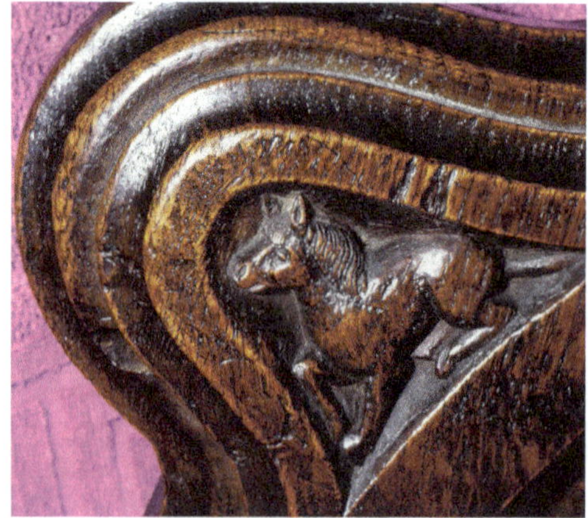

Delightful little pony. Elbow, 1520. Beverley Minster.

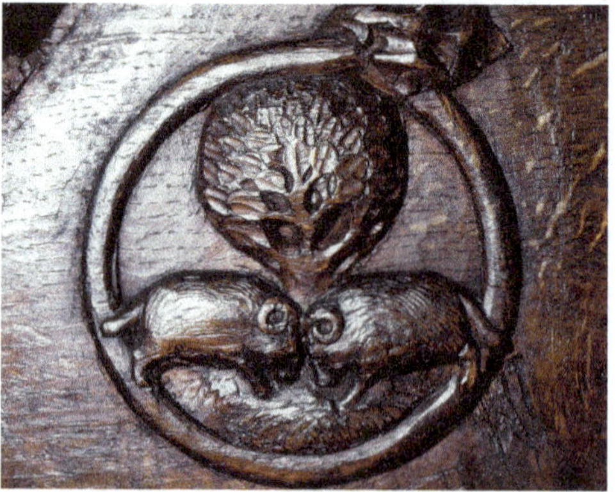

Two tubby little sheep with long tails butting each other beneath a tree. Supporter, 1520. Beverley Minster.

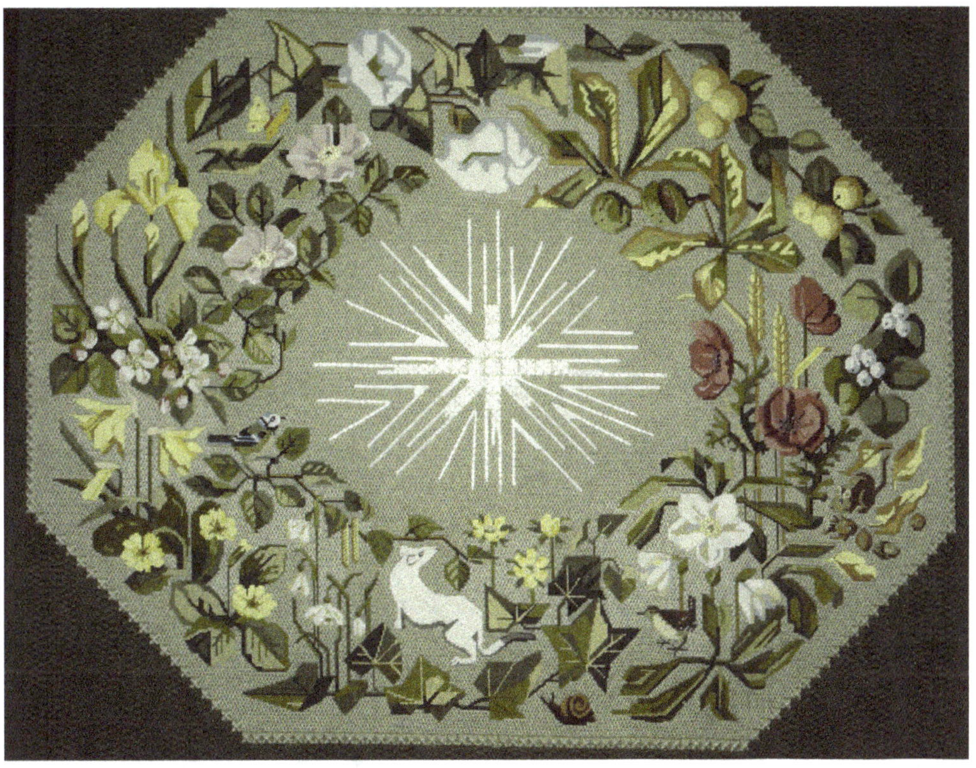

Stoat, mouse, Blue Tit, wren, snail, fruit and flowers. Altar frontal. Bubwith.

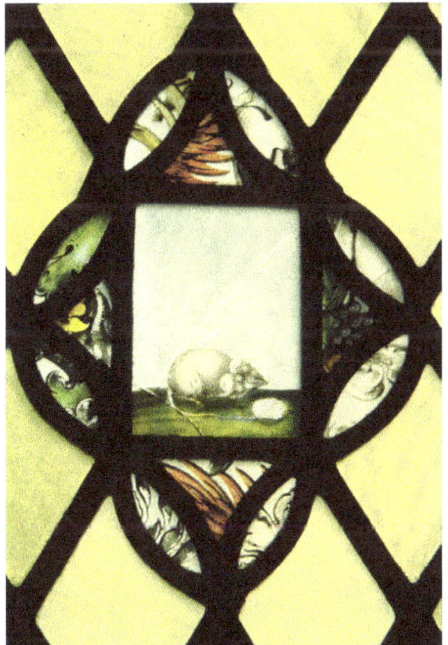

A tiny mouse with a lump of cheese. Flemish glass, late 17th century. St Helen, York.

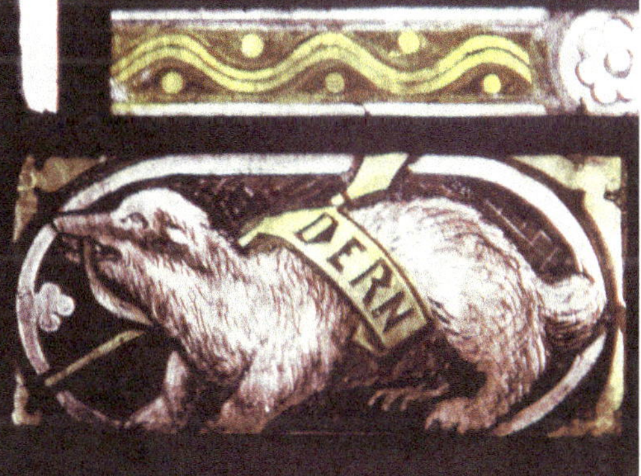

An otter with a banner. Window, 1873. Ripon.

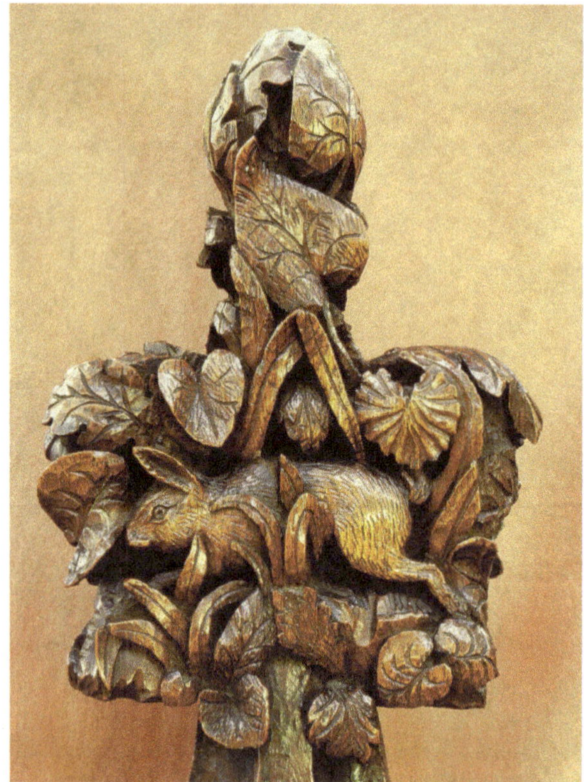
Rabbit among foliage. Poppyhead, 1858. Rothwell.

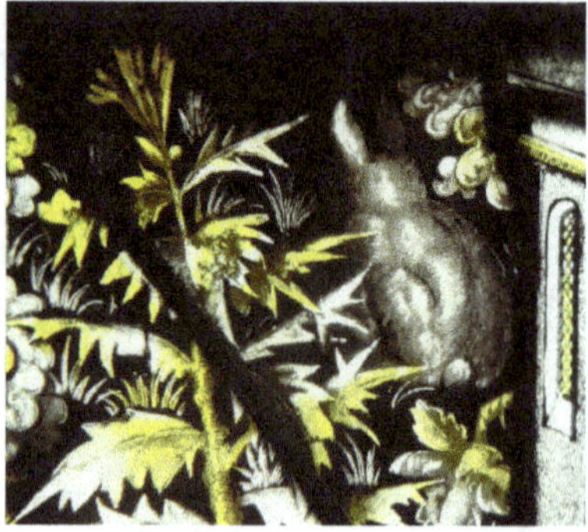
Rear view of a hare. Window, 1870. Wakefield Cathedral.

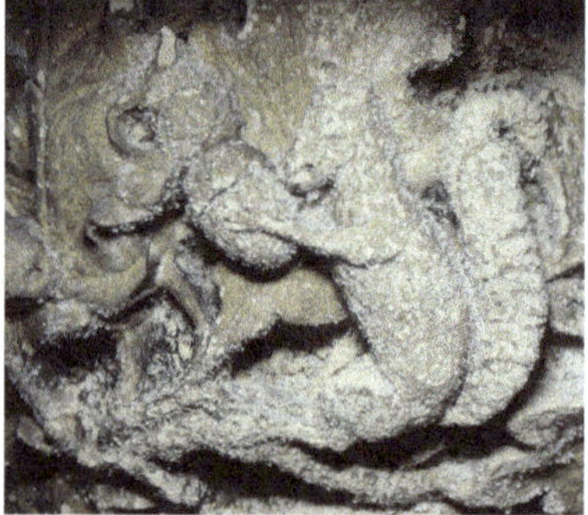
Red Squirrel eating an acorn. Capital, circa 1250. Selby Abbey.

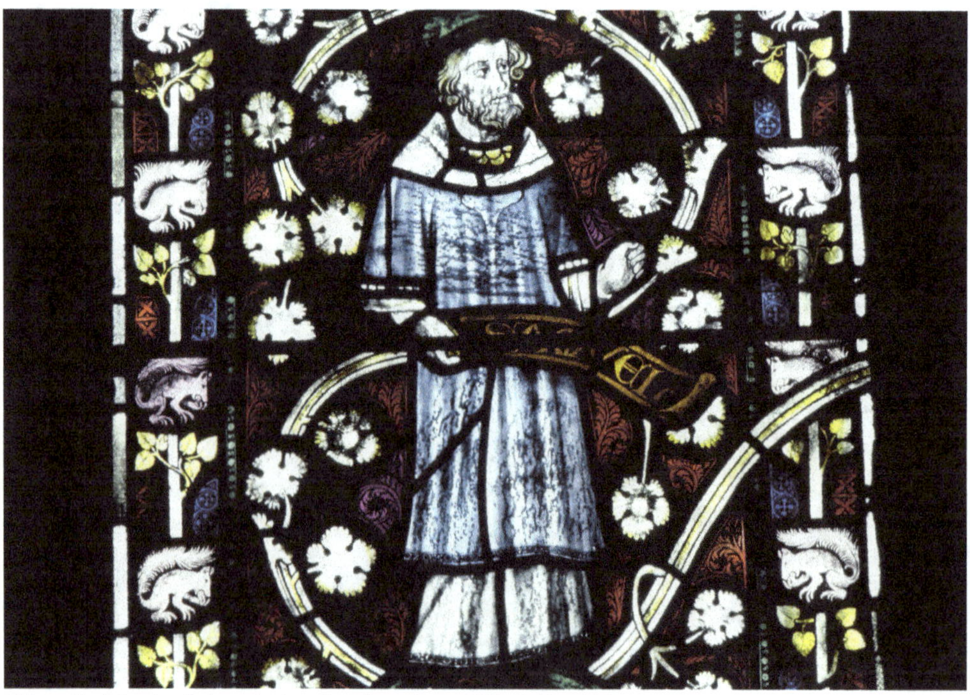
White Red Squirrels in window border, circa 1325. Selby Abbey.

PLANTS in YORKSHIRE CHURCHES

Apple
Barley
Beech
Bluebell
Bramble and blackberries
Bryony, Black
Buttercup
Cinquefoil
Clover
Columbine
Convolvulus
Crocus
Currants
Daffodil
Daisy
Fig
Fir cones
Flax
Frogbit
Fungi
Fuchsia
Geranium
Harebell
Hart's-tongue
Hawthorn and haws
Hazel
Herb Bennet
Holly
Honeysuckle
Hop
Horse-chestnut
Iris
Ivy and berries
Juniper
Leek
Lily
Lily-of-the-valley
Madonna Lily
Mallow
Maple
Marguerite
Mulberry?
Narcissus
Nuts
Oak and acorns
Olive
Palm
Pansy
Passion-flower
Periwinkle
Pineapple
Pine cones
Pinks
Polypody
Pomegranate
Poppy
Primrose
Reedmace
Rose Wild
Shamrock
Snowdrop
Strawberry
Sycamore
Thistle
Tulip
Vine and grapes
Violet
Water-lily
Wheat
Wheat sheaf
Winter Aconite
Wood Avens
Wood Anemone
Wood-sorrel
Yellow Flag

The Roman goddess of flowers was called Flora and her festival or Floralia was celebrated either at the end of April or beginning of May. She was said to be the West Wind's bride whose gentle breath was the origin of all the flowers.

Plants worldwide have, over the centuries, either accidentally or deliberately been introduced into this country and many have become naturalised. The beliefs, traditions and medicinal uses came with them from their country of origin. Pagan meanings and superstitions were replaced as some of the plants became 'Christianised' and today they are part of our cultural background and heritage.

Plants were selected for a number of reasons – for religious purposes; for their imagined magical or medicinal properties; as heraldic symbols; for their familiarity or because their shape fitted the object being carved.

Foliage is a common motif and may signify life and the goodness of creation, spring, fertility and rebirth. Usually flowers and trees symbolise the root of virtue from which arise good works. The Tree of Life, a tree of no known species, is often carved over Norman doorways illustrating creation, fertility and regeneration. However, from 1250 onwards identifiable leaves are found, often concealing animals, birds and men. The Green Man or Jack 'o the Green with foliage issuing from his ears, nose or mouth is one such figure. He is said to have been a fertility symbol from a pagan era.

Trees which Bede suggests are said to have provided wood for the Cross are cypress, cedar, pine or box. There is a legend which states that a seed from the Tree of Knowledge was planted in Adam's mouth and it is from this that the tree from which the Cross was made grew.

"Nailed were His feet to Cedar,
To Palm His Hands,
Cypress His body bore,
Title on Olive stands"

Oak, mistletoe and aspen are also said to have been used.

Churches were and still are decorated with flowers and foliage. During Lent and on Our Lady's Feast days lilies were used. The Annunciation is commemorated on Lady Day and many of the species dedicated to her are prefixed by 'Lady'. Others include almond, carnation, and Cedar of Lebanon, columbine, daffodil, daisy, hawthorn, iris, marigold, peony, pomegranate, primrose, rose, sage, violet, strawberry and possibly forget-me-not. Some of these plants can be found carved, painted or embroidered in churches.

On Palm Sunday, box, willow and yew were favoured. The latter is a symbol of immortality and was also used at Easter. The name Easter is derived from Eostre who was the ancient goddess of Spring. In late December the Romans celebrated the feast of Saturnalia decorating their temples with evergreen foliage. Holly, ivy and fir trees, all evergreens, are part of the traditional Christmas celebrations.

Sacred to the Druids and revered by the Celts, oak is a familiar species, but wheat and vine symbolising the Eucharistic bread and wine are the two most often seen. Vineyards were not uncommon in Medieval England and carvers would be familiar with both the living plant and the biblical text" I am the vine, ye are the branches".

Depicting the attributes and emblems of saints, animal and bird motifs are fairly common but flowers are rarely illustrated. Saint John the Great has, in addition to a scallop shell, a gourd, whilst Saint John the Lesser has a teasel as his attribute. In memory of her martyrdom under Diocletion Saint Dorothea may be pictured with a basket of apples or some other fruit. She was sarcastically asked by the judge's secretary, Theophilus, to send him some fruit and roses from Paradise. Shortly after her execution an angel presented Theophilus with a basket containing apples and roses saying "from Dorothea in Paradise". The legend of Saint Elizabeth of Hungary also features red roses. She was known for her good works but forbidden by her husband to give to the poor. Seeing her carrying a bundle which unknown to him concealed bread, he asked her to show him what was in the bundle. "Only flowers, my lord" said Elizabeth and a miracle had changed the bread into roses.

Apple In the Old Testament story of the Temptation, the fruit of the Tree of Knowledge is identified as the apple. The fruit is a symbol of earthly love and of death.

Barley In Palestine barley was the staple food of the poorer classes. Jesus said "I am the bread of life" (John 6: 35).

Black Bryony It was probably for its decorative appeal, rather than its magical and medicinal properties that Black Bryony was chosen as a subject for carving.

Bluebell The bluebell is rarely found in churches, although it was believed that all evil would vanish if a whole bluebell plant was hung above the threshold. It may signify fertility when depicted with its seed capsule.

Bramble In Christian tradition, the bramble is the emblem of Christ and the Virgin Mary. It was the bush which burned without being consumed (Exodus 3:2) and traditionally, it was a branch from the bush which Christ used to drive the moneylenders from the Temple and to drive the donkey which He rode on His way to Jerusalem.

Buttercup These flowers were part of the May Day rites, protecting milk and butter and keeping evil away from farm livestock. Bulbous Buttercup is sometimes known as St Anthony's turnip.

Cinquefoil Commonly known as Five-fingers from the shape of its leaves, it was thought to represent the five wounds of Christ. Herbalists called it the little powerful one or potentilla and it was hung in the byre or round the necks of cattle, where it was a protection against witchcraft. It was regarded as a cure for malaria - the ague of the Fenlands.

Clover The Druids used this as a charm against the evil eye. A four-leaved plant hidden in a cowshed protected against magic and wearing one averted the evil eye. It can be difficult to establish whether 'three-leaved' leaves are clover or the emblem for the Holy Trinity. It is sometimes said to be the shamrock traditionally used by Saint Patrick. This plant was once used as a charm against sorcery and was 'Christianised' by the saint, who is said to have explained the Holy Trinity, the three in one, by employing a three-leaved clover.

Columbine The generic name *Aquilegia* may be from the Latin *Aquila*, an eagle, the flower spur resembling an eagle's claw. Its common name of columbine is from *Columba*, a dove, and, as the shape of the flowers look like doves in flight they became a symbol of the Holy Ghost. The flower is usually depicted with seven petals instead of the normal five, to portray the seven gifts of God: - council, fortitude, Godly fear, knowledge, learning, piety and wisdom. It does not appear to have been used as a Christian symbol after the 16th century. It is one of the badges of the House of Lancaster.

Convolvulus This is an evil plant as evinced by some of its colloquial names - Devil's Guts, Devil's Garter and Devil's Nightcap.

Daffodil The Virgin Mary is compared to several plants. In one hymn, 'the blossoming daffodil stands for chastity wherein God has enclosed all preciousness'. One of the more common names for the daffodil is Lent Lily. In this species the outer petals are paler than the inner corona. The scientific name for the genus is *Narcissus*, after a Greek youth who fell in love with his own reflection. At his death he changed into the flower which then became a symbol of youthful death.

Daisy Daisies are a symbol of the innocence of the Holy Child and of the Virgin. Mythologically, it is believed that when each tear Mary Magdalene wept in repentance fell to the ground, it turned into a daisy. When Saint Augustine of Canterbury first came to England, it was said that he spent quite a lot of time walking in the countryside. He compared daisies to the spirits of the blessed in the courts of heaven. Children came to him with daisy chains and he taught them about paradise by showing the sun in the centre surrounded by white rays of goodness and purity. In paradise, all righteous souls would be united like the daisies which grew together in the meadows. Daisies were popular flowers in the Middle Ages, implying freshness and innocence, yet they are symbols of death, 'pushing up the daisies' is a euphemism for death.

Dandelion One of the bitter herbs (Exodus 12:8) may have been the dandelion.

It is a Christian symbol of grief and resurrection.

Ferns Bracken was considered by many people to be a holy plant because when the roots of the plant are cut, marks are found which are said to resemble the Greek letter X, meaning Christ.

Hart's-tongue The flourishing of spiritual knowledge and the healing powers of the Tree of Life are represented by this fern. In Christian myths the fern provided a pillow for Christ when He had nowhere to lay His head. Two hairs were left on the stem which the plant treasures to this day.

Spleenwort No symbolic significance.

Fig On realising that they were naked after eating the fruit of the Tree of Knowledge (Genesis 2:17) Adam and Eve used fig leaves to cover their nakedness.

Frogbit No symbolic significance.

Fruit trees Trees bearing fruit could be interpreted as symbols of fertility.

Fungi Mushrooms and toadstools were works of the devil.

Geranium Many carvings of leaves are called 'geranium' type. Meadow Crane's-bill, one of our wild geraniums, is sometimes known as Grace of God. The prophet Mohammed is said to have hung his shirt on a plant in order to dry it, and when he removed the shirt the geranium was revealed.

Hawthorn After vine and barley, hawthorn must be one of the most commonly carved plants to be found in churches.

> *"Under a thorn*
> *Our Saviour was born"*

Christ's crown of thorns was believed to have been made from this bush. Benedict and Saint Francis of Assisi threw themselves into thorn bushes to still sexual feelings said to be generated by the ascetic way of life of hermits. The clergy are reminded that they are servants of 'One crowned with thorns', by the clerical tonsure. The 'Green Man', a pagan divinity signifying nature worship, is frequently depicted with hawthorn issuing from his mouth. Often known as May or Whitethorn it was an essential part of the May Day celebrations symbolising the change from spring to summer. May Day was the time when witches and warlocks wove their spells. It was believed to be a powerful protection from a wide range of evils including lightning.

Hazel Often mistaken for beech, hazel symbolises justice and truth. It is the 'magic' wood used by diviners.

Herb Bennet See Wood Avens

Holly A pre-Christian festival held in December used holly and ivy in its fertility rites. The holly was the male element and the ivy the embracing female element. Planted outside a house, holly wards off witches, so it is a protective plant. There is an old rhyme which states:-

> *'The holly bears a berry red,*
> *The ivy bears a black 'un,*
> *To show that Christ His blood did shed,*
> *To save our souls from Satan'.*

It is a symbol of suffering especially Christ's Passion. It is one of the plants said to have been employed to make the crown of thorns. Used in decorations at Christmas it is associated with the Nativity. A 15th century carol includes the following verse:-

> *'Holly and his mery men*
> *They daunsen and they sing;*
> *Ivy and her maidens*
> *They wepen and they wring'.*

Hop This plant symbolises bitterness.

Iris Iris, almond and lily are all emblems of the Virgin Mary. Yellow Flag *Iris pseudacorus* was believed to have the power to avert evil and may be the heraldic form of the French fleur-de-lys. Bearded Iris *Iris germanica* is one of the flowers dedicated to Mary.

Ivy Ivy is an ambivalent symbol. Being an evergreen it symbolises immortality, and because it clings to a support it signifies fidelity. Like the buttercup and hawthorn, it was part of the May Day ceremonies having magical powers to keep evil at bay from animals and protecting milk and butter, but it is an evil plant because whatever it embraces is killed. One of the latest plants to flower, it is used with holly to decorate churches at Christmas. It was sacred to Bacchus and in the past was valued for its medicinal properties. Containers made from ivy wood were believed to make the medicine contained within them more effective.

Juniper Juniper is said to denote longevity, protection and fecundity. It is another plant which, according to Christian legend, sheltered the Virgin Mary and Jesus when they were fleeing from Herod. There was a belief in the Middle Ages that the branches when burnt produced a pungent smoke which kept evil spirits at bay and flushed out witches. Juniper branches were hung in Scottish cowsheds as a talisman against the evil eye. Some authorities suggest that the ball flower (a type of stylised decoration) represents the berries of this tree.

Lily In Christian legend it is stated that the lily sprang from the tears which Eve shed as she left the Garden of Eden. The flower or the leaves can represent the seven gifts of the Holy Spirit: - purity of body, purity of heart, meekness, Godly fear, holiness, self-discipline and steadfastness. Its touch lessened pride, its scent invoked pity, its fruit calmed anger, its taste and juice strengthened wisdom and intellect against lust and gluttony and its colour gave endurance. The emblem of the Virgin Mary is the lily and it is an attribute of all virgins. The white petals represent the body of the Virgin Mary and the yellow anthers represent her soul. The flower was used on all feast-days of Our Lady and also in Lent. The Madonna Lily *Lilium candidum* is the species usually illustrated and it represents immaculate purity. The bowl in which the lily often stands is emblematic of the Virgin's womb. The fleur-de-lys may be the heraldic form of this plant.

Lily-of-the-valley Humility and purity are symbolised by this plant. The Song of Solomon mentions the Lily-of-the-valley but this may be a reference to the Madonna Lily.

Maple Maple has been used as a decorative motif since the 12th century. It was valued for its medicinal and magical properties and was often thought of as a type of oak.

Marguerite Known as Saint John's Flower, Maudlin Daisy (after Mary Magdalen) and Our Lord's Mint, the Marguerite is also called the Eye of Christ. It used to be hung on doors and round the necks of cattle to keep away lightning.

Mistletoe This is an evergreen plant which is parasitic on trees. It became a symbol of life and love because in winter it draws its sustenance from trees. Primitive man believed that it incorporated a living spirit within it so it became an object of pagan rites and worship. The Christian Church in Britain banished it because of this association. The Druids of pagan Britain, long thought of as witches, attributed great powers to this plant. It was venerated by them when it was found (which it rarely is) growing on oak. It occurs most commonly on apple. The Druids are now thought to have been herbal medicine men and they called the plant All-heal. The berries were prescribed to soothe nerves, to calm hysteria or epileptic fits and to reduce blood pressure. It was recommended by Culpepper. It was 'Christianised' in Europe, and to many monks it was the wood of the Holy Cross. The present day custom of kissing under the mistletoe is associated with the pagan belief that it was a lucky plant. In antiquity it was a protective talisman. Before descending to the Underworld with Cumaean Sibyl, Aeneas plucked the 'golden bough'.

Myrtle The myrtle is a symbol of divine generosity and of love. Myrtle groves are symbols of peace and of the Gentiles who became followers of Christ.

Nuts Any tree bearing nuts signifies the Church. The outer casing of the nut represents Christ's Flesh. The shell is the Cross on which the Flesh suffered, and the kernel is the hidden Divinity.

Oak The oak represents strength and durability, thus signifying the firmness of the Christian faith and fidelity in love and marriage. Before the arrival of Christianity, the oak like the mistletoe, was a sacred tree. In antiquity it was sacred to Zeus, Jupiter and Thor. The Druids revered it and for this reason Bishop Boniface rests his foot on a fallen oak when baptising, thus symbolising the conversion of the pagan. An old German legend states that Boniface was sent to Germany to convert the pagan tribes to Christianity. As he and his monks were walking through some woods one evening they found villagers about to sacrifice a young boy to their god Odin. The boy was tied to an oak tree so Boniface freed the lad and felled the oak. The Cross on which Christ was crucified was thought by some to have been made from the wood of an oak tree. Therefore, in the Middle Ages, this wood was believed to ward off evil spirits.

Olive The olive and the dove are symbols of peace and friendship. They occur in association with Noah's ark (see Dove under birds). To Christians, a sprig of olive signifies the making of God's peace with man. The oil is the oil of blessing, consecration and unction. In 1968 a fragment of a cross used for the crucifixion of a youth was discovered. The cross was made from olive wood.

Pansy Heartsease, *herba trinitas* or Herb of the Blessed Trinity is rarely found in churches.

Passion-flower Epitomising Christ's Crucifixion, the passion-flower's five anthers represent the five wounds, the three-branched style the three nails, the receptacle the pillar of the Cross, the filaments the crown of thorns and the calyx the nimbus (halo).

Pear This is a rarely used symbol of the Virgin Mary.

Pine Pine cones are a symbol of everlasting life and in Japan of longevity.

Pinks The Incarnation of Christ is symbolised by carnations and pinks.

Pomegranate In classical mythology Persephone was carried off by Hades. Demeter scoured the earth for her missing daughter and when told of her whereabouts forbade the earth to bring forth fruit, thus threatening famine. Zeus agreed that Persephone could leave Hades providing she had not eaten in the underworld. Hades agreed to let her go but tempted her into eating a pomegranate. She had then to spend the winter months, when nothing grew, with Hades, and the fertile months with Demeter. The pomegranate became a symbol of fertility and the resurrection in association with Persephone who returned every spring to regenerate the earth. The tough outer case of the fruit around the numerous seeds was the unity of many under one authority, either church or secular. It is a symbol of afterlife and a promise of immortality. According to Bede it may also signify Christ. Ornamental pomegranates decorated the hem of the High Priest's robe (Exodus 28:33).

Poppy In Cornwall, the Field Poppy is known as Devil's Tongue. It is a rare symbol of fertility and also infers sleep and death.

Potentilla See Cinquefoil

Primrose Although in the Middle Ages primroses were often known as Saint Peter's Keys or the Keys to Heaven, they appear to be of no special significance. In the north of England they are sometimes called Lady's Candlestick.

Reedmace The 'bruised reed' of Ezekiel (29:6-7) symbolises the weak. Before His Crucifixion, the soldiers gave Christ a reed as a mock sceptre. This could have been reedmace, reedgrass or some other moisture-loving plant.

Rose Long before Christianity, roses had been sacred to the goddess of love, to Venus in Italy and to Aphrodite in Greece. In the Song of Solomon (2:1-2), 'I am the Rose of Sharon' was taken to be one of the wild roses or *Rosa gallica* of medieval gardens - a yellow-centred, perfumed red rose. Roses in general symbolise triumphant spiritual love. A red rose signifies martyrdom and a white one, purity. A chaplet of roses is represented by a rosary, and Christ's Passion or the brevity of earthly life can be symbolised by the rose. Saint Ambrose retelling an earlier legend tells how roses grew without thorns until the Fall of Man. The Virgin Mary is the 'rose without thorns', that is, sinless. Bernard of Claivaux was one of the first to attribute the rose especially to Mary. He says that "Eve was the thorn that brought death to the world, but Mary is the rose, the source of salvation for all mankind". It was said of Mary that the rose was white through her virginity and love of God, and red through her charity and by her compassion for those who were near to her. A golden rose was the badge of Edward 1, a red rose an emblem of the House of Lancaster and the white rose an emblem of the House of York and the badge of Edward 1V. *Sub rosa* or under the rose, a reference to the plaster decoration in ceilings, is an emblem of silence.

Snowdrop Consecrated to the Virgin Mary, snowdrops are emblems of purity and chastity. Formerly on one day each year the images of Mary were removed from altars and their places were taken by snowdrops.

Strawberry In antiquity the fruit is the fruit of Venus. In Christian tradition, the Wild Strawberry, with both fruit and flowers, is a symbol of the good fruits of the Holy Spirit, whilst a leaf on its own stands for the Holy Trinity. The fruit is an emblem of the Virgin Mary. In Britain, the leaf is a symbol of rank - ducal coronets are ornamented with strawberry leaves. The maker's mark of Sir Ninian Comper is a Wild Strawberry plant.

Sycamore Sycamore is a symbol of the Cross. The sycomore of the Bible is a species of fig and the sycamine is a mulberry.

Thistle Thistles are a symbol of penitence, sin and earthly sorrow. Our Lady's thistle or the sacred Milk Thistle refers to the following legend. The white veins prominent on the leaves of the plant were said to be marked by the Virgin's milk when she suckled the Child. Children suffering from the 'terror' and other demonic diseases were dosed with a preparation made from the plant, and an ointment made from thistles and known as Magdalene salve was used in the later Middle Ages. Milk Thistle was likely to have been the 'thorn' amongst which grain fell in the parable of the sower (Matthew 13:7). It infests field margins and grows very quickly. In 1370 the Order of the Thistle, a knightly order, was founded by Louis 11, Duke of Bourbon, on the occasion of his daughter's marriage. The badge of Scotland and of the Stuarts is represented by a thistle.

Tulip An emblem of Christ and symbolic of a chalice.

Vine Of all the plant species encountered the vine is the most frequent. It is a symbol of Christ, of Christ's Blood, of Eucharistic wine and of life. The vine and grape are common symbols of Christ and the Christian faith. Christ described himself as the true vine, and at the Last Supper the fruit of the vine, symbolising Christ's atoning blood became the Eucharistic wine. Corruption and evil represented by toads were, in medieval England, believed to be repelled by the plant.

Violet The violet is a symbol of the humility of the Son of God assuming human form. Because humility is one of the most admired of Christian virtues, like the lily of chastity and the rose of charity, the violet of humility is an emblem of the Virgin Mary.

Wheat Wheat is a symbol of God's goodness and provision, of thanksgiving when portrayed in a sheaf and of the Eucharist when depicted with grapes or birds. It was used by Christ to show that spiritual fruitfulness has its origins in the death of self.

Wild Arum Said to have more colloquial names than any other English plant, Wild Arum also has some of the rudest, particularly in reference to certain parts of the anatomy of ecclesiastics, for example:- Parson's Billycock, Priest's Pilly (pintle) and Priest's Pintle (penis). The plant is a medieval symbol of fertility and a remedy for poison.

Wood Avens The upper leaves with the three leaflets and the flower with the five yellow petals signify the Holy Trinity and the five wounds of Christ. This plant is sometimes called the Blessed or Holy Herb from its supposed power to render the devil harmless. Its roots are fragrant and were thought to repel moths as well as the devil. It is also called Saint Benedict's Herb or Herb Bennet because on one occasion, it is said, a monk presented the saint with a cup of poisoned wine, but when the saint blessed it the glass shattered and the monk's crime was exposed.

Wormwood Aromatic and with a bitter taste, wormwood was used as a symbol of bitterness, calamity and sorrow. Its medicinal properties include repelling worms, moths and fleas, and the ability to cure dropsy and jaundice.

Yew Formerly sacred, yew symbolised life and immortality. It was planted in many churchyards and frequently alongside cottages and farmhouses. Planting yews may be a survival of a veneration of yews as strong enduring evergreen trees. It was a tree to worship for its powers of protection from prevailing winds, rain, gales and evil spirits. If a yew was on a site when pagan temples were purified for Christian use, it was allowed to remain. The yew at St John the Baptist at Tisbury in Wiltshire is said to be three thousand years old, and that at Fortingall, near Loch Tay four thousand years of age. Medieval churches were decorated with yew at Easter. Yew foliage was cut as 'Palm' for Palm Sunday and came to symbolise the message of eternal life in the Christian religion. It may have been the yew tree to which Boniface refers in the German legend (see also under Oak). The monks had been carrying lighted candles and they placed them on the branches of an evergreen fir tree. Boniface told the people "From this night, this tree shall be your holy emblem. It is the wood of peace, because your houses are built from it. It is the sign of eternal life, because its leaves are always green. It points to heaven, and so from this day it will be called the tree of the Christ-Child".

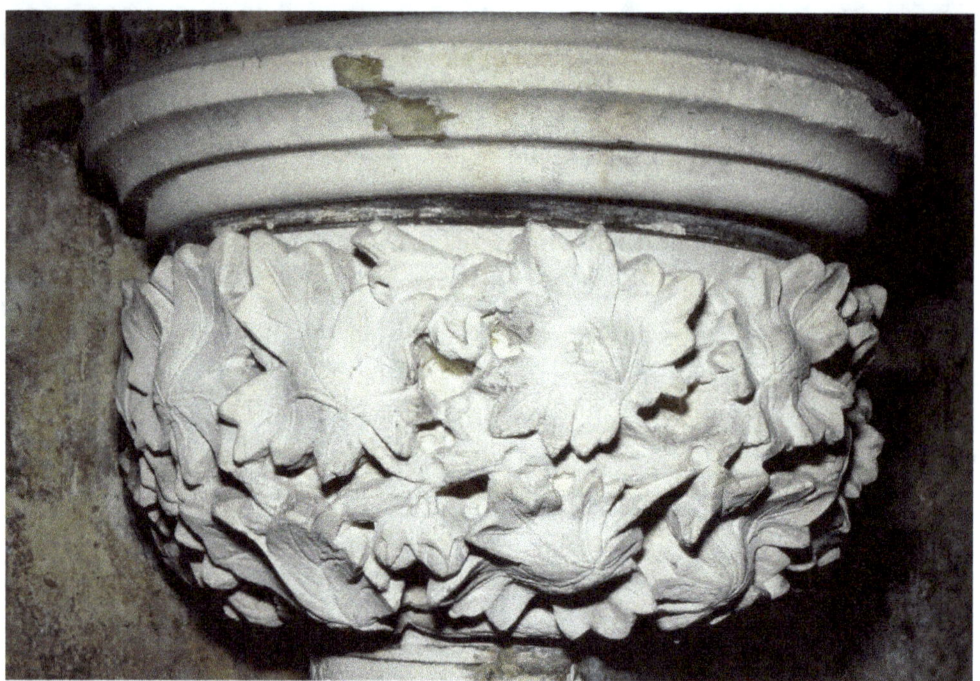

Hazel. Capital, circa 1250. Selby Abbey.

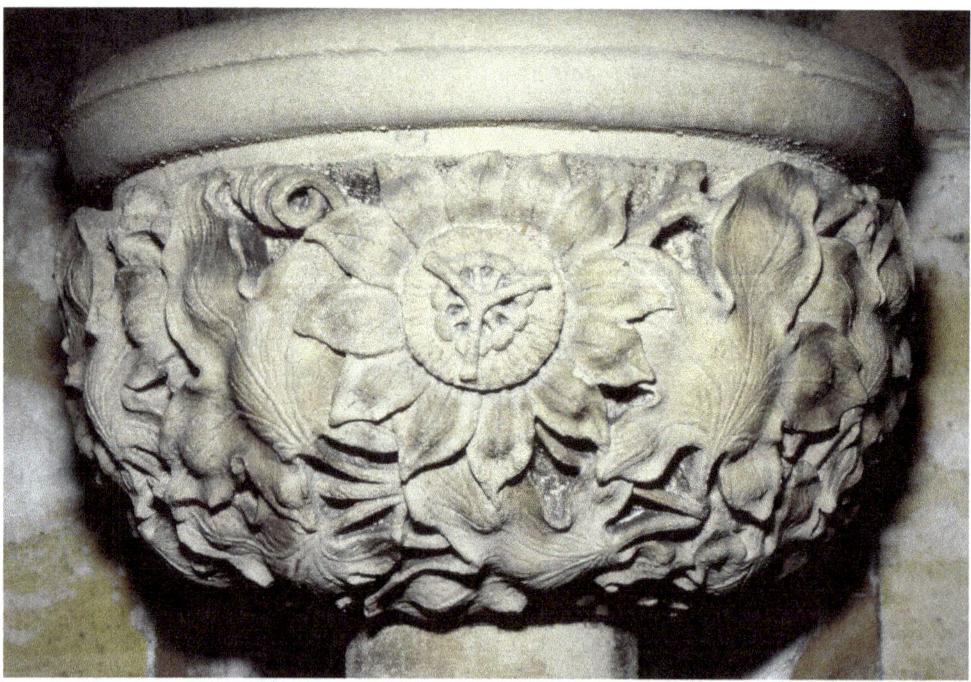

Passion-flower. Capital, circa 1250. Selby Abbey.

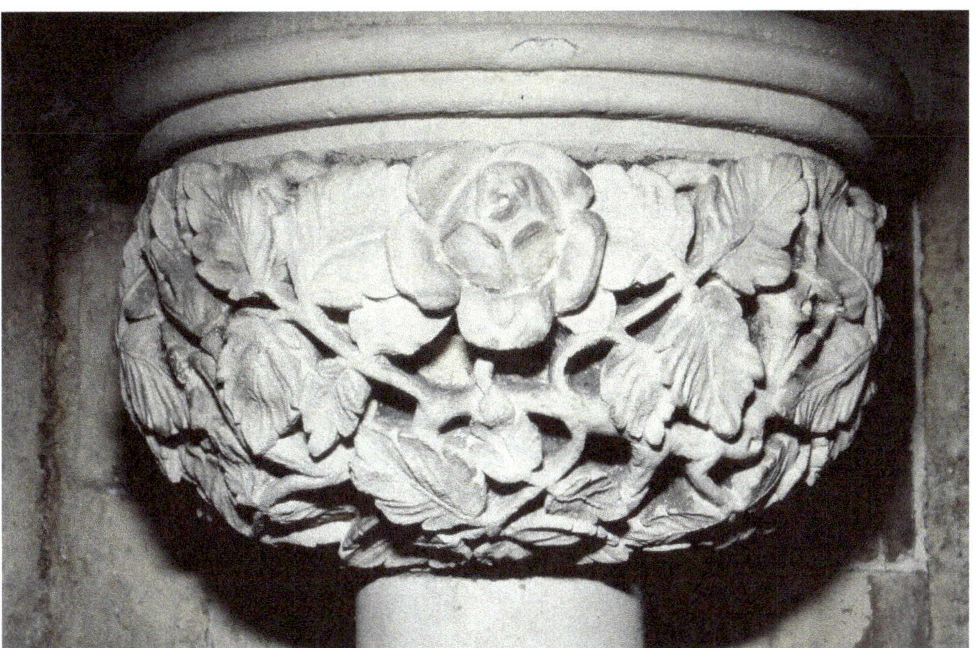

Rose. Capital, circa 1250. Selby Abbey.

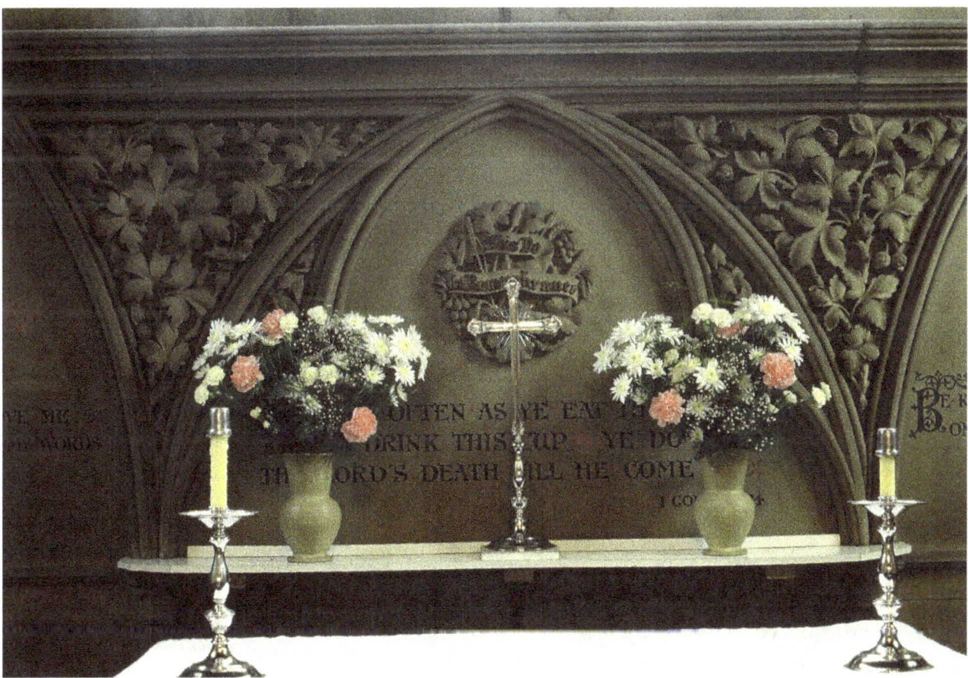

Maple, strawberry, corn and grapes. Reredos, circa 1860. Helme.

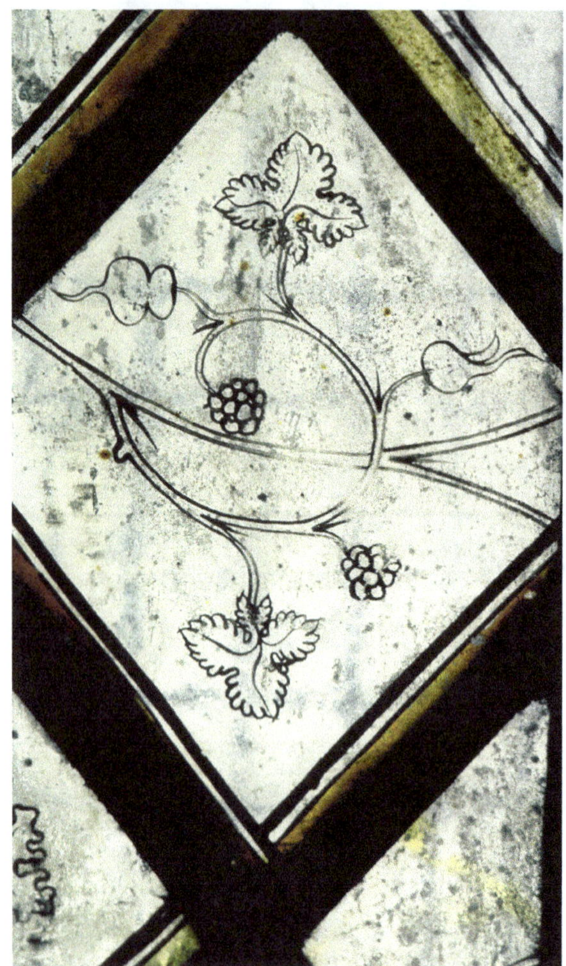

Bramble. Quarry, circa 1320. Acaster Malbis.

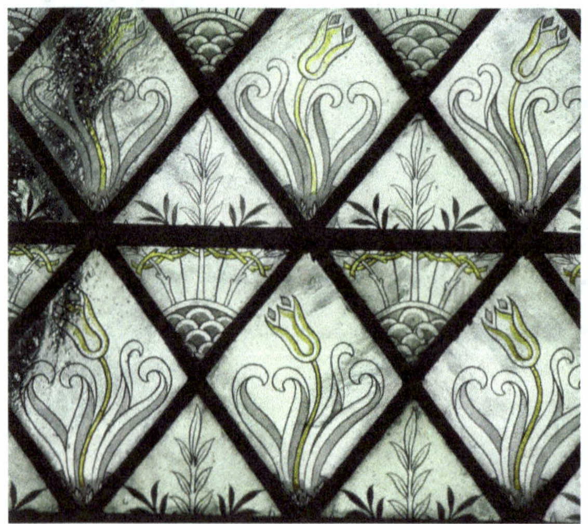

Quarries. Tulips. Lockwood.

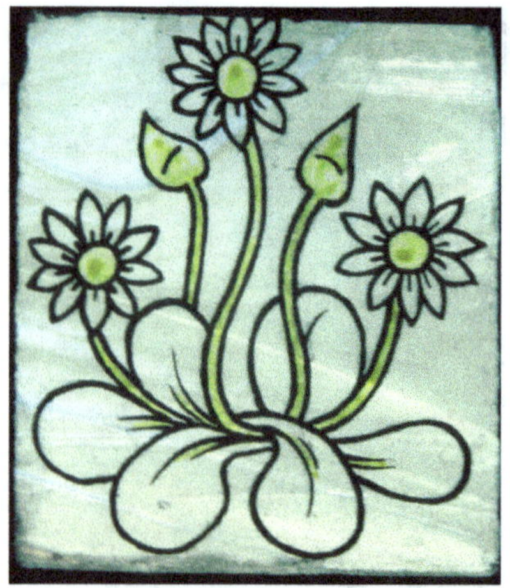

Crude Daisies. Window, circa 1870. Leeds.

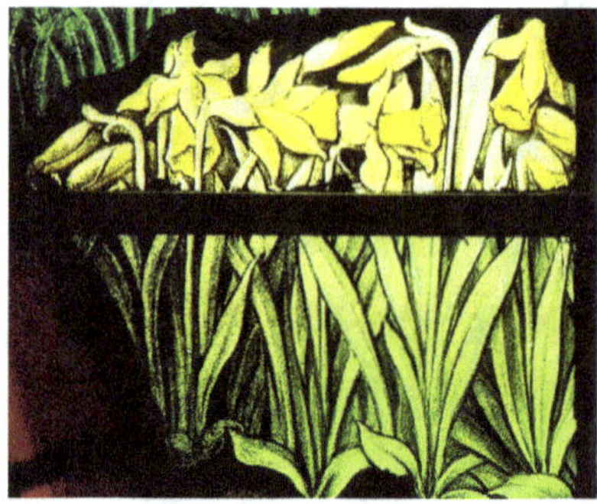

Wild Daffodils. Window. Lepton.

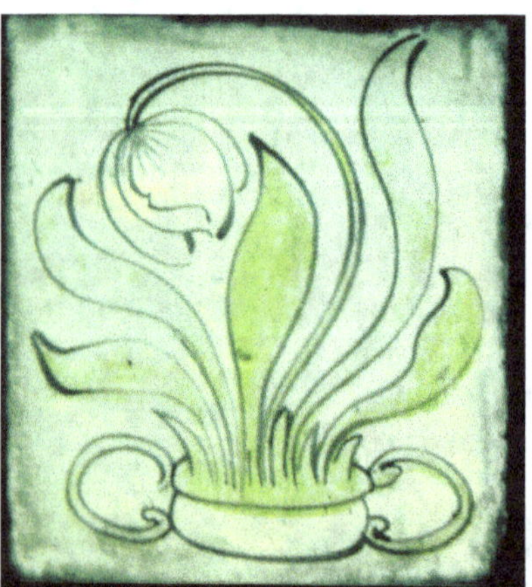

A tulip perhaps.
Window, circa 1894-97. Leeds.

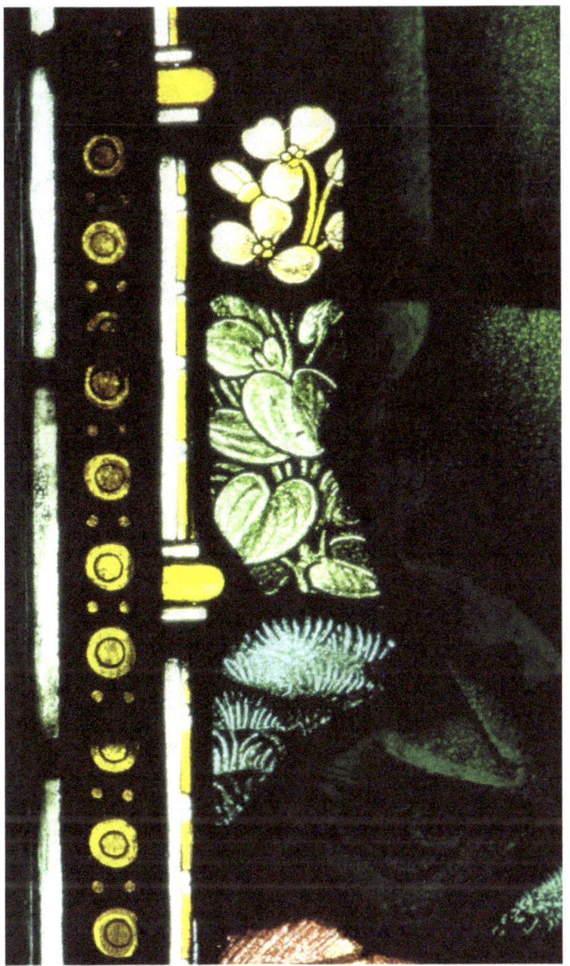

Frogbit. Window border. Hepworth.

Pomegranate. Window, circa 1894-97. Leeds.

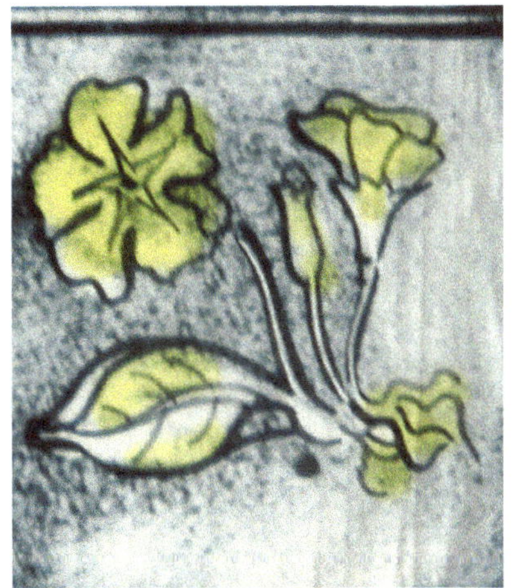

Primrose. Window, circa 1894-97. Leeds.

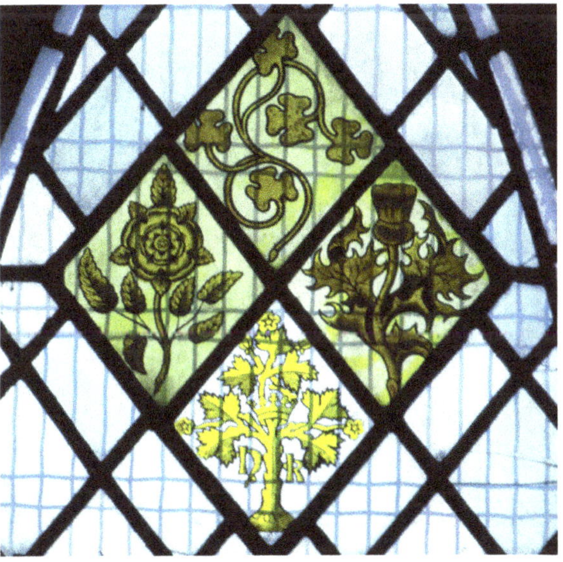

Clover, rose, thistle and a crowned bush with the initials NK. Quarries within a quarry, 15th/16th centuries and Victorian. Ryther.

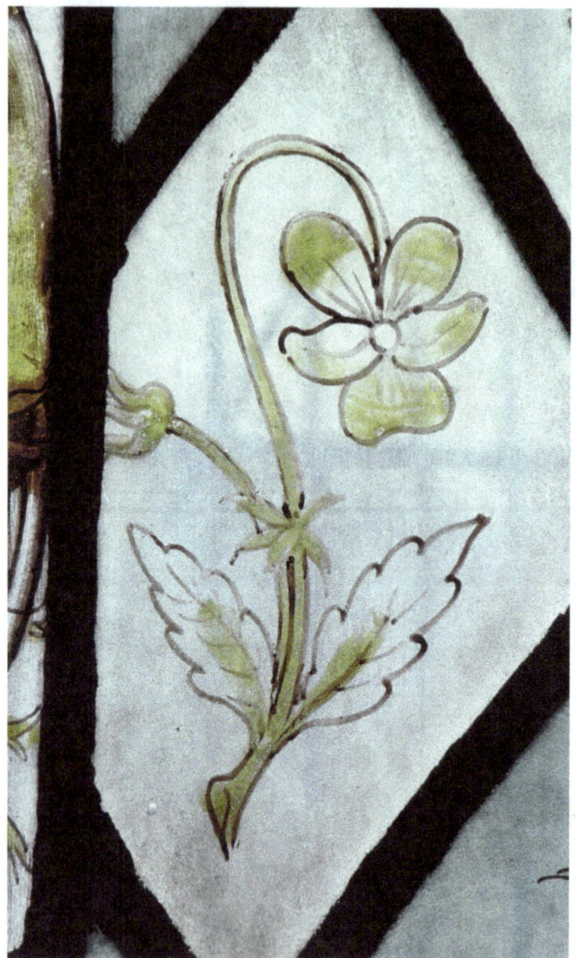

Pansy, a rare subject to find in a church. Quarry, 1905. Bolton on Swale.

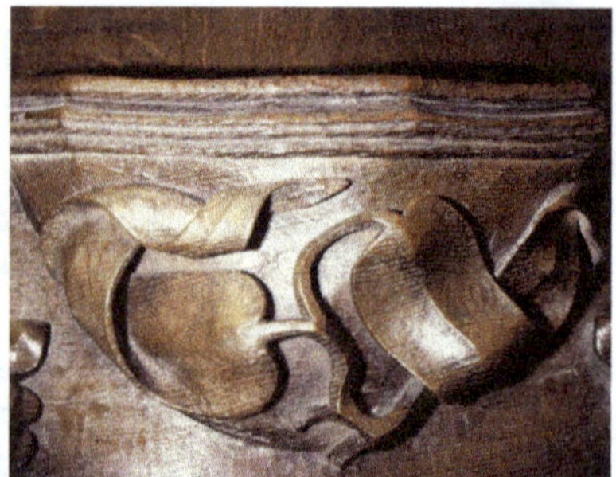

Hart's-tongue. Misericord, 1490. Ripon.

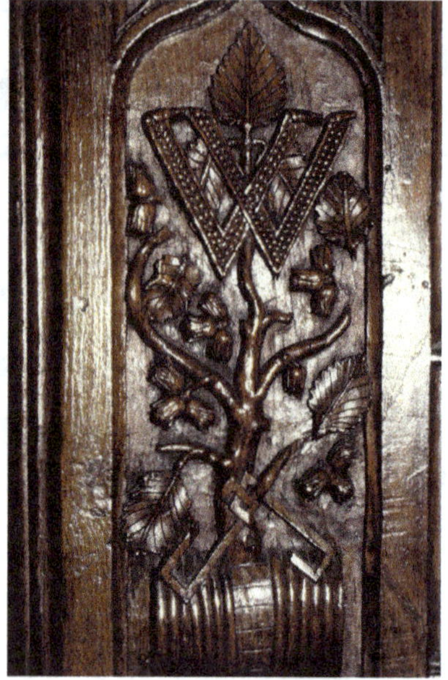

Hazel on a barrel, a rebus on Hazelton. Screen, 1506. Aysgarth.

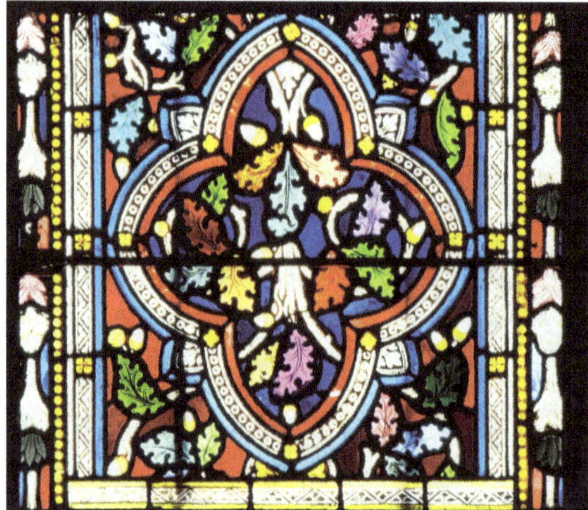

Oak leaves and acorns. Window. Cawthorne.

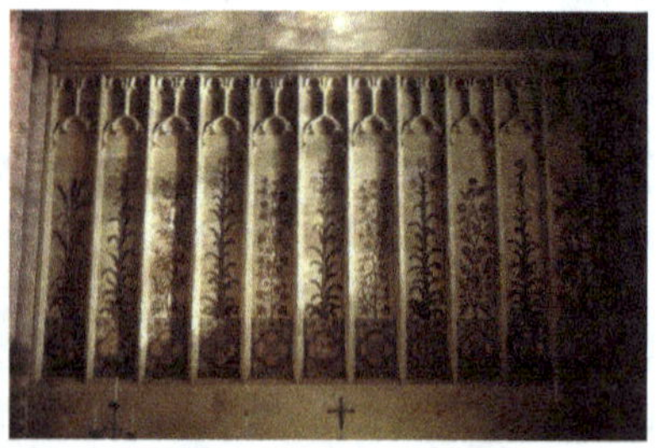

Wall Painting, 1880. Bolton Abbey.

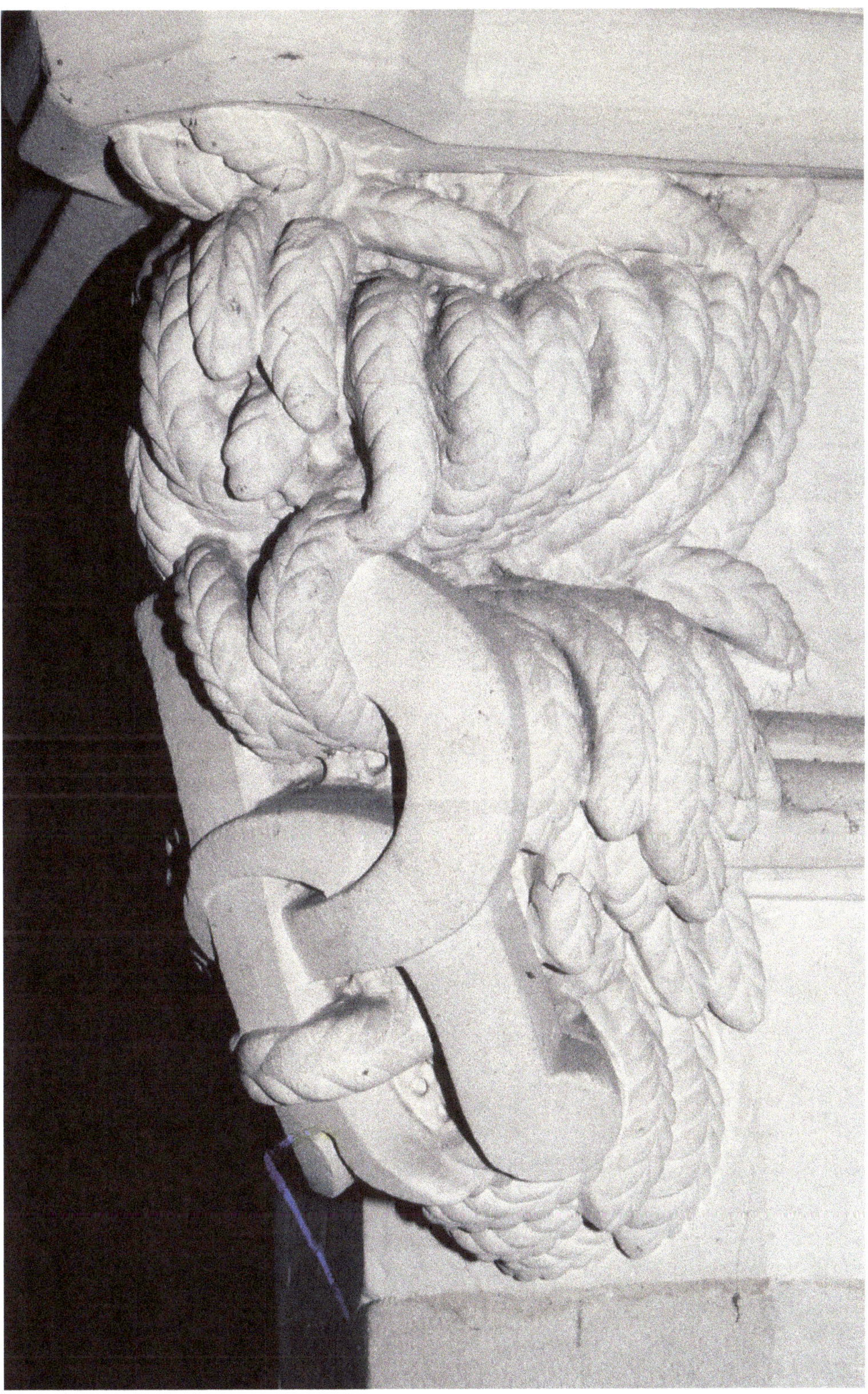

Wheatsheaf of huge proportions. Capital. Thirkleby.

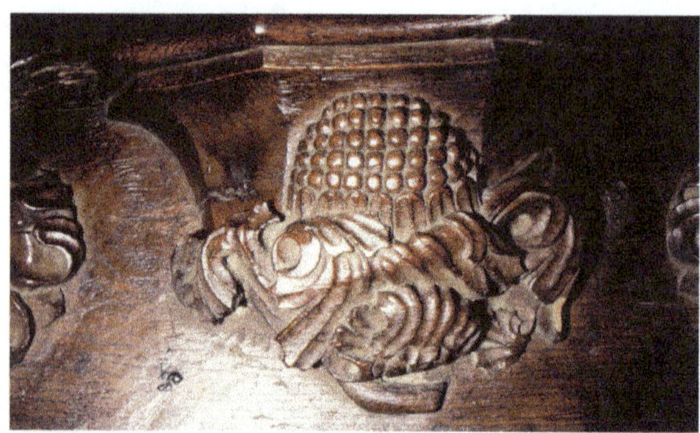

Stylised Ox-eye Daisy. Misericord, 1515. Richmond.

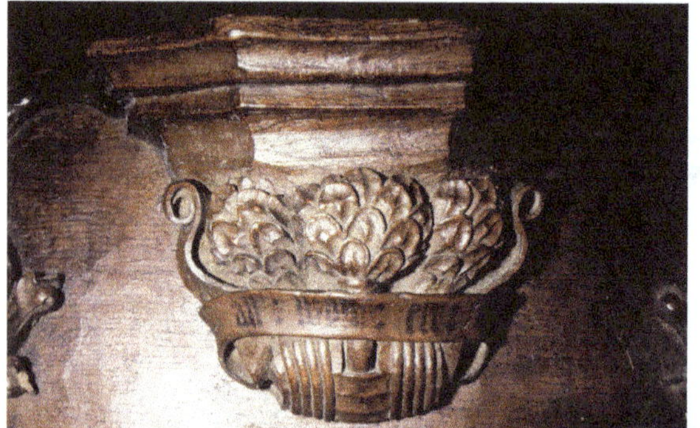

Stylised pine cones. Misericord, 1515. Richmond.

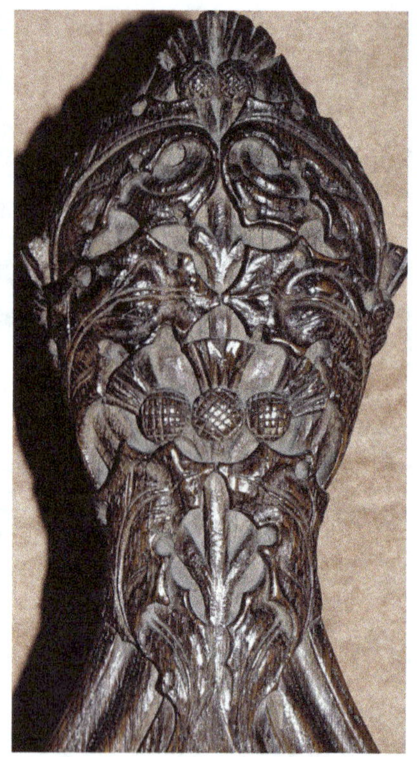

Thistle. Poppyhead, circa 1600s. Howden.

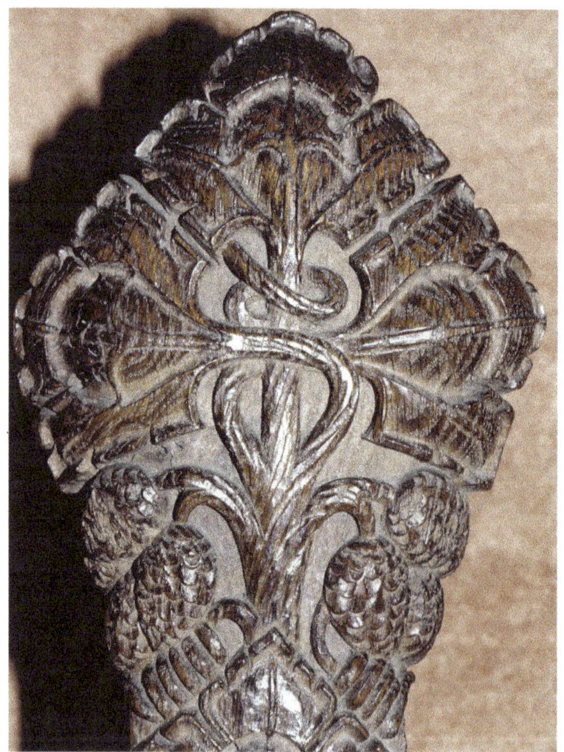

Hop with tendrils. Poppyhead, circa 1600s. Howden.

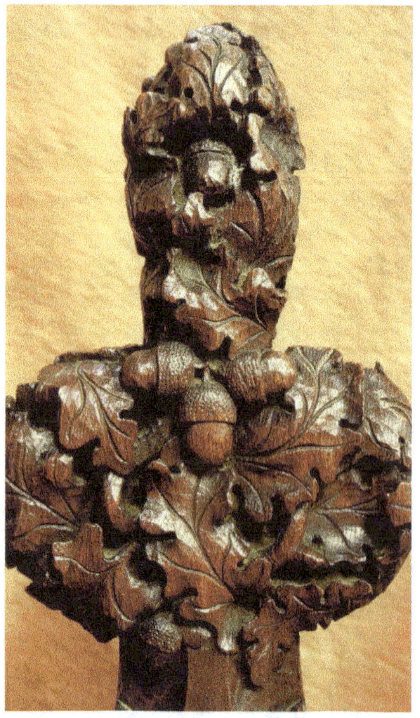

Oak leaves and acorns. Poppyhead, 1858. Rothwell.

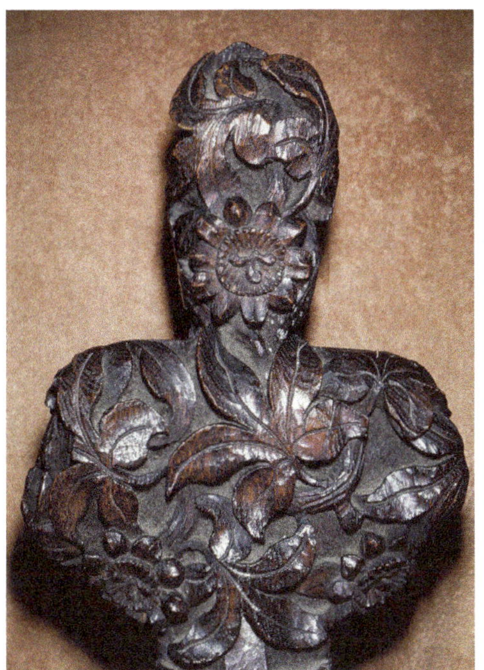
Passion-flower.Poppyhead, 1858.
Rothwell.

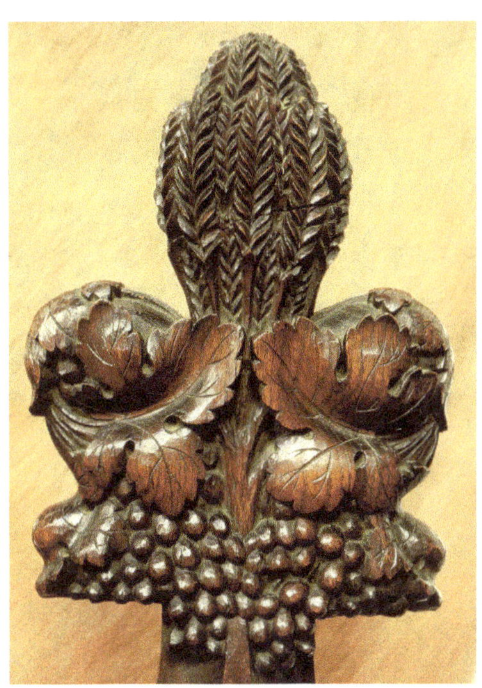
Vine and wheat. Poppyhead, 1858.
Rothwell.

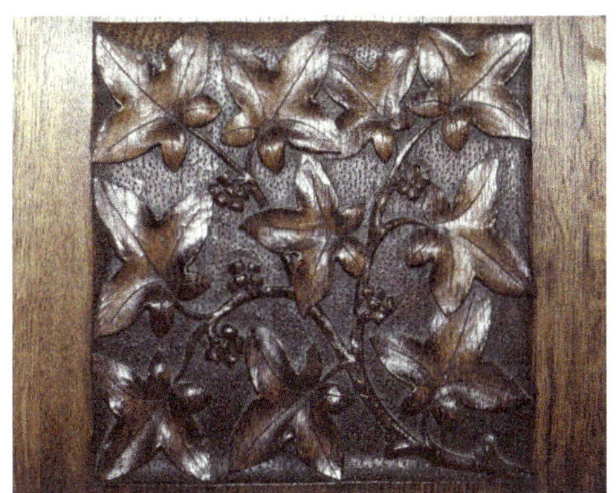
Ivy leaves and berries. Seat. Helme.

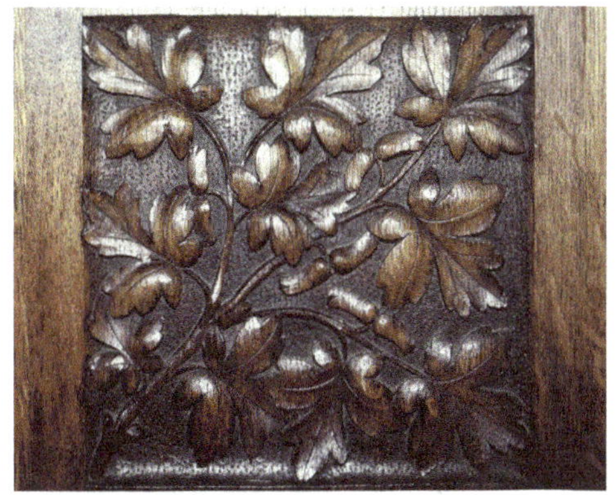
Maple leaves and keys. Seat. Helme.

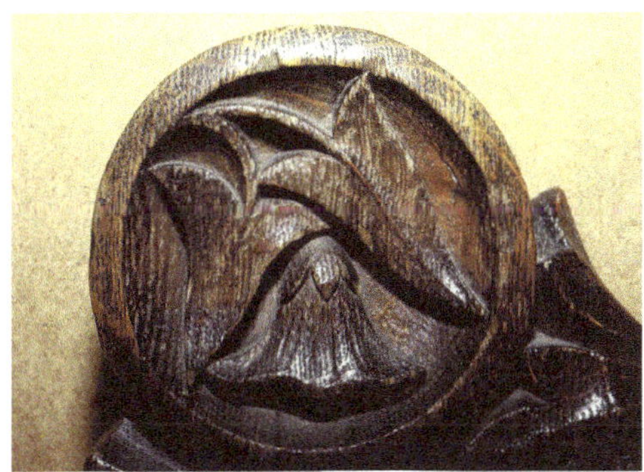
Convolvulus. Elbow. Helme.

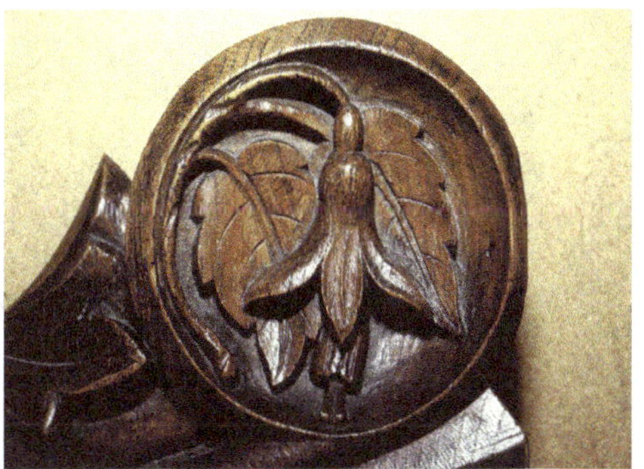
Fuchsia. Elbow. Helme.

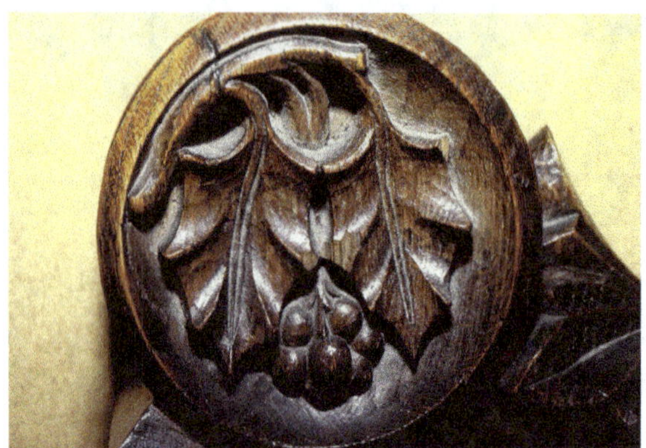
Holly and berries. Elbow. Helme.

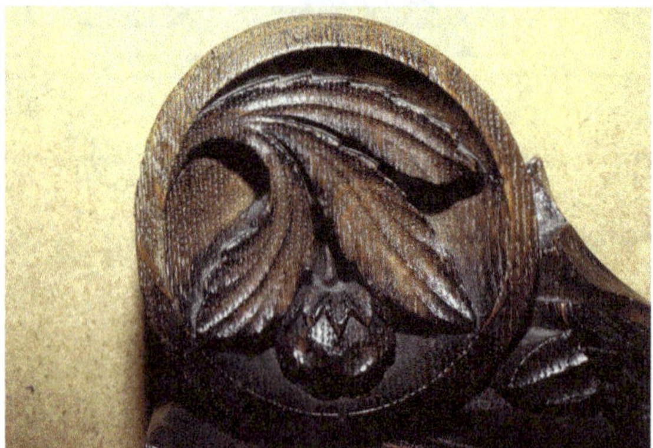
Strawberry. Elbow. Helme.

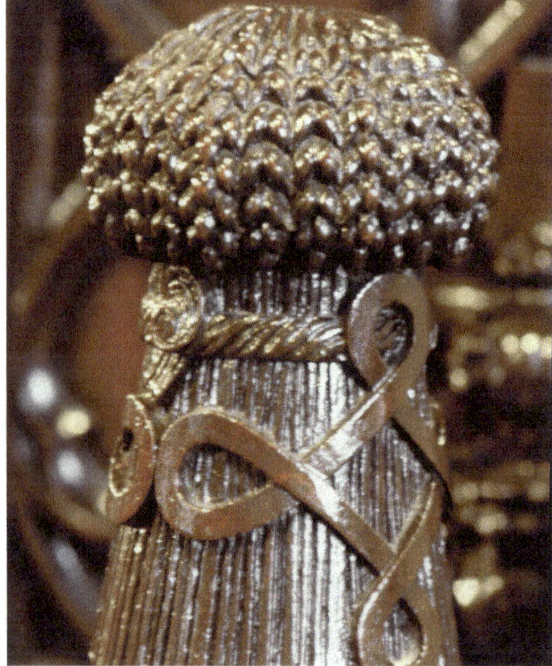
Wheatsheaf. Pulpit finial. Armitage Bridge.

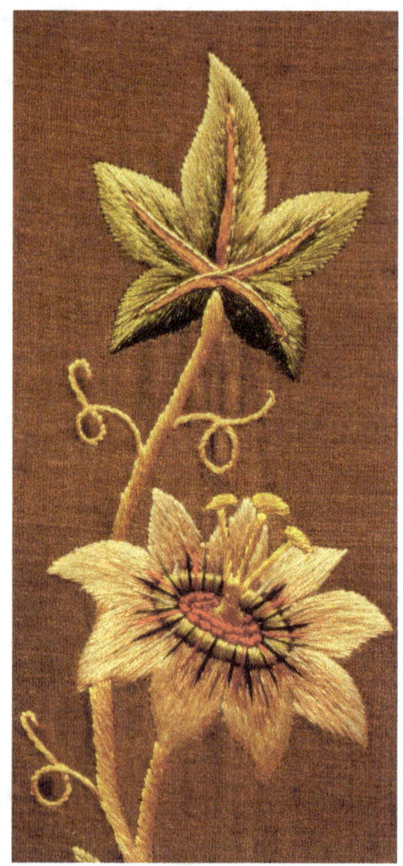
Passion-flower. Altar frontal. Greenfield.

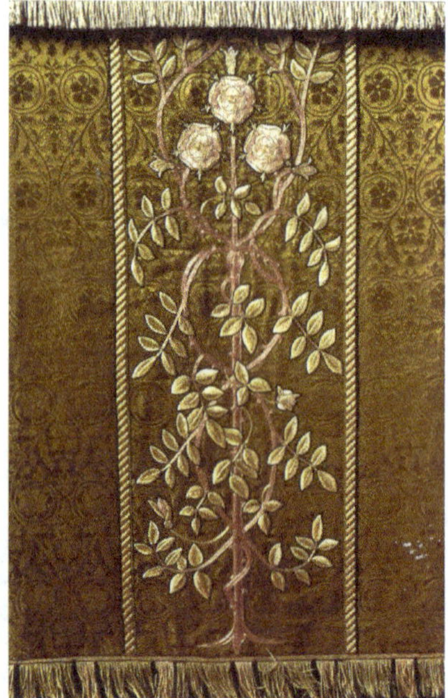
Roses. Altar frontal. Emley

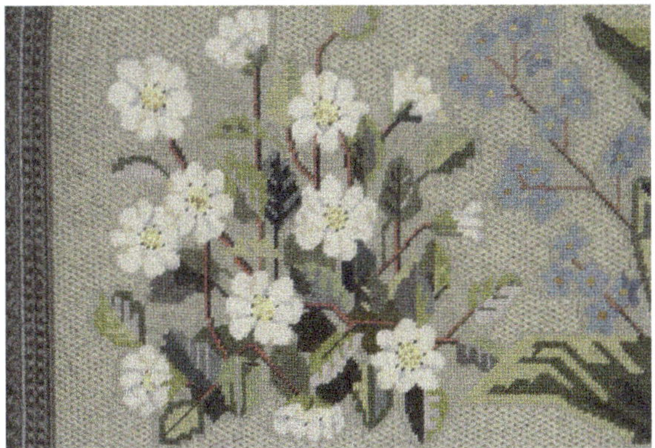

Mountain Avens representing Russia. Kneeler, 1981 York Minster.

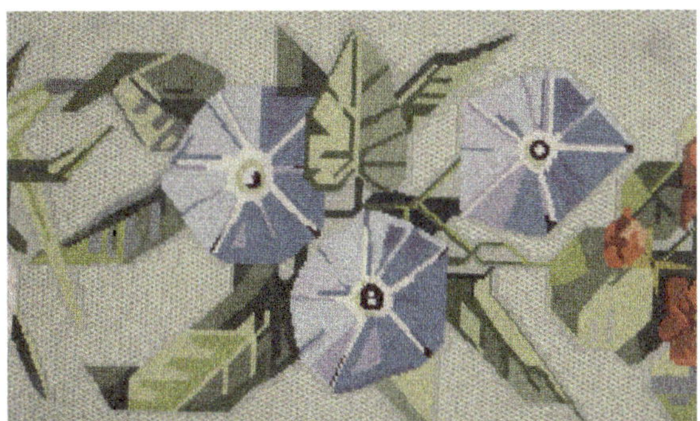

Morning Glory, representing C. and S. America. Kneeler. 1981. York Minster.

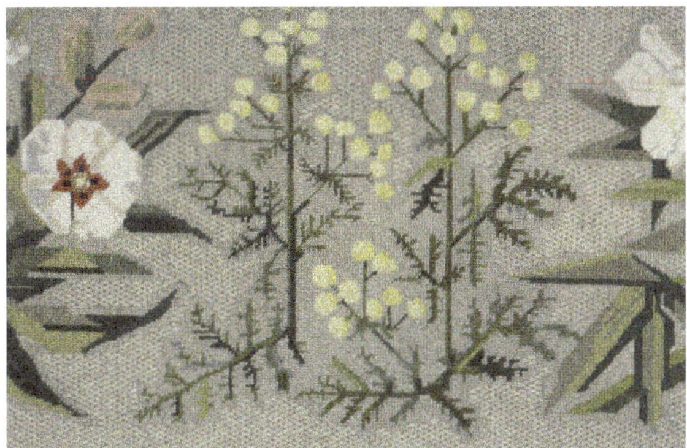

Tansy representing Europe. Kneeler, 1981. York Minster.

OTHER CREATURES in YORKSHIRE CHURCHES

Alligator/Crocodile	Grasshopper	Sea-anemone
Bee	Jellyfish	Sea- horse
Beetle	Lamprey	Slug
Butterfly	Lizard	Snail
Chameleon	Lobster	Snake
Cicada	Mayfly	Spider
Crab	Mite	Stickleback
Crayfish	Moth	Stingray
Cuttlefish	Newt	Sturgeon?
Dragonfly	Octopus	Swordfish
Fish	Periwinkle	Tortoise
Flying fish	Pike	Turtle
Frog	Salamander	Worm

Moths and butterflies, fish and snakes are often found but other insects, aquatic fauna and amphibians are not well represented and when they do appear they are seen more as decorative or heraldic motifs rather than as symbols in religion. When they do occur, their symbolism tends to have originated in the Bible and classical mythology, but beetles, lizards and snails may signify human decay.

Bee The bee is a survival of a pagan symbol of immortality. Various monastic orders carried out the rearing of bees. They supplied honey and wax for culinary and sacred purposes and were an ever present example to the brothers of diligence, watchfulness and order. A beehive or a swarm of bees is a reference to Ambrose, Bishop of Milan. According to the *Golden Legend*, when Ambrose was a baby in his cradle a swarm of bees flew into his mouth and out again and then ascended to heaven. This story is told of others who were noted for their eloquence, and they were said to have lips flowing with honey. The Cistercian monk, Saint Bernard of Clairvaux, was known as Doctor Mellifluus, a reference to the scientific name for the Honey Bee.

Beetle In Britain and most of the Germanic countries the Seven-spot Ladybird was dedicated to the Virgin Mary. It was directly dedicated to God in Latin countries. The seven spots on the wings are representative of the seven virtues of the Virgin Mary; the lady stands for Our Lady and the red colour of the wings are said to be the red of the Virgin's cloak.

Butterfly or **Moth** In Greek literature, Psyche, the soul personified, was often portrayed as a butterfly. In pre-Christian times there was a belief that a butterfly issued from and hovered above the mouth of the person who had just died. To Christians, the butterfly was the resurrection of the human soul. Each stage in the life-cycle of the insects is symbolic. The caterpillar represents life, the chrysalis death and the adult insect, resurrection. Up to and including part of the 17th century no distinction was made between moths and butterflies, moths were known as butterflies of the night.

Caddis fly No symbolic significance

Centipede No symbolic significance

Chameleon This reptile is an attribute of air one of the four elements. Pliny believed that the chameleon neither ate nor drank but lived on air.

Crab With its sideways movement the crab symbolised one who was devoted to an earthly life, its pleasures and luxuries. It was an 'unclean' food.

Crocodile Biblically speaking the crocodile was an 'unclean' fish, but it was honoured by the Egyptians as the living representative of God. It was thought to be tongueless and the lack of a tongue was likened to the Divine Word which needs no voice. The nictitating membrane, allowing the crocodile to see without itself being seen, was likened to God. In Job (41:1-34) the Leviathan is thought to be the crocodile. Mythologically, eclipses were supposed to have been caused by the creature wrapping its coils round the sun and this is referred to in Job (3:8). The creature is an attribute of Saint Theodore the warrior and may also symbolise death and hell. As far as is known all carvings in old English churches are of crocodiles and not alligators.

See also Elephant and Otter under Mammals.

Dragonfly This insect may signify baptism, as the larval stage is aquatic and the adult stage is aerial.

Fish Water creatures having fins and scales were 'clean' according to Mosaic Law (Deuteronomy 14:9-10) and could be eaten by the people. The fish is one of the earliest symbols of the Christian and is the traditional symbol of the Christian soul. The letters of the Greek word for fish - Ichthys - were taken as an acronym for Iesous Christos Theou Hyios Sotor, Jesus Christ, of God the Son, Saviour. Fish which are depicted eating each other are symbols of greed.

Fly The god of flies, Boal-zebub, whose symbol was a fly, could either bring or send away plagues of flies. In times of pestilence as soon as a sacrifice was offered to the 'Disperser of Flies', the flies were believed to perish and the pestilence to cease. Flies, like mice, were recognised as bringers of disease and it was common practice to display images of undesirable insects in order to keep them at bay. A painted fly would serve as a talisman against real flies.

Frog The second of the plagues of Egypt was said to be frogs, but it is more likely to have been toads. The food was contaminated and in Egypt toads are toxic but frogs are not. The croaking of the frog was likened to the croaking of the heretic and thus it represented heresy and corruption, and may also be indicative of those who grab at the ephemeral pleasures of this world.

Grasshopper Locusts are grasshoppers and they were the only species of insects regarded as 'clean'. The eighth plague was that of locusts. Punishment was sent or threatened by God through locusts. Christian Mission is signified by grasshoppers.

Lizard In classical mythology, Ceres (Greek, Demeter) the goddess of agriculture, turned a boy into a lizard because he called her greedy. In the Middle Ages, when a Christian moral was found in many classical myths, the lizard stood for the Synagogue and Ceres for the Church. The bestiary lizard goes blind as it ages and creeps into a hole in a wall facing east. Its sight is restored when it stretc.hes itself towards the rising sun. It is a symbol of regeneration and the illuminating influence of the Gospel. It is also an attribute of Logic, one of the seven liberal arts.

Lobster According to Mosaic Law (Leviticus 11: 9-12) any creature which lived in water and had neither fins nor scales, was an 'unclean' food and as such, the people were forbidden to eat it.

Moth See Butterfly.

Octopus No symbolic significance.

Scorpion From its treacherous and often deadly sting the scorpion is a symbol of Judas, evil, and infidelity.

Sea-horse In early Christian art, the 'great fish' which swallowed Jonah was represented as the hippocampus. This is an example of a classical image being adapted to Christian use as sea-horses drew the chariots of Galatea and Neptune.

Snake or **Serpent** These creatures are symbols of evil and chaos and are the biblical synonym for deceit and the devil, but they can also signify fertility, wisdom and the power to heal. The snake was sacred to Hygeia the goddess of healing, to Asclepius the Greek god of medicine who had a snake as his insignia and to Hippocrates the Greek physician.

The serpent was said to have four characteristics. It sloughed its old skin by scraping through a narrow crack in rock, and thus it became a symbol of baptismal regeneration, i.e. the putting off of sin by man. Its second characteristic was that when it went to a spring to drink it left venom in its hole. The third characteristic was to be afraid of a naked man and to flee from him, but to attack the man if he was clothed. The final characteristic was that when attacked, it sought to protect its head by exposing its body. This trait was applied to Christians, who should endure for Christ's sake.

The asp resists the wiles of the snake charmer by laying one ear to the ground and blocking the other ear with its tail. 'They are like the deaf adder' (Psalm 58:4-5) was interpreted as shutting one's ears to satanic suggestions. The association of the snake and wisdom is found in the Bible (Matthew 10:16). A snake with a tail in its mouth is signifying eternity.

Shrimp Like the crab and the lobster, the shrimp is an 'unclean' food.

Snail There is an ancient belief that the visible trail left by snails meant that they were gradually melting away (Psalm 58:8).

Spider A spider with a fly signifies covetousness. One with a chalice or monstrance is a symbol of Bishop Norbert. This an allusion to the story in which he found a poisonous spider in the cup of sacramental wine as he was about to receive it. He drank the wine and was unharmed. In Cornwall it was considered to be unlucky to kill a spider because the web spun by the creature over Jesus in the manger hid the child from Herod. In both Christian and Islamic folklore a spider spun its web across the entrance to the cave where the Holy Family had taken refuge. The hunters did not search the cave believing that the web would have been torn had anyone taken shelter in there.

Toad Like frogs, toads are representative of heresy. They are attributes of death when found in conjunction with either a skull or a skeleton.

Tortoise The tortoise of Leviticus is one of the many 'unclean' animals which were forbidden food to the Israelites. May you be turned upside down like a tortoise (and die) is a curse.

Whelk Figures are frequently found rising from whelk shells. These figures may be pilgrims, armed men, grotesques or monsters. Sometimes a vine bearing grapes is found and this may be a symbol of Christ.

Woodlouse No symbolic significance.

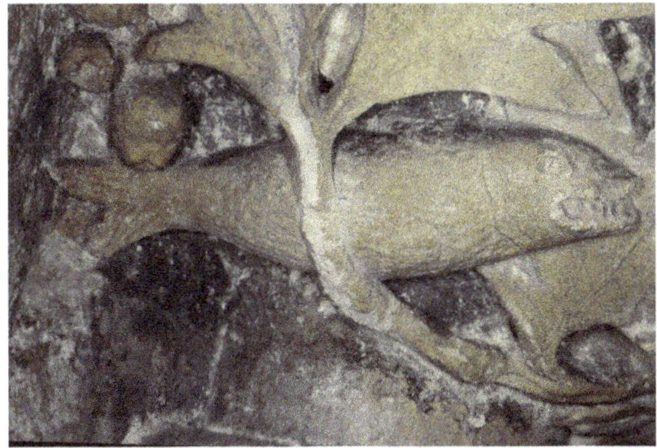

Fish with a mouthful of teeth. Capital, circa 1250. Selby Abbey.

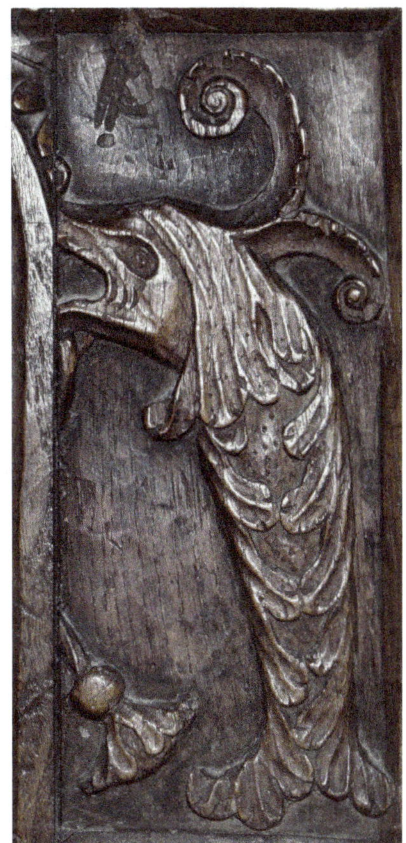

Possibly a fish. Stall end, 14th/15th century. Hemingborough.

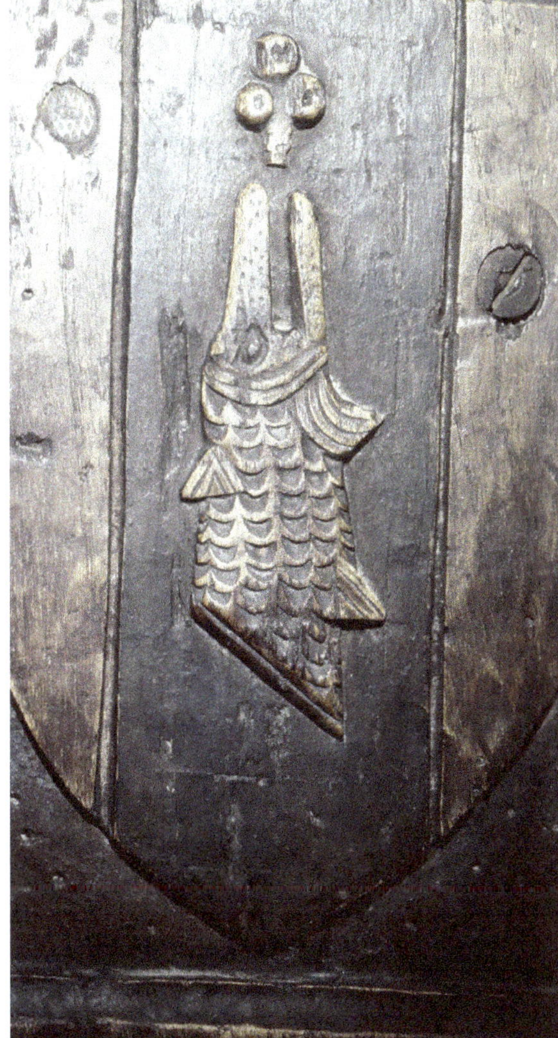

Fish, possibly a Sturgeon. Stall end, 14th/15th century. Hemingborough.

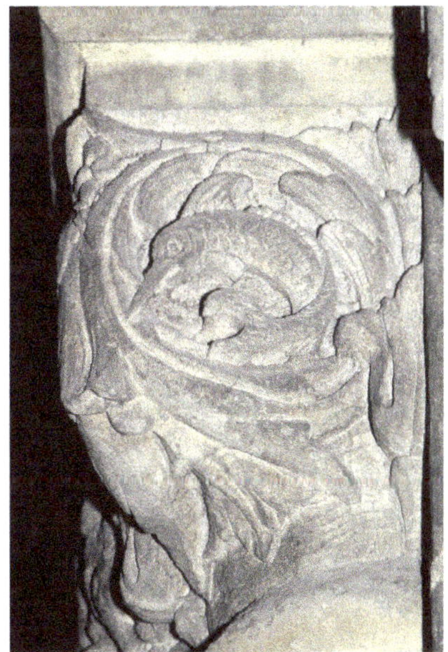

Swordfish. Capital, 1924-61. Ampleforth.

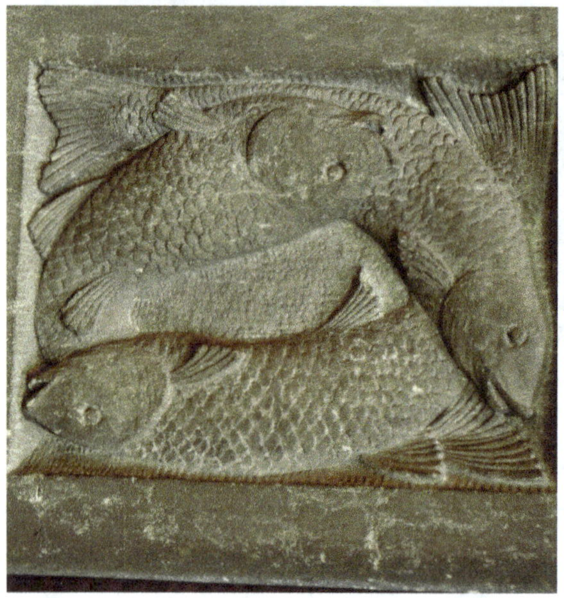

Three fish in a circle. Font, circa 1824. Woodhouse.

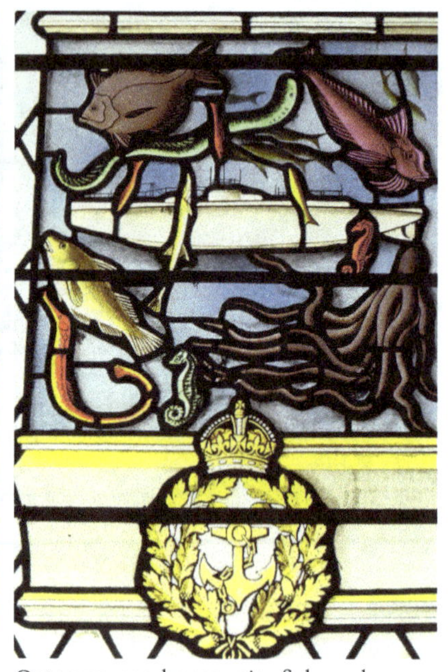

Octopus, sea-horse, pipefish and rockling. Window. Hemingborough.

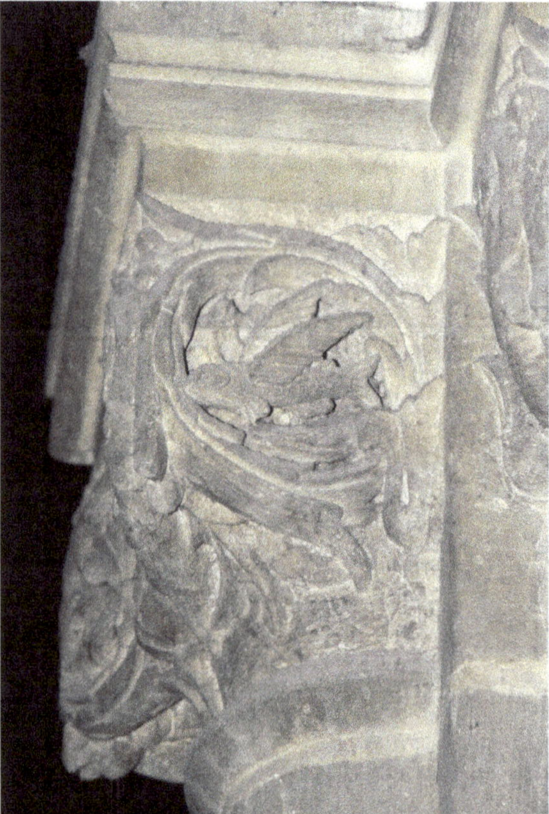

Flying fish. Capital, 1924-61. Ampleforth.

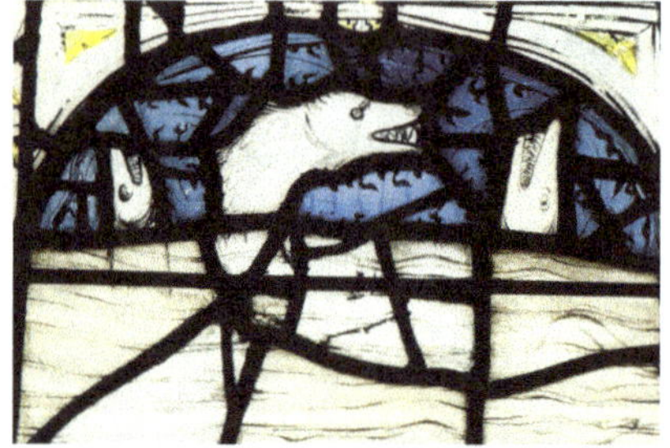

Lamprey. Window, circa 1420. All Saints, North Street, York.

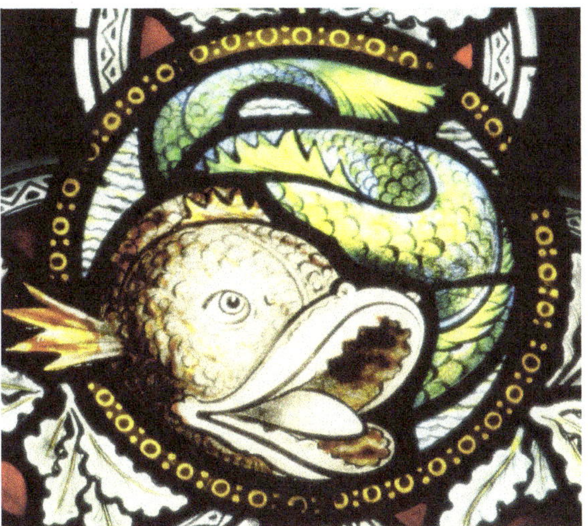

Fish with tongue. Window. Hunsingore.

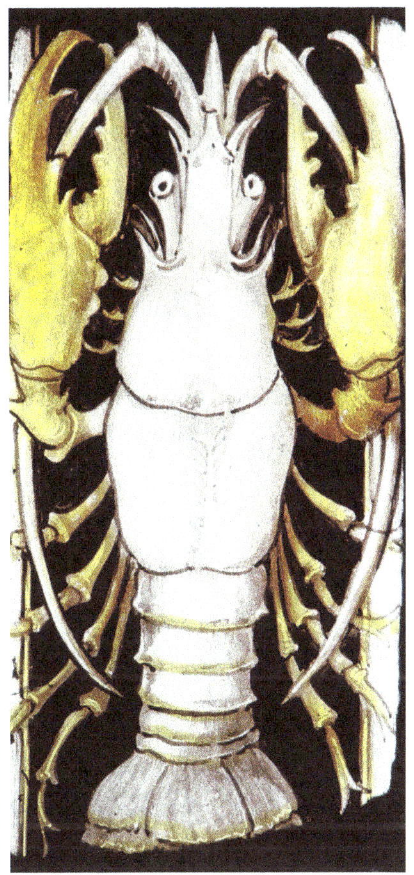

Lobster. Window, 1905.
Bolton on Swale.

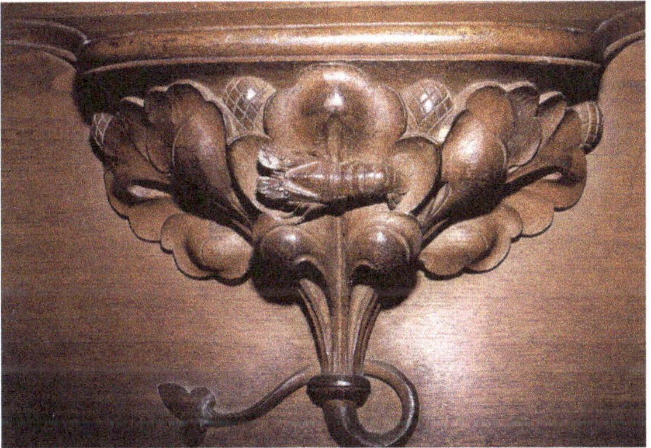

Crayfish. Misericord, 1872-78. Studley Royal.

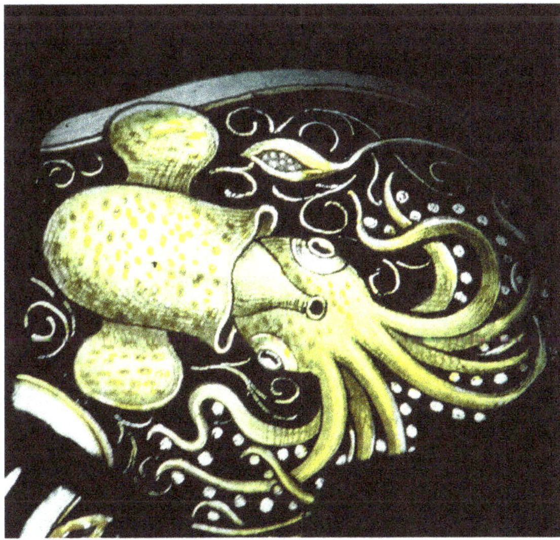

Cuttlefish. Window, 1905. Bolton on Swale.

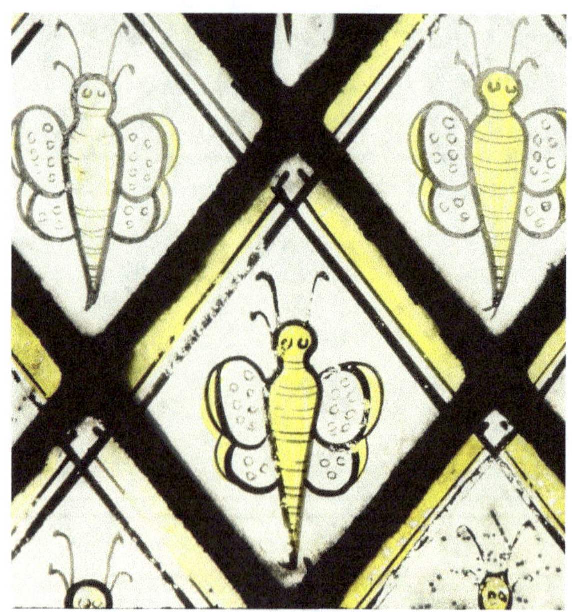

Butterflies with two pairs of antennae.
Quarries, circa 1300s and Victorian. St Denys, York.

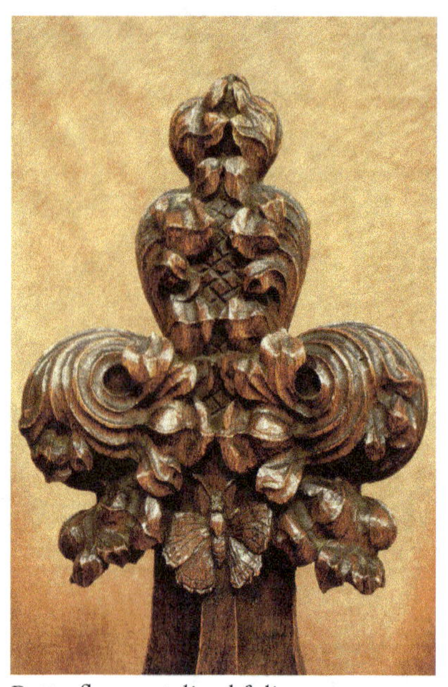

Butterfly on stylised foliage.
Poppyhead, 1858. Rothwell.

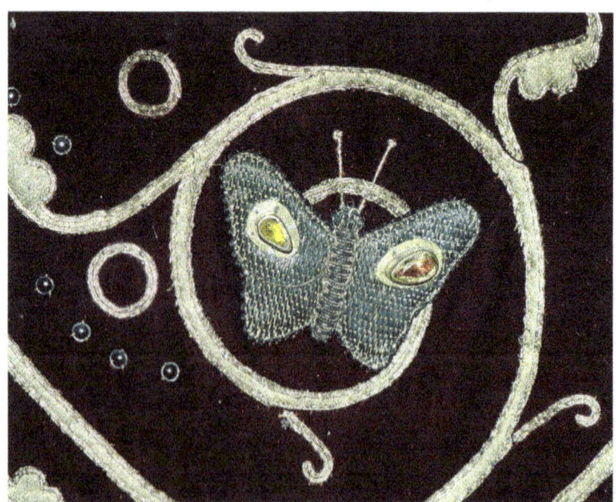

Butterfly embroidery. Altar frontal, 1872-76. Skelton.

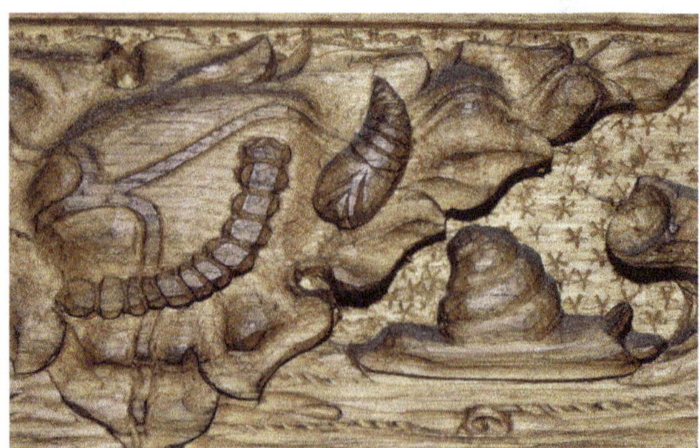

Larva, pupa and snail. Screen. Emley.

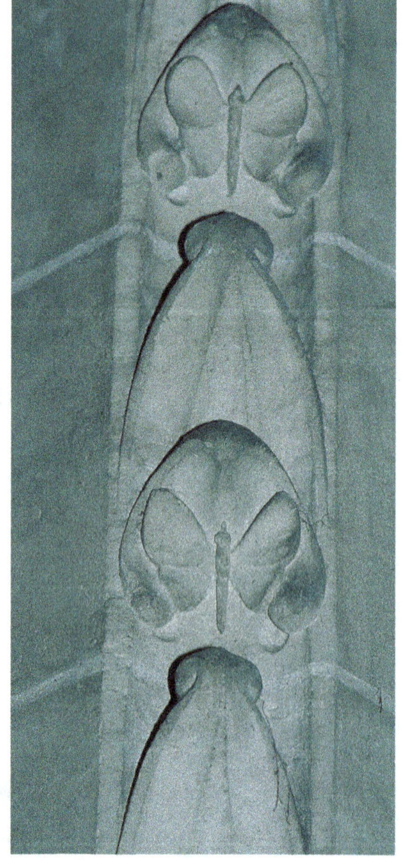

Butterfly. Pillar,1872-78. Studley Royal.

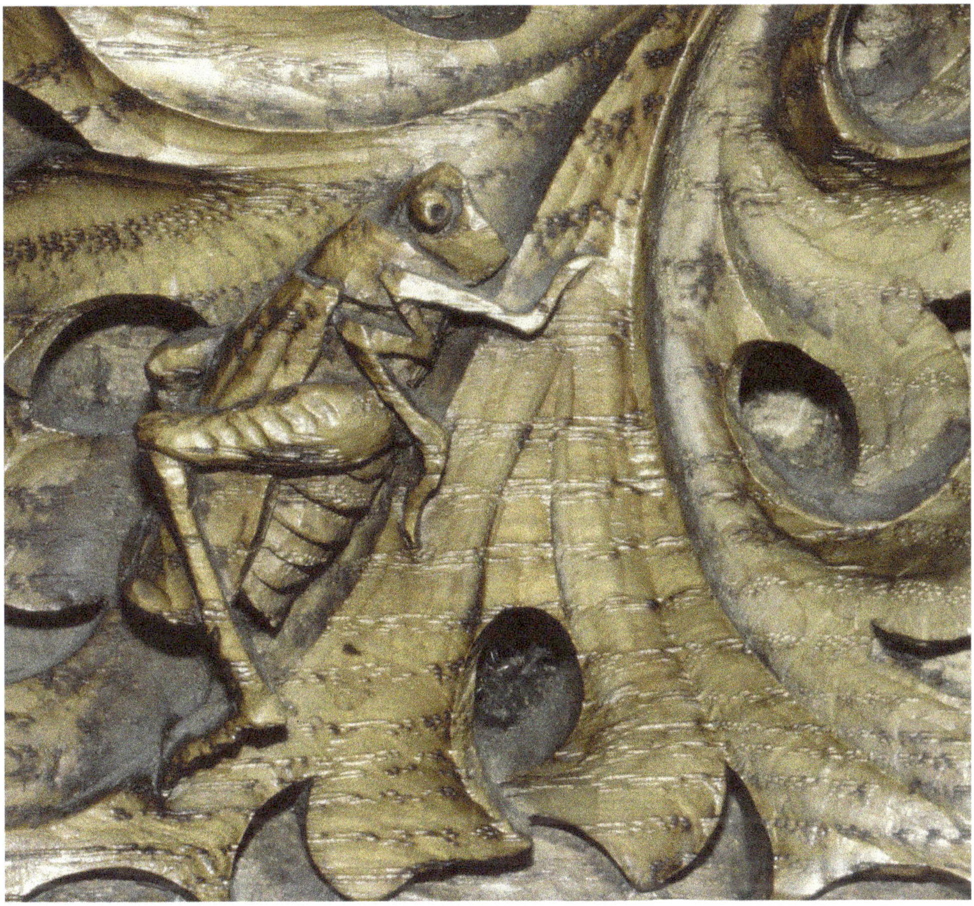

Grasshopper. Altar, circa 1930. West Tanfield.

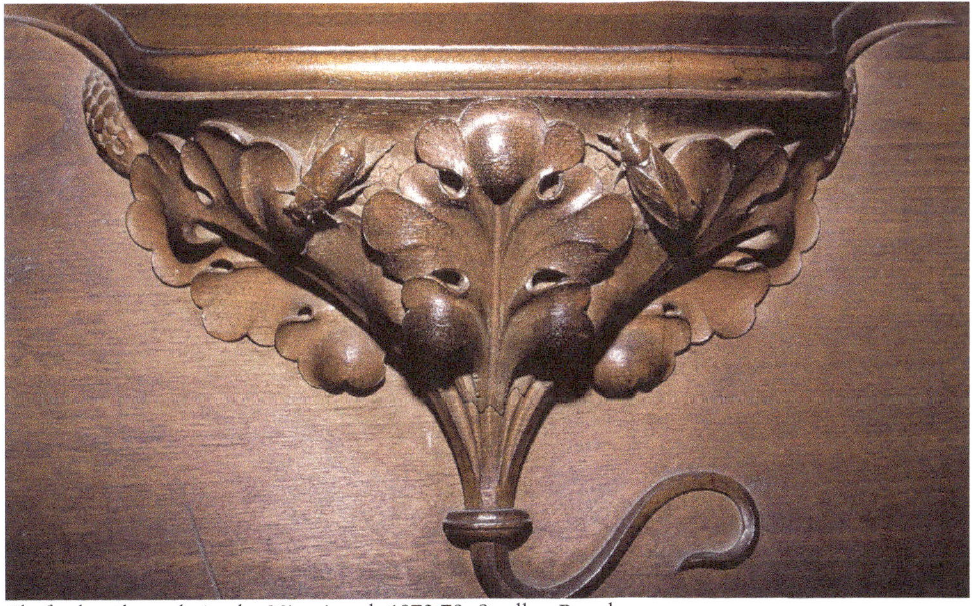

Chafer beetle and cicada. Misericord, 1872-78. Studley Royal.

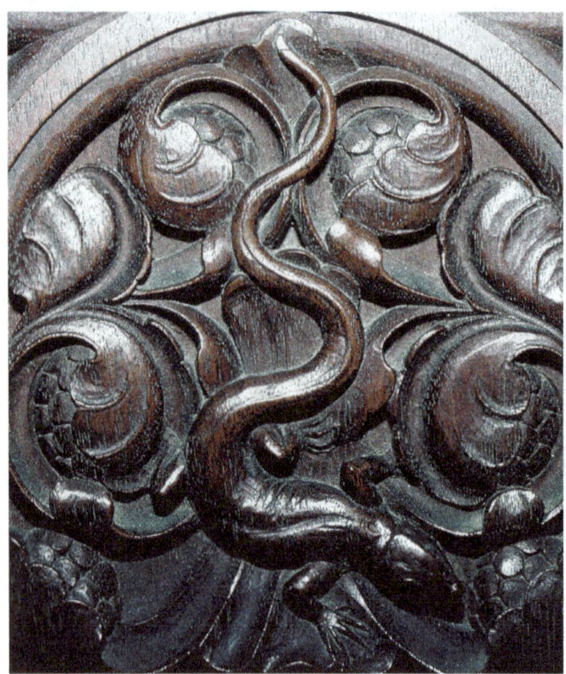

Lizard. Choir stall, 1872-76. Skelton.

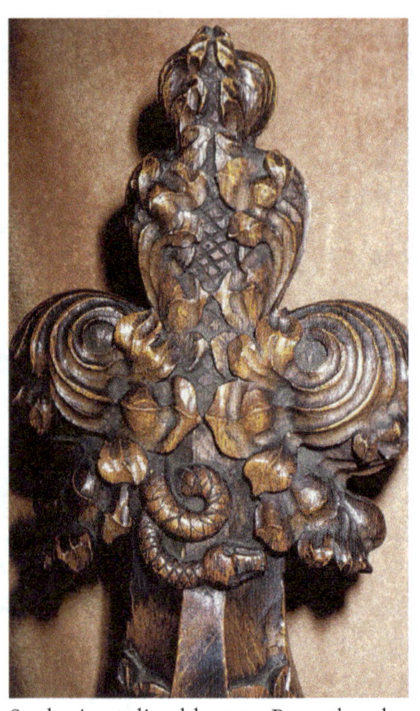

Snake in stylised leaves. Poppyhead, 1858. Rothwell.

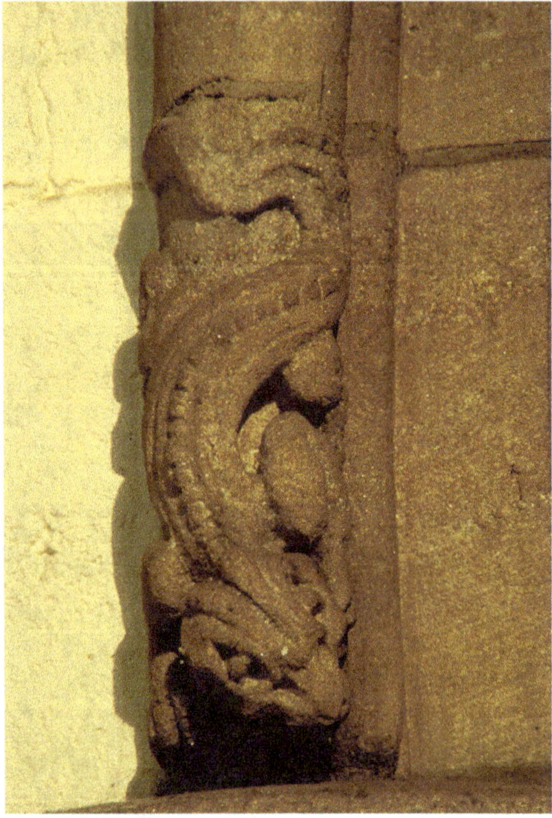

Lizard peering down pillar. Headingly

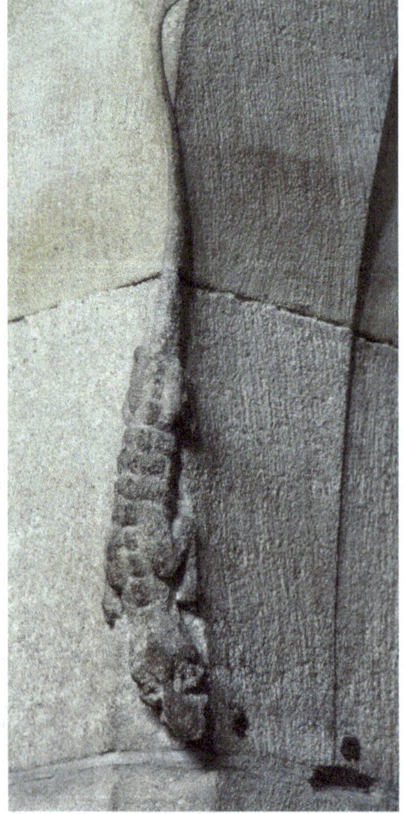

Lizard running down pillar. Headingly

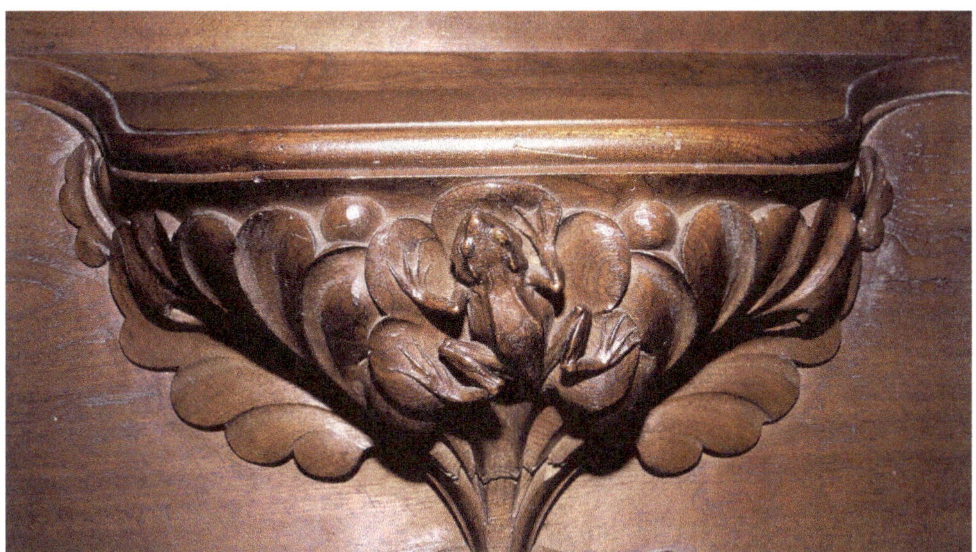

Delightful dorsal view of a frog. There should be five toes on the hind feet. Misericord, 1872-78. Studley Royal.

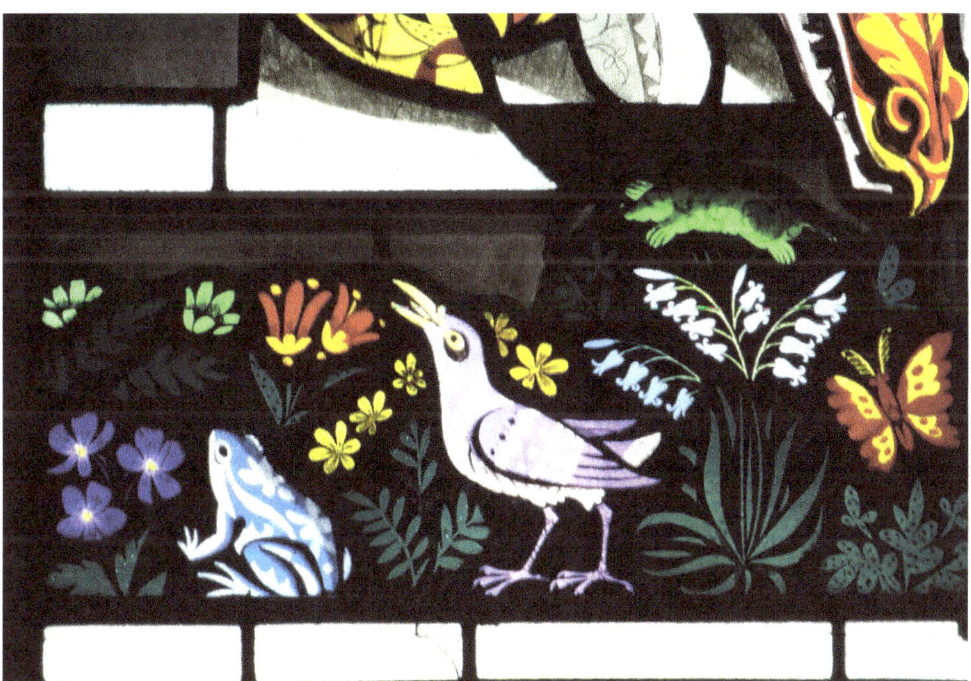

Delightfully coloured bird, frog and butterfly. Window border, 1930. Adel.

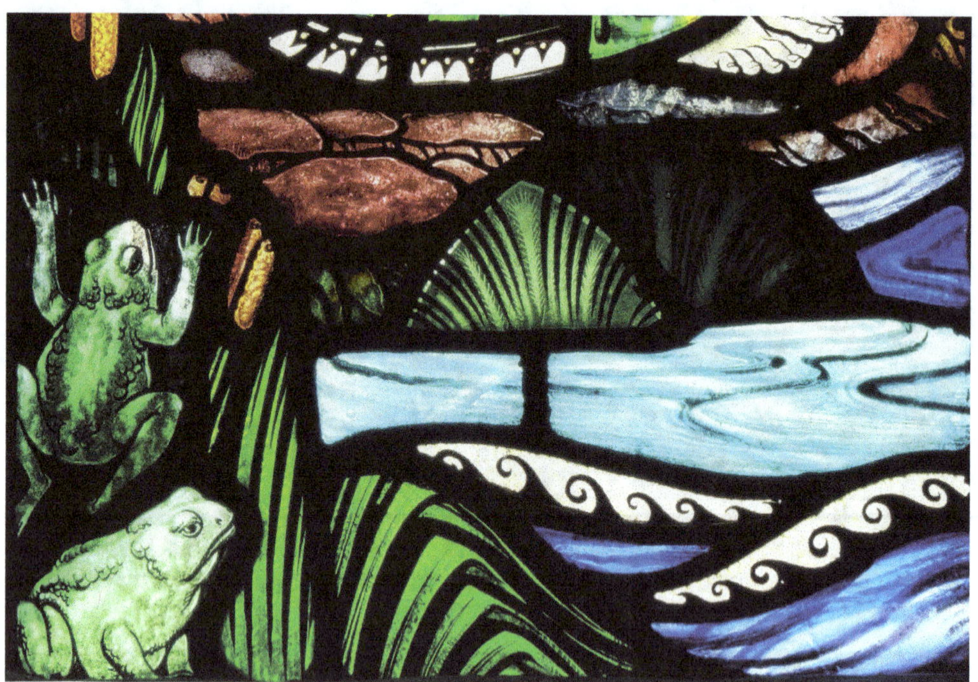

Two frogs. Window, 1951. Penistone.

FABULOUS/MYTHICAL BEASTS in YORKSHIRE CHURCHES

Amphisbaena
Aspido Chelone
Basilisk
Blemya
Caladrius
Centaur
Dragon
Green Man
Griffin
Harpy
Mermaid/Siren
Salamander
Unicorn
Wodehouse
Wyvern

Books of Beasts or bestiaries have been described as religious natural history books and medieval moralising treatises. The earliest bestiary was probably compiled about the end of the 4th or early part of the 5th century by a Greek monk of Alexandria. Later bestiaries were derived from and quote as their author 'Physiologus'. This was the standard guide to scientific knowledge and the name translates as the 'Naturalist or 'Natural Philosopher' and was based upon moralising tales.

Some of the creatures described are hybrid images: for example, the centaur is part man part horse; the griffin part lion part eagle whilst the unicorn is a horse with the spiral tusk of a narwhal.

The books were one of the main sources of inspiration for the carvers and even though some of the subjects would have been familiar to them, e.g. the bat, they are often anatomically incorrect and have been carved from book illustrations rather than from actual specimens.

Around the south doorway at Alne are medallions with carvings of animals taken from a bestiary source. We know this because the titles appear on the medallions as they do in manuscripts.

Amphisbaena A symbol of deceit and evil, the amphisbaena was thought to be a serpent with a second head at the tip of its tail. By sticking one head into the mouth of the other, it had the ability to bowl along in either direction like a hoop. It is now known that the mythical amphisbaena was founded on fact. It is a limbless tropical lizard which, when danger threatens, lifts its tail menacingly to look like a head.

Aspido Chelone This beast is a representation of the devil that deludes the pleasure seekers of this world and then destroys them. See Whale under Mammals.

Basilisk Called the little king of reptiles because the comb on top of its head resembled a crown, the basilisk, dating from the 14th century, was said to have hatched from the egg of a seven year old cock. The egg was laid in a dunghill and was hatched by either a toad or a serpent. It had the head, wings and feet like those of a cock, the body and tail like those of a serpent, and a lethal glance. The only animal which could attack it in safety was the weasel, and this was only possible if the weasel had previously eaten rue. The basilisk was the devil and the weasel represented humanity, which, by digesting the Old and New Testaments, obtained protection. From the moment of the basilisk's birth, it hid itself from human eyes because if seen first by man it would die, but if it saw a man first then the man would die. Whoever wished to kill the creature held a crystal ball before his own face and this deflected the deadly venom from the basilisk's eyes, hurling it back upon the beast which was then killed with its own poison. The explanation for this was that the creature was the devil and the only way Christ could overcome such evil was by entering a vessel clearer than crystal, i.e. the Virgin's womb.

This creature is not to be confused with the Green Basilisk Lizard also known as the Jesus Christ Lizard from its ability to run on water, and which is native to the rain forests of Central America.

Blemya This is represented as a grotesque human with eyes and a mouth in a headless chest. It may also be a head on legs. It is a symbol of gluttony, evil and corruption.

Caladrius The caladrius was said to be a pure white bird capable of absorbing human sickness and whose excrement was a cure for those with failing eyesight. It had the power to foretell if a sick person would live or die. If the disease were fatal the bird would look away from the patient, but would look at him or her if the patient was going to survive. Because it was pure white without marks or blemishes it was likened to Christ who was without sin. He came to save the Jews who rejected Him and so He turned away from them like the caladrius does to the dying man, and turned to the Gentiles bearing their sins and healing their illnesses. The only recorded example is found at Alne on one of the stone carved medallions surrounding the south doorway.

Centaur This fabulous beast was half man half horse. The man represented Christ and the horse His vengeance on those who had betrayed Him. A centaur shooting arrows signifies Christ as the Avenger or Harrower of Hell. The arrow is sometimes described as the fiery dart of the wicked, as the triumph of animal passions, or as men torn between spirituality and bestiality.

Dragon The dragon has the head of an animal, the wings of a bat, four legs with talons like those of an eagle, and the barbed tail of a serpent with which it kills with a single blow. It is an evil creature and a symbol of the devil. Classical sources state that the dragon and the elephant are enemies. On sighting an elephant the dragon springs up and tries to suffocate it. The fight continues until the elephant, weakened by loss of blood, falls, and in doing so lands on the dragon crushing it to death. The bestiary dragon is an enemy of the doves which shelter in The Tree of Life found in India. The birds live in the branches and eat the fruit which the tree bears. Dragons are afraid of the tree and go to the side not in shadow. If a dove ventures beyond the tree, the dragon will catch and eat the bird. The tree represents God, its shadow Christ the Son, the dove the Holy Spirit or the Christian and the fruit, wisdom. A dragon on its back in the stocks depicts Satan's degradation. In the legend of Saint George and the Dragon, Saint George was a native of Cappadocia and a tribune in the army of Diocletian. One day, journeying to join his legion, he came to a city in either Libya or Syria where a dragon had been devouring flocks and herds belonging to the citizens. When this food supply became exhausted the people had to supply the monster with their children who were chosen by lot. The lot fell upon Cleodolinda the daughter of the king. Saint George saw her weeping as she went on her way to the dragon. He fought the beast pinning it to the ground where it was bound with Cleodolinda's girdle, it was then led to the city where it was killed. After this event the citizens became Christians. Saint George was martyred for trampling on an anti-Christ edict of Diocletian's. Both Saint George and Saint Michael can be found fighting dragons. Saint George is usually depicted on horseback, whilst Saint Michael bears a pair of wings. Saint George was developed from an ancient Egyptian religion, which, on April 23rd. celebrated the death of Typhon who murdered his brother Osiris.

Green Man or **Jack in the Green** A foliate head pre-dating Christianity probably Celtic in origin, this is a symbol of renewal and rebirth; a uniting of the human and vegetable kingdoms. In the earliest representations he appears as a head with hair and features formed from a single leaf or many leaves. In later forms he is represented with foliage issuing from his mouth and sometimes from his ears and eyes to simulate hair as it curls round his face. In a third depiction the face is placed in the centre of vegetation to represent either flower or fruit.

Griffin Supposed to be the offspring of a lion and an eagle and the most noble of land and air animals, the griffin had the body and legs like those of a lion, and the head and wings like those of an eagle - a combination of the noblest of birds and beasts. It was hostile to horses, would tear humans to pieces and was known for its great strength and ferocity. It was an ambivalent symbol standing for Christ, covetousness and persecution. Like the lion, it represented either good in its nobility or evil in its ferocity and in the French bestiaries it was symbolic of the devil. It was said to guard hidden treasures and so became a symbol of watchfulness and was adopted as a badge by Edward III. According to the Flight of Alexander legend, Alexander having reached the end of the world, wished to see its extent and to visit heaven. He harnessed two starving griffins to the chair on which he sat. Meat was fixed to the ends of two spears in the hope that in chasing food, the griffins would fly higher and higher in a vain attempt to obtain it, rather in the fashion of the proverbial carrot dangled in front of a donkey. This legend was interpreted as how man should hunger for the beauty of heaven.

Harpy The harpy was part woman and part bird, a dirty and avaricious monster derived from the Greek harpy, meaning snatcher. She is the ancient counterpart to the modern femme fatale, and depicts an unscrupulous but irresistible woman who uses her femininity to satisfy her desires and in so doing destroys the object of her cravings.

Mermaid A mermaid has the top half of a woman and the tail of a fish. She may be derived from an ancient fish-tailed goddess who turned her lovers into dolphins. Mermaids and sirens by their sweet music were believed to lure sailors to their deaths. 'Beware of those who speak sweet words but whose deeds are evil'. They are symbolic of the temptress, luring men away from the path of salvation to their destruction on the rocks of passion. If a mermaid is illustrated holding a mirror (a sign of self-centredness) she represents deceit, lust, luxury and pride. If she is holding a fish (sole) she signifies a soul either caught by the enchantment of evil, or a soul in the grip of earthly passion. She may also be found holding a brush and comb, or suckling either lions or dolphins. If the former it signifies vanity, the latter lust.

Mermen are rarely found. They represent Dagon, a Philistine god of agriculture whose temple at Gaza was pulled down by Samson.

Salamander This is a reptile-like creature which is in impervious to and lives in and on fire and with the power to extinguish flames. It is a symbol of the righteous man who overcomes temptation. It produces deadly venom with which it infects fruit and anyone who eats the fruit dies. This is equated to man who is unscathed by the deadly poison of evil and temptation.

Siren True sirens differ from mermaids in that they are female in form from the waist upward and bird-like in their lower parts. Sirens were derived from

Near Eastern mythology and were supposed to be the daughters of Achelous and Terpsichore. The sirens originally had wings, but after quarrelling with the Muses they were deprived of them and were vanquished. Like mermaids they lure sailors to their deaths by singing sweet music. Greek and Latin poets said that listeners forgot everything, even forgetting to eat, and so they died of starvation. Because sirens entice sailors they represent the temptations of the flesh.

Unicorn This animal is a symbol of Christ because of its purity. The earliest description of the unicorn occurs about four hundred BC. In the centre of its forehead it had a horn which was credited with the power to detect and be an antidote to poisons, to purify what ever it touched and to be an aphrodisiac. The same aphrodisiacal powers are attributed to the horn of the rhinoceros and may have been developed from stories of the unicorn's horn. The animal could run so swiftly that no hunter was able to catch it so the following stratagem was employed. A virgin was sent into the wood on her own and on seeing her, the unicorn would leap into her lap and embrace her, whereupon the hunter, who had been hiding behind a tree, approached and captured the creature. An alternative method of capture was for the hunter to stand in front of a tree and as the unicorn charged, step aside at the last moment so the horn became embedded in the tree trunk. These stories represent the incarnation and death of Christ at the hands of the Jews. The unicorn on its own symbolises Christ, the virgin and the unicorn together symbolise the incarnation and passion and the single horn represents the oneness of the Father and Son. The virgin signifies Our Lady, the unicorn resting its head in her lap symbolises the incarnation, and the unicorn's death at the hand of the hunter is Our Lord's death and passion. Although said to be the size of a kid, the animal is usually illustrated as being much larger.

Wodehouse The wodehouse was a wild man who lived in trees in India. Until he had killed a lion and used its skin as a garment, he was naked. He symbolised unregenerate man. A wodehouse fighting a dragon was the Christian soul fighting human passions.

Wyvern Wyverns were evil creatures, similar to dragons, but they had two legs instead of four. When lions are depicted with wyverns, the lions are a symbol of goodness.

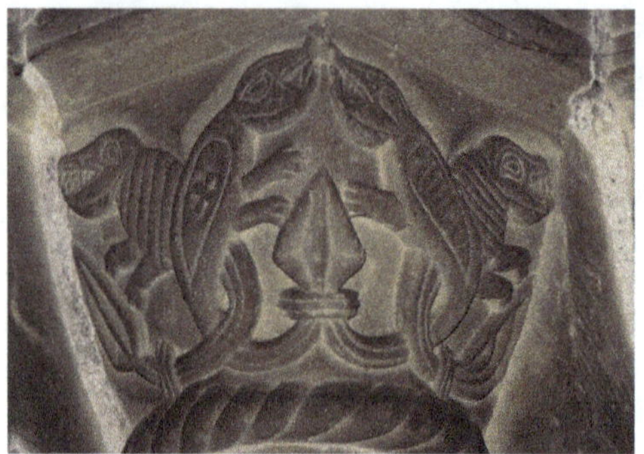
Christianised and pagan salamanders. Capital, Norman. Adel.

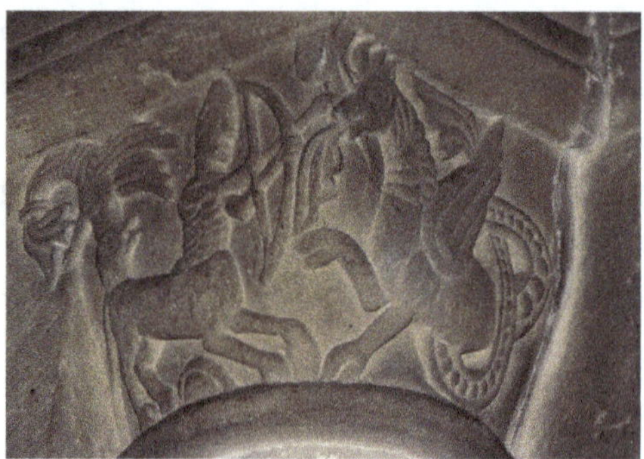
Centaur fighting a dragon breathing fire. Capital, Norman. Adel.

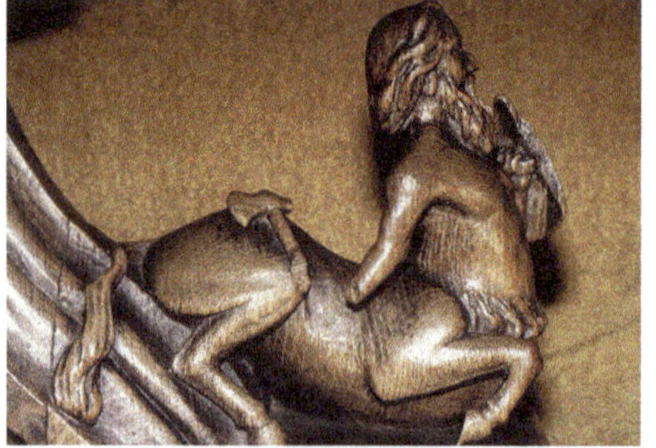
Centaur right view. Elbow, 1490. Richmond.

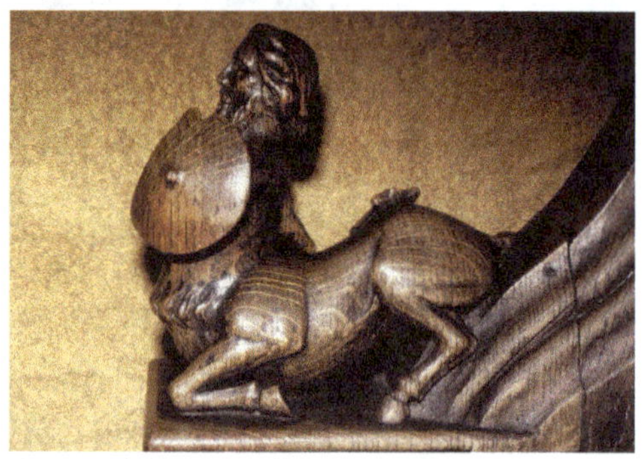
Centaur left view. Elbow, 1490. Ripon.

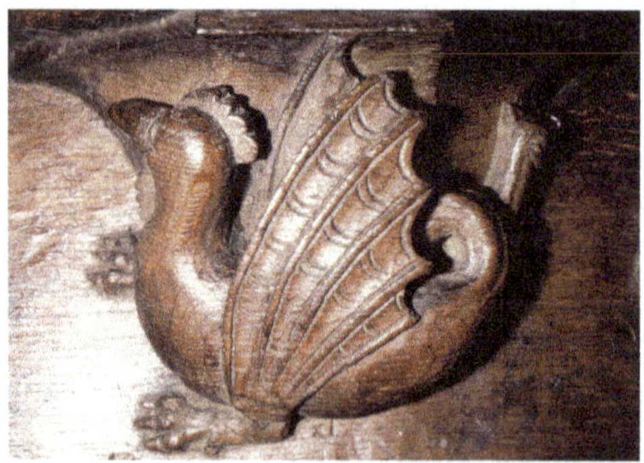
Basilisk with a face in its tail. Misericord, 1515. Richmond.

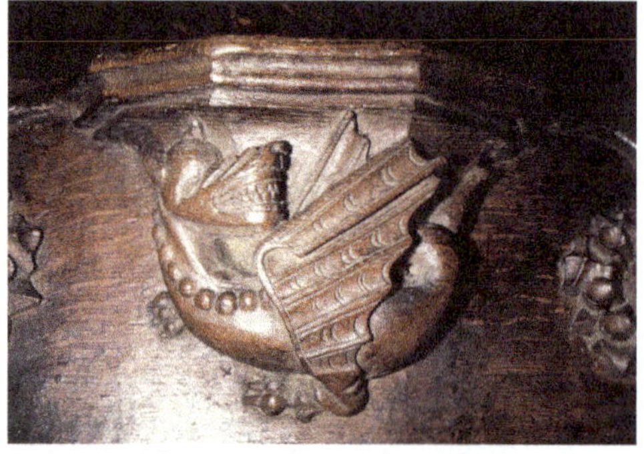
Dragon with enormous teeth. Misericord, 1515. Richmond.

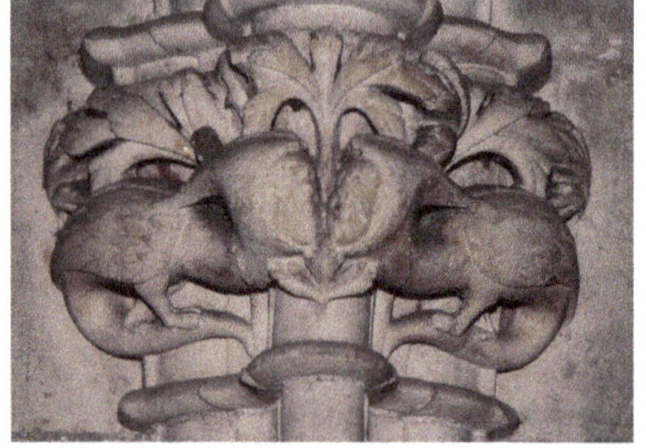
Two grotesques. Capital, 1280-90. York Minster.

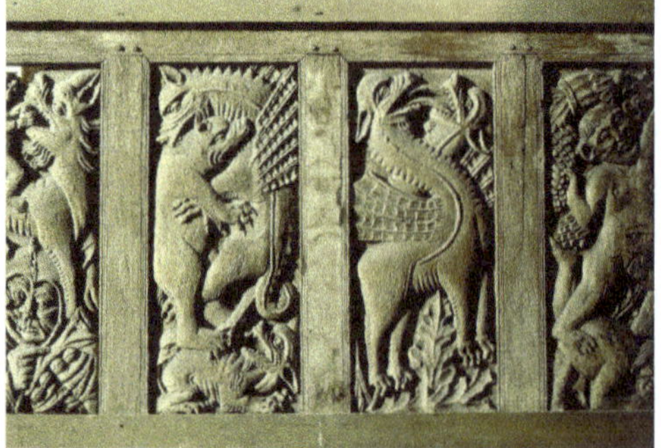
Crisply carved monsters. Panel, 1520-30. Hemingborough.

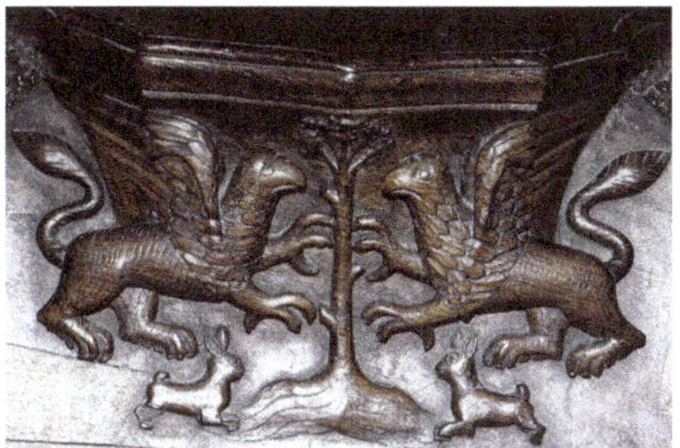
Griffin between the Tree of Life with two rabbits. Misericord, circa 1445. Beverley St Mary.

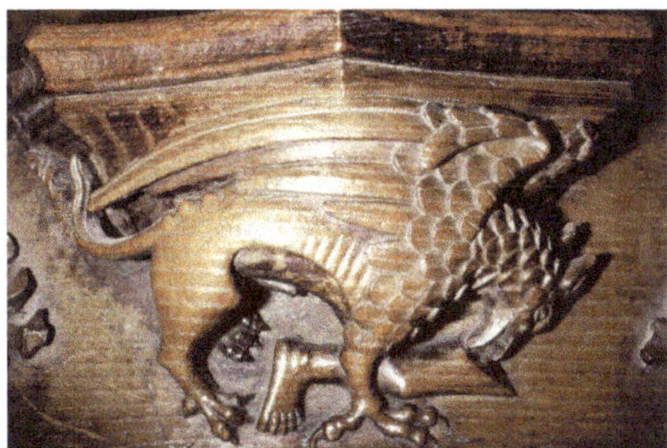
Griffin devouring a human leg. Misericord, 1490. Ripon.

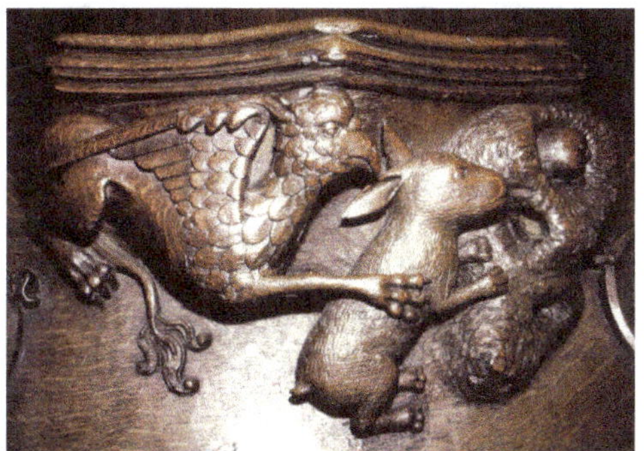
Griffin catching rabbit as another flees into burrow. Misericord, 1490. Ripon.

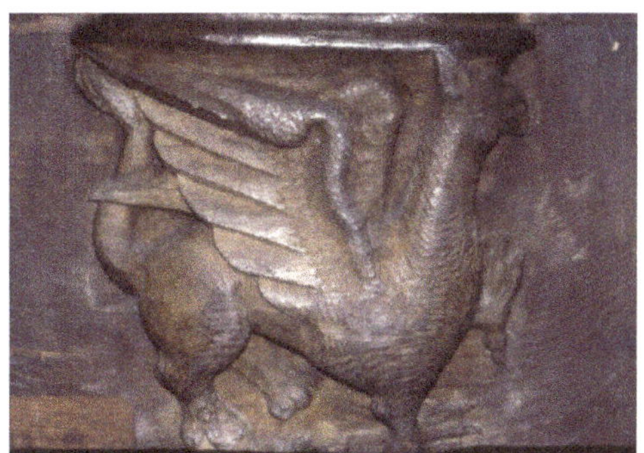
Griffin. Misericord, late 15th early 16th century. Old Malton Priory.

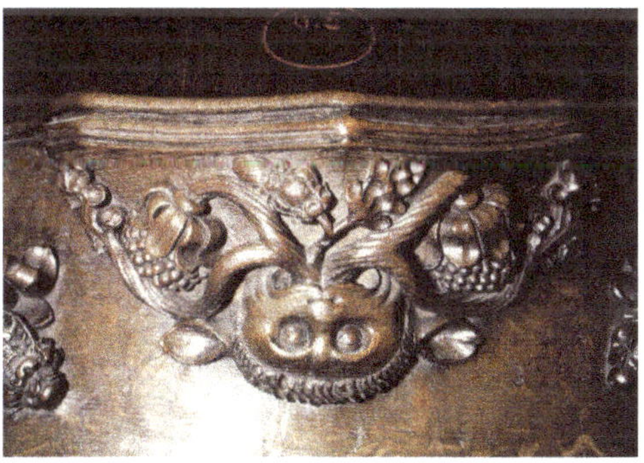
Green Man mask, upside down. Misericord, 1489-94. Ripon.

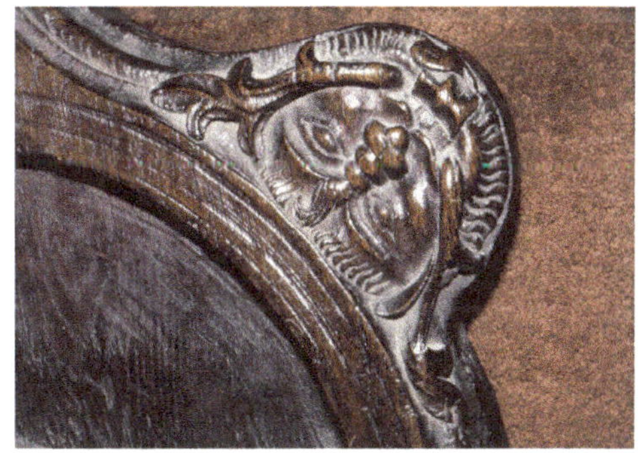
Green Man face. Elbow, 16th century. Richmond.

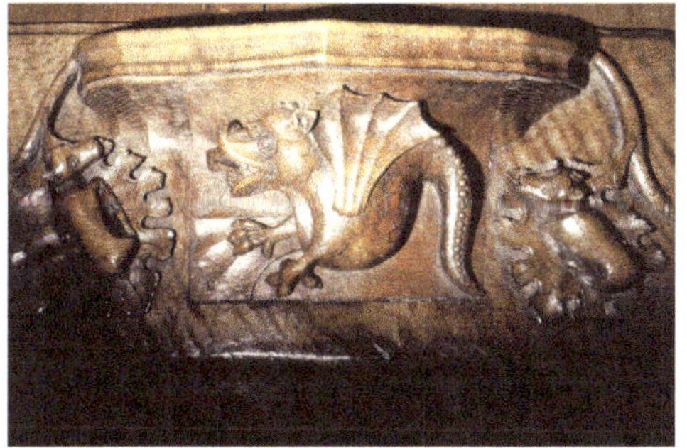
Wyvern snarling at two dogs or sheep. Misericord, 1490. Ripon.

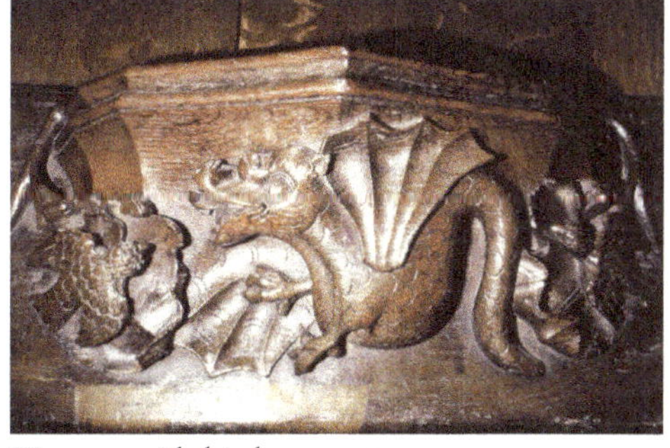
Wyvern with bird supporters. Misericord, 1490. Ripon.

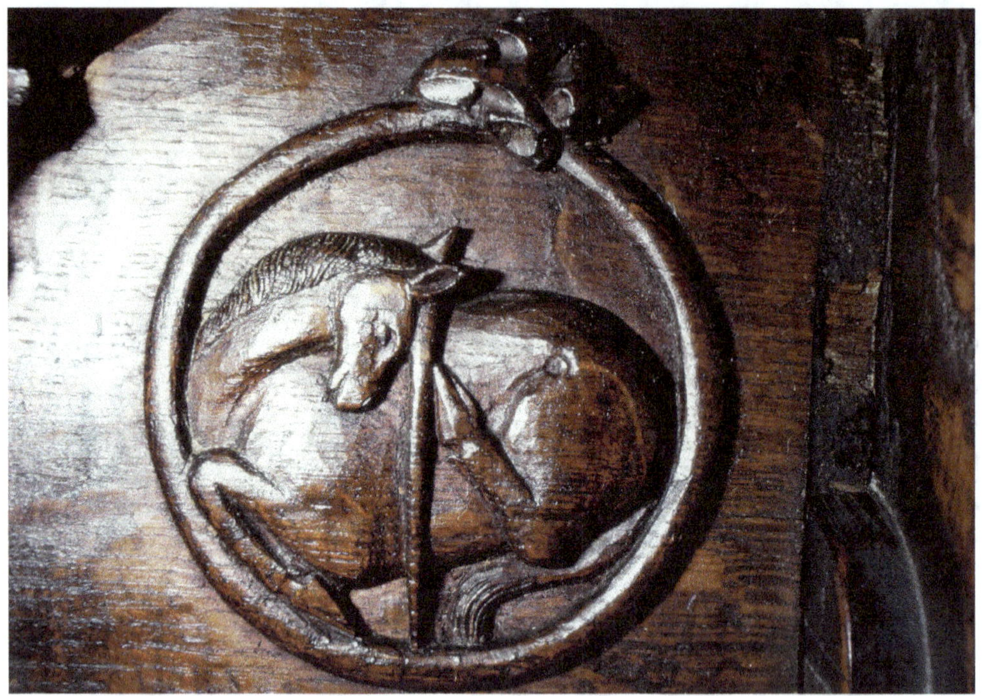

Unicorn scratching its head. Supporter, 1520. Beverley Minster.

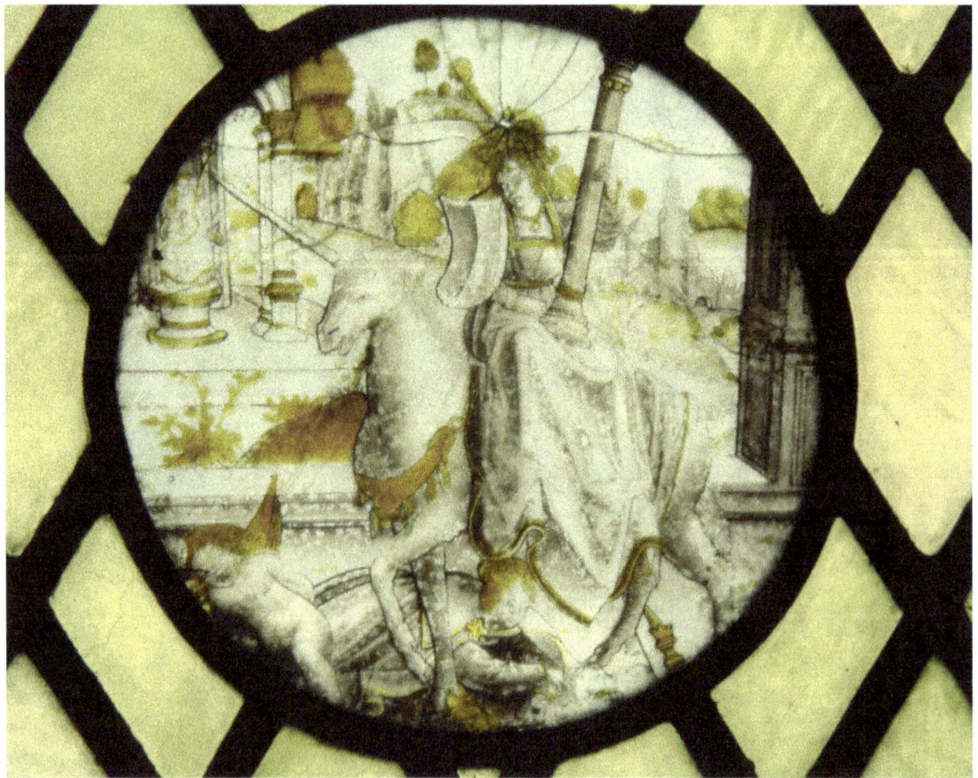

Lady riding a unicorn. Flemish roundel, late 17th century. St Helen, York.

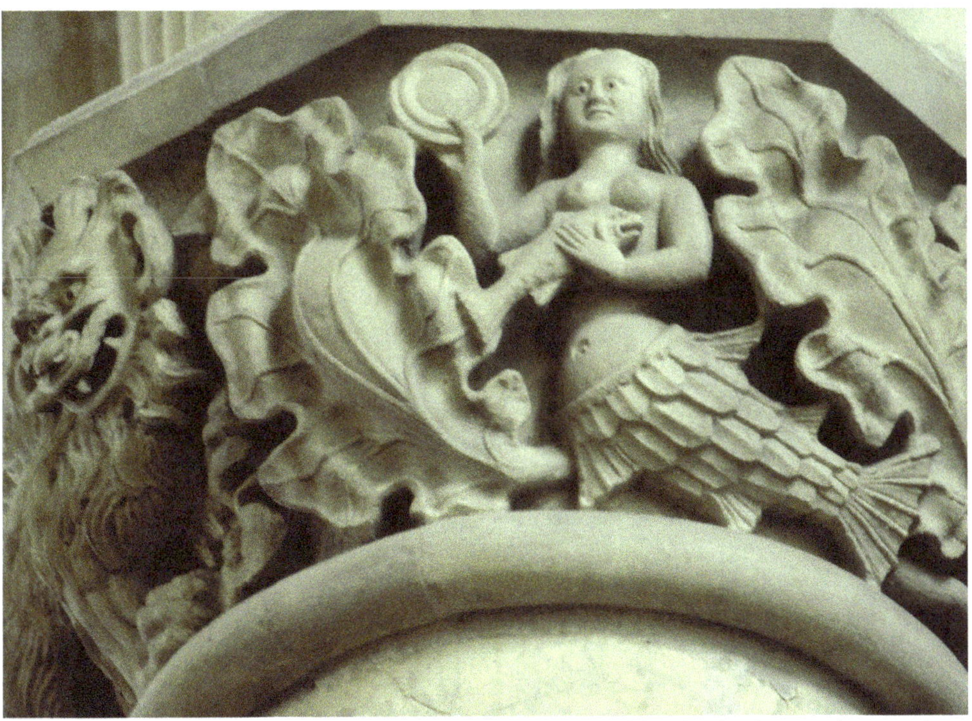

Mermaid with mirror and fish signifying lust or a soul captured for the devil. Capital, circa 1400s. York Minster.

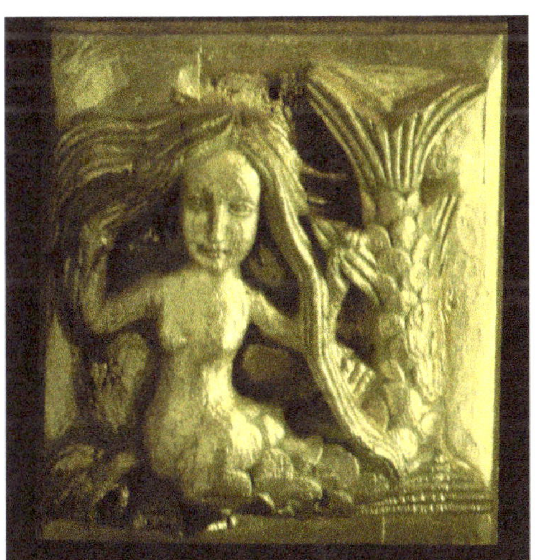

Charming mermaid holding her hair and tail. Roof boss, 13th/14th. centuries. Selby Abbey.

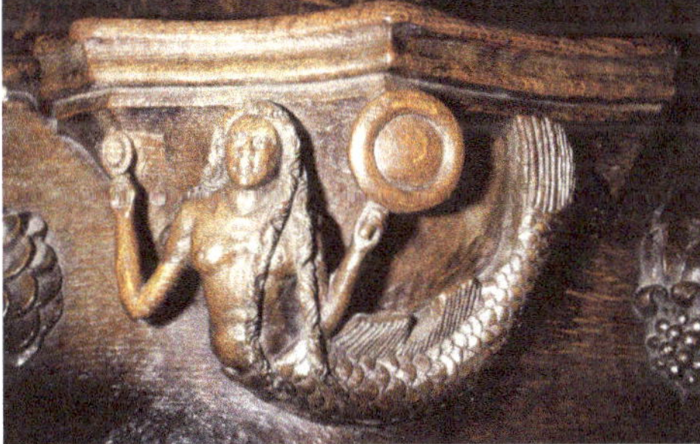

Mermaid with beautiful ringlets holding a brush and mirror personifying Vanity. Misericord, 1490. Ripon.

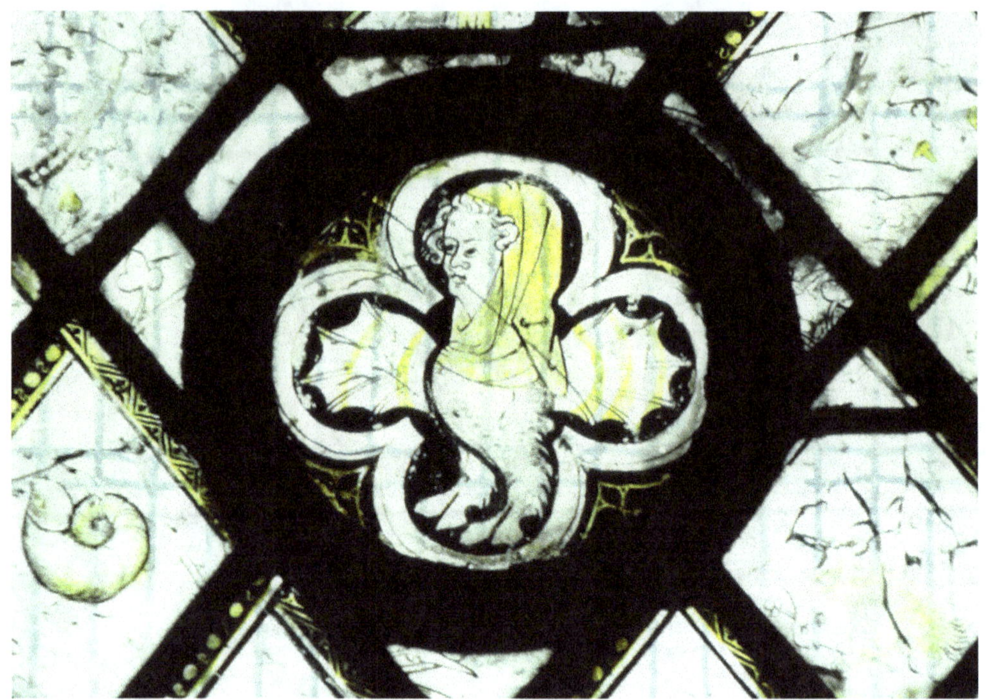

Cloven-hoofed harpy with wings. Roundel, mid 14th century. Dewsbury.

MISCELLANEOUS SUBJECTS

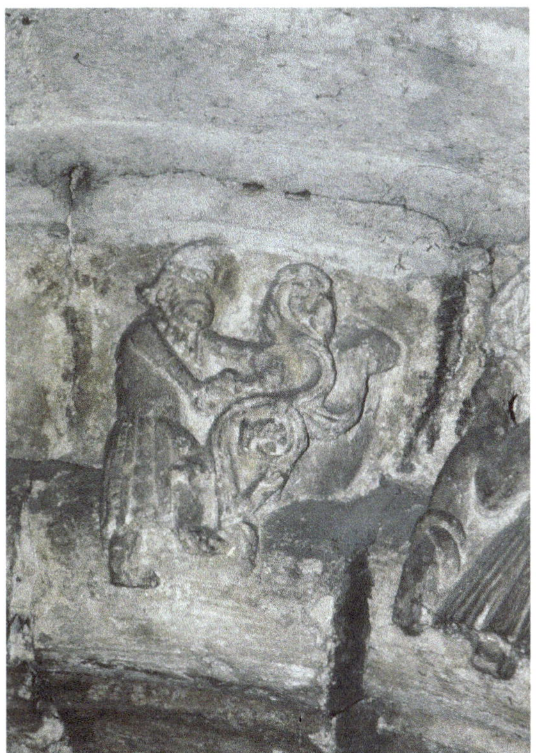

Man pruning a vine, illustrating March. Voussoire, circa 1160. Riccall.

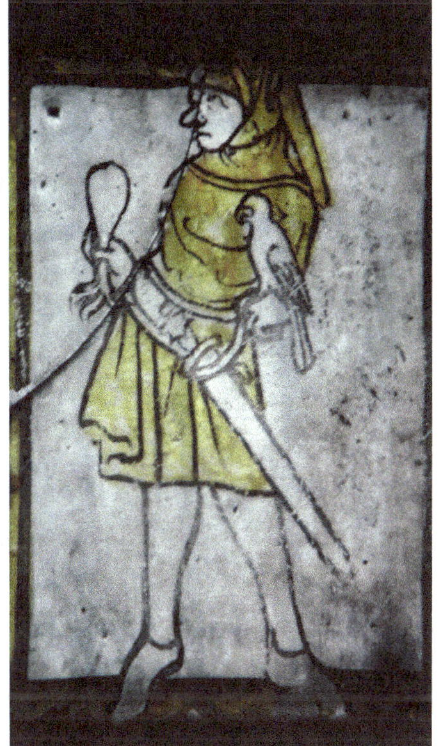

Man holding a hawk llustrating May or October. Window, 14th century. Ledsham.

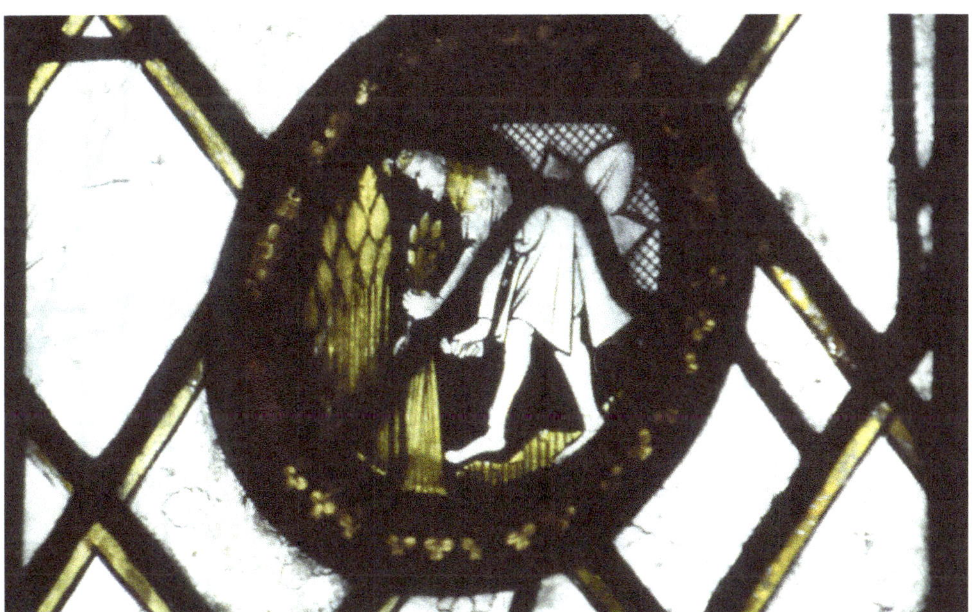

Harvesting, August in the Occupations of the Month. Roundel, 1350. Dewsbury.

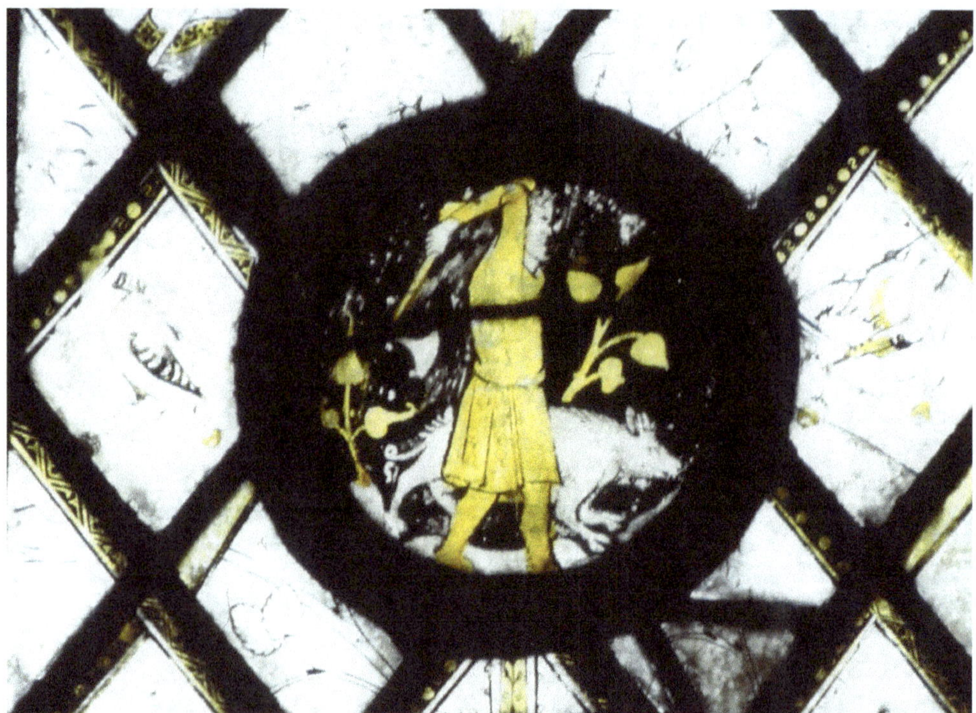

October or November in the Ocupations of the Month. Knocking down acorns to feed the pigs. Roundel, 1350. Dewsbury.

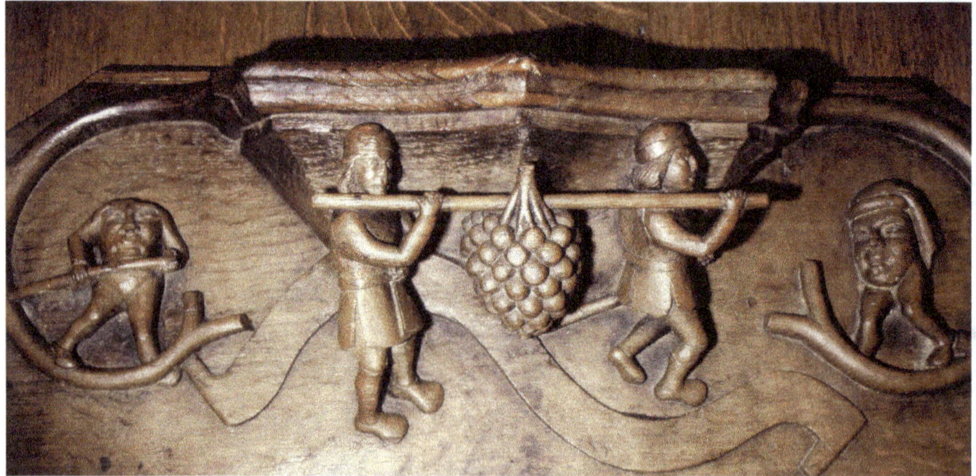

Spies from Canaan bearing a huge bunch of grapes. (Numbers 13:23-25). Blemya supporters. 1490. Ripon.

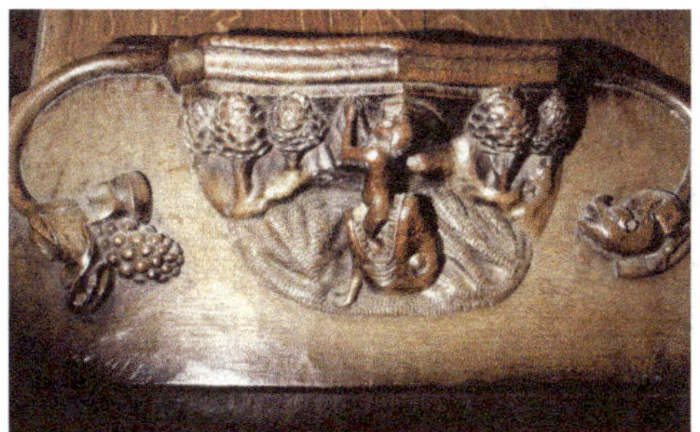

Jonah sallowed by the big fish. Misericord, 1490, Ripon.

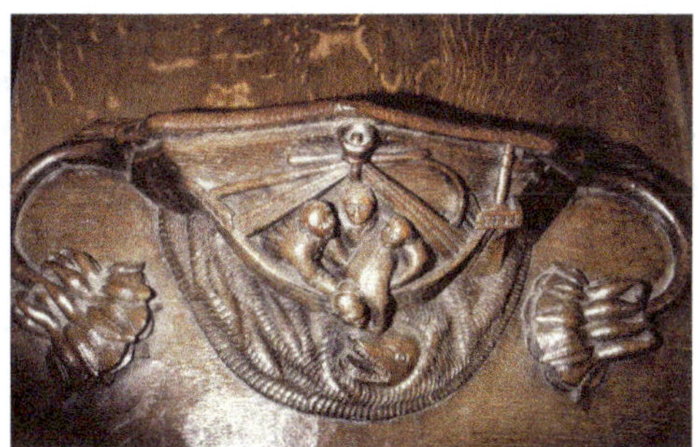

Jonah returned to dry land. Misericord with columbine supporters. 1490. Ripon.

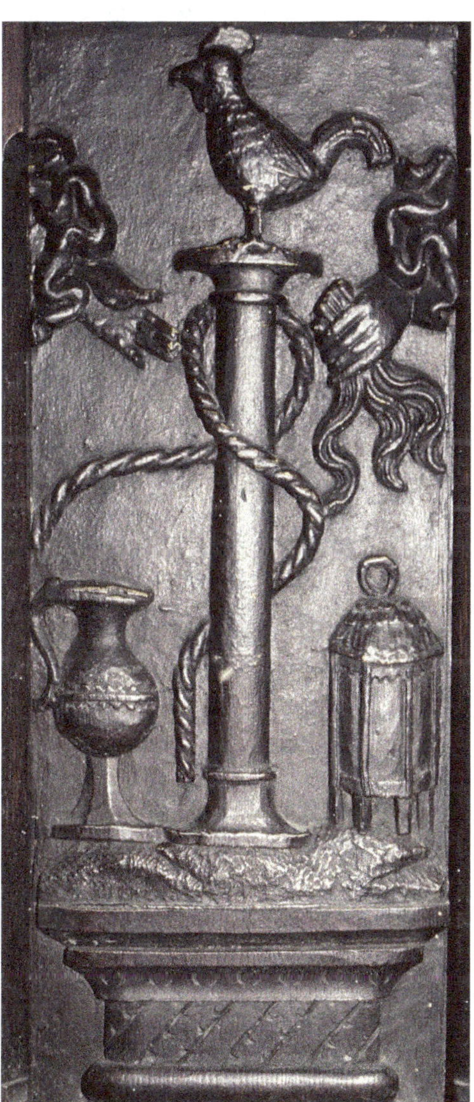

Cock on the Pillar of flagellation. Screen, Jacobean. Kirkby Wharfe.

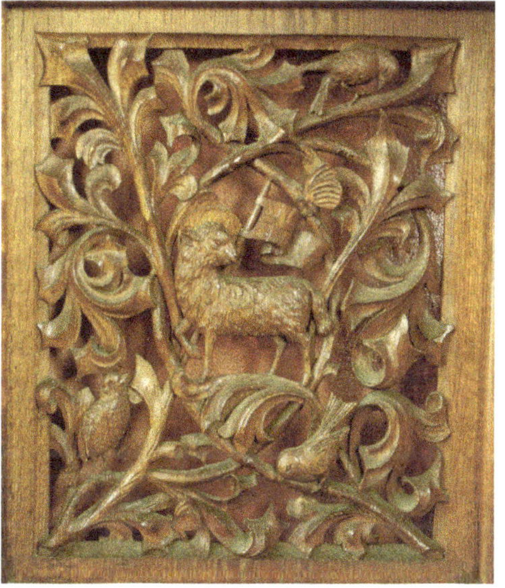

The Agnus Dei with three birds and two butterflies. Altar rail. circa 1930. West Tanfield.

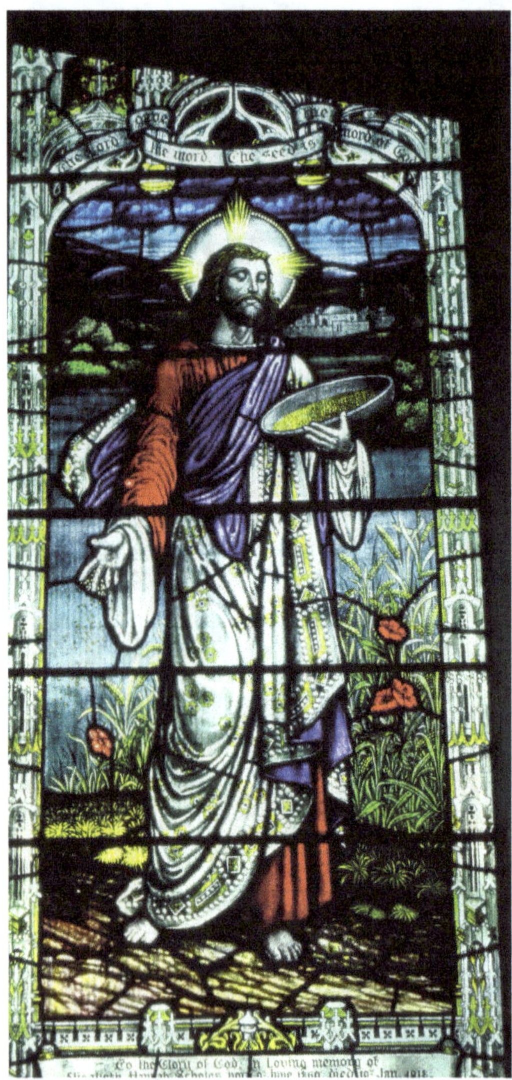

The Sower, (Luke 8:11-12), poppies and wheat. Window, 1919. Lindley.

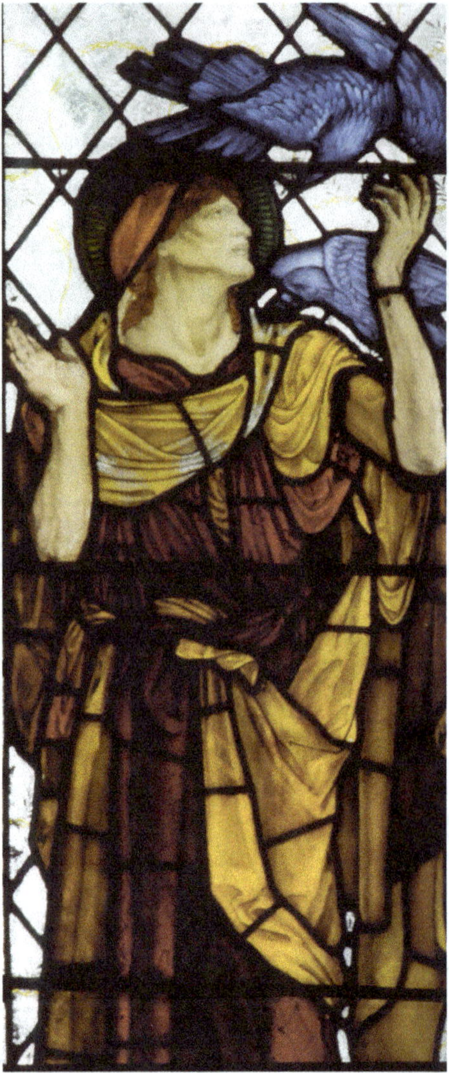

Elijah in the desert being fed by ravens. (1 Kings, 17:4). Window. Kirkheaton.

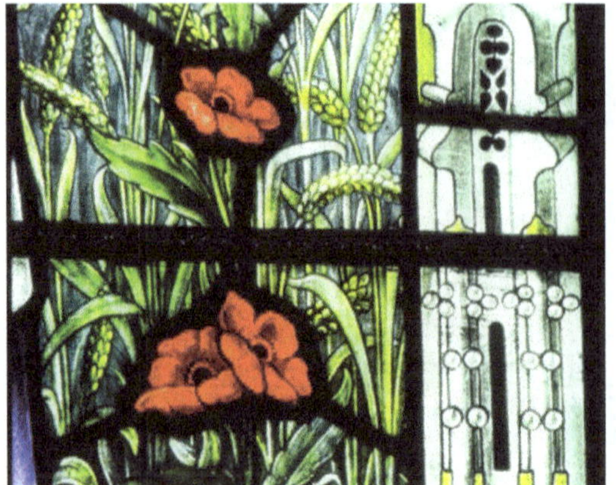

Detail of poppies in wheatfield.

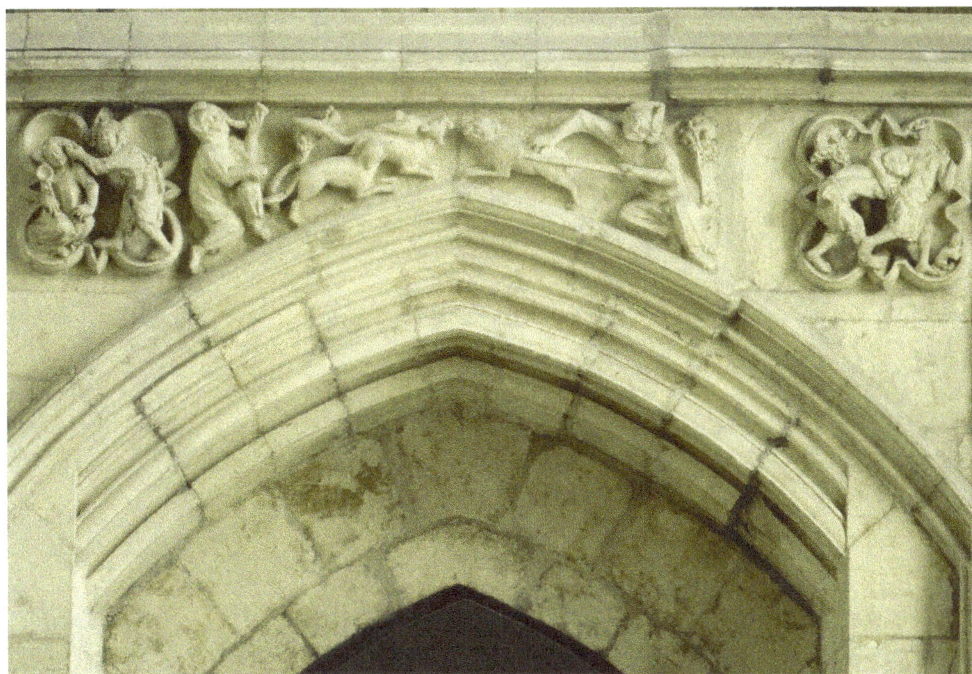

Domestic violence, boar hunting and wrestling. Tympanum. York Minster.

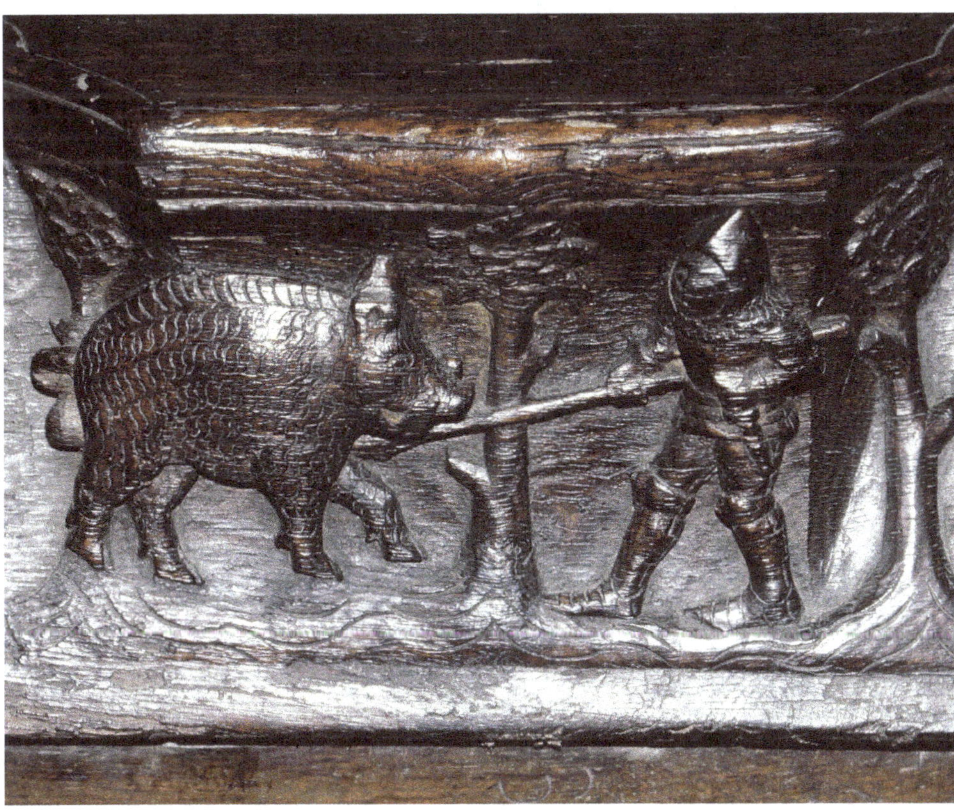

Boar hunting. A knight spears the boar and draws his dagger to kill the animal. Misericord, 1445. Beverley St Mary.

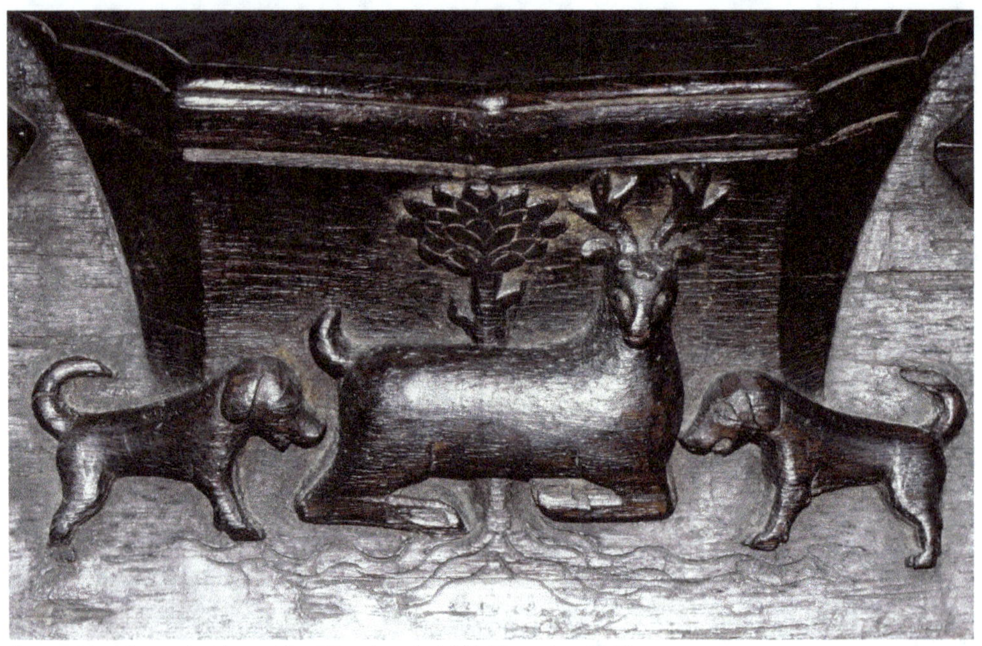

Stag with a hound either side. Misericord, 1445. Beverley St Mary.

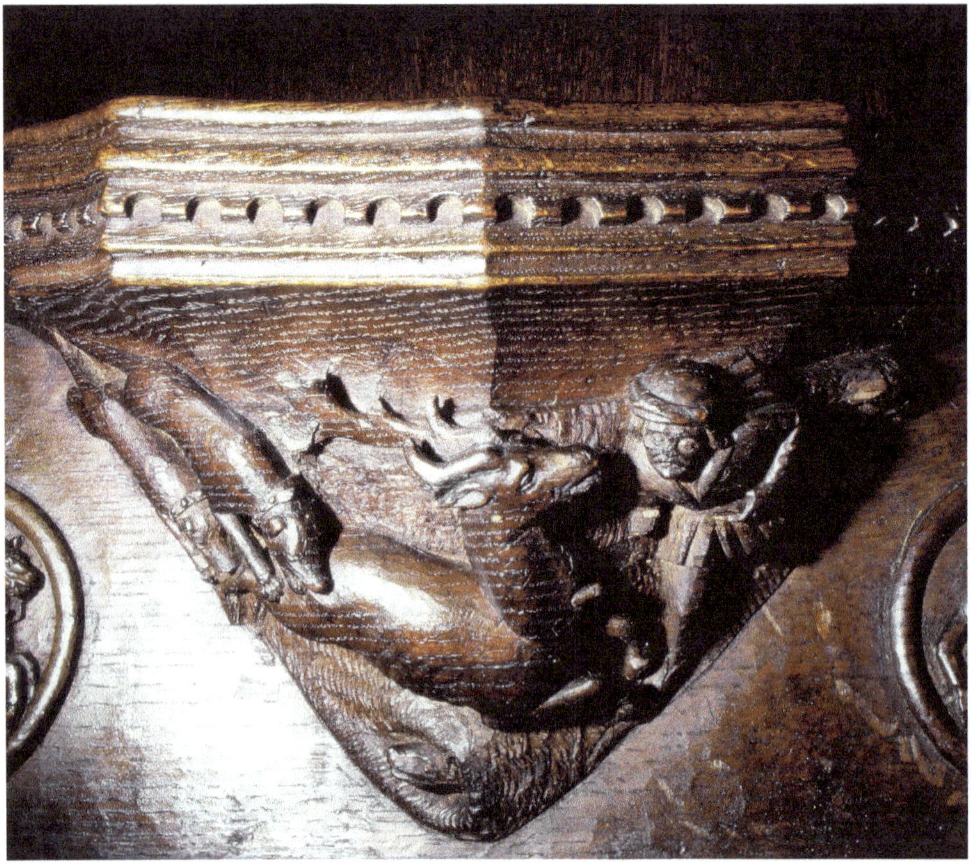

Stag hunting scene. Misericod, 1520. Beverley Minster.

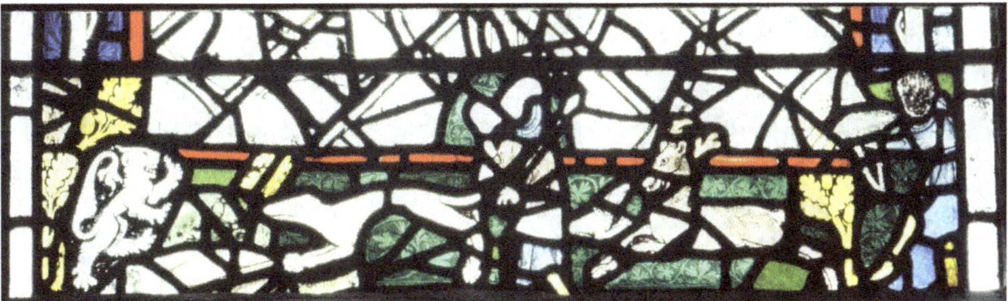

Stag hunting. Window border, 1310-20. York Minster.

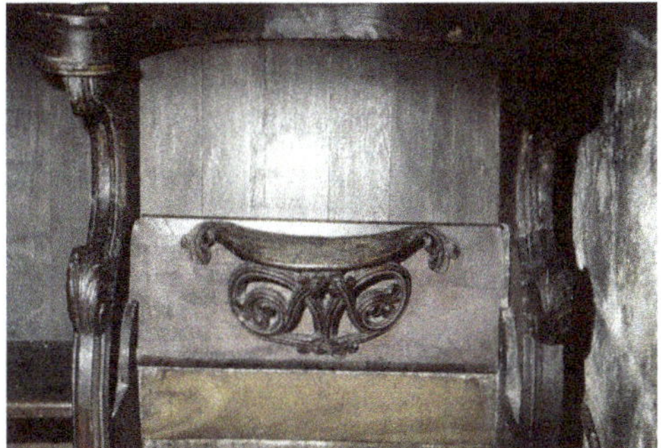

Misericord believed to be the oldest in the country. circa 1200. Hemingborough.

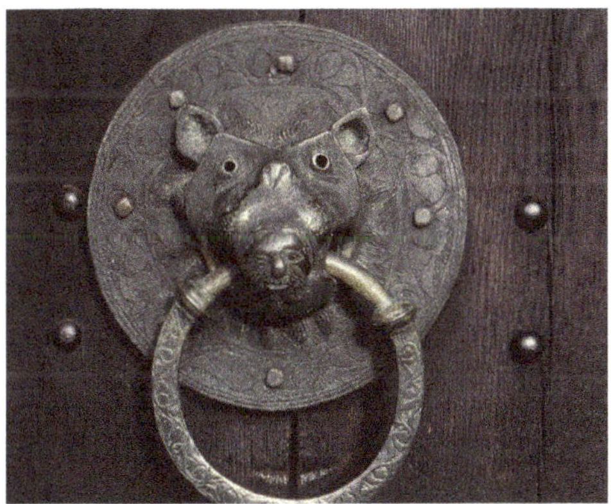

Closing ring. Door, copy of 13th century original. Adel.

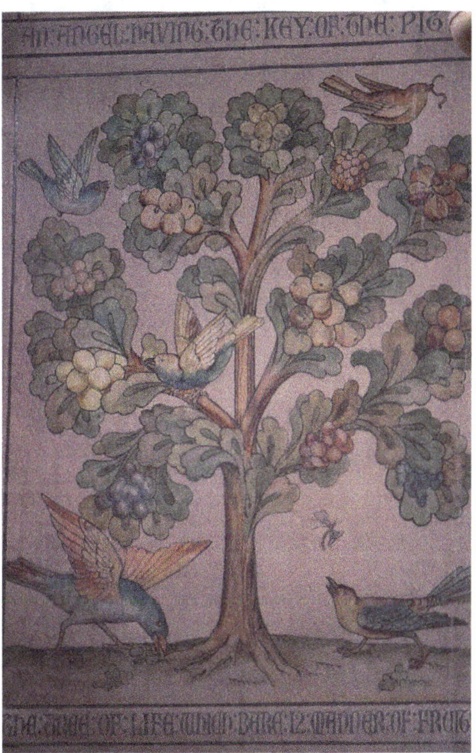

Wall painting depicting The Tree of Life. Revelation 22 verse 2. Studley Royal.

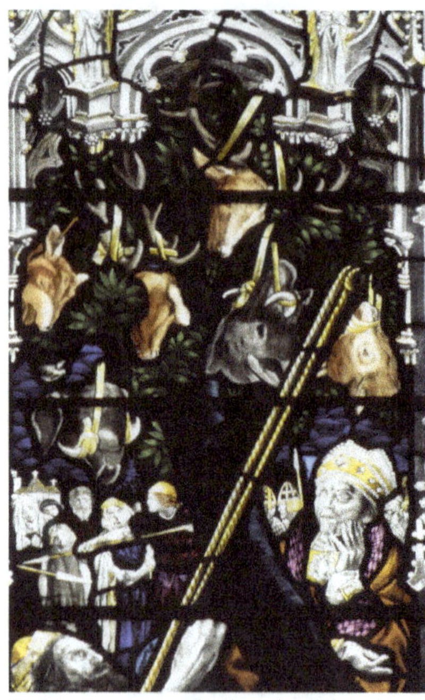

St Germanus with the dead heads of animals. Window. Selby Abbey.

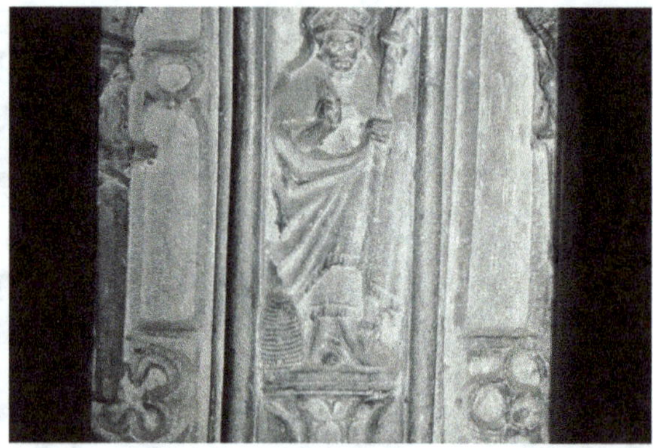

St Ambrose with beehive. Brus Cenotaph, 1520-30. Guisborough.

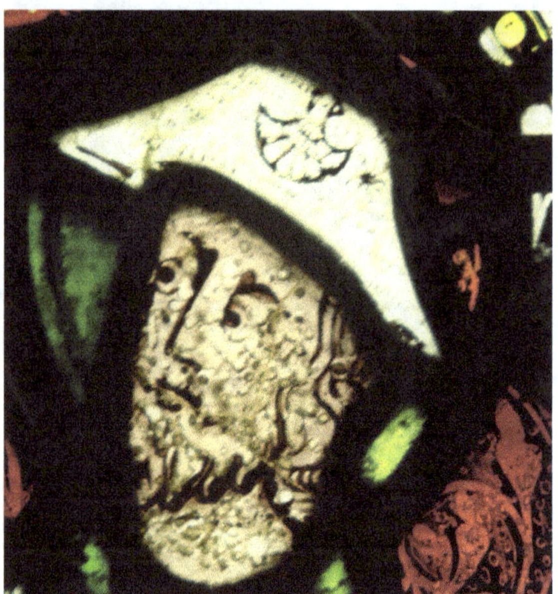

Spider on St James's hat.
Window, 15th century. St Cuthbert, York.

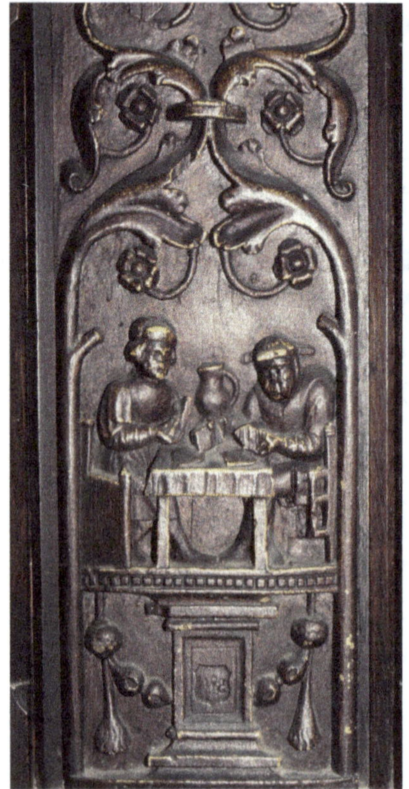

The card players. Screen, 16th century. Kirkby Wharfe.

GLOSSARY

Agnus Dei A representation of a lamb bearing either a cross or a flag as an emblem of Christ.

Altar A table or other raised structure at which the Eucharist is celebrated.

Altar frontal A hanging usually of richly embroidered material which hangs in front of the altar. The colour varies according to the season of the church year.

Altar rails Low palings enclosing the altar and providing kneeling places for communicants.

Amphisbaena A mythical serpent with a head at each end of its body enabling the creature to see in and move in either direction. A symbol of deceit.

Aspido Chelone A sea tortoise. Chelone are tortoise, terrapins and turtles.

Basilisk A fabulous reptile half cock half serpent hatched from the egg of a cock and with a glance that can kill. Weasels, providing they have previously eaten rue can attack it in safety.

Bench-end In a church the vertical section at each end of a bench, pew or seat, Usually but not always carved. Animals, birds and plants are often depicted, with medieval ones being richly carved.

Bestiary A book of animals real or mythical with a moralising story attached to them.

Blemya Monsters with faces in their headless bodies.

Boss Decorative, circular carvings at the intersection of vault ribs.

Breadstone A stone upon which bread was placed for the poor, particularly used at Christmas when diners would leave food to be distributed by the clergy on Boxing Day.

Caladrius A mythical white bird which could prophecy death or cure to a sick person.

Capital The head or top of a column or pillar that acts as a support for everything above it. Capitals are often carved and the styles vary with the date of the church.

Cartoon A full scale design usually for stained glass windows.

Centaur A mythical creature in the form of a horse but with a human head, arms and body in place of an equine head and neck. It is symbolic of Christ departing to deliver souls from Hell when shown shooting an arrow. The man typifies Christ and the horse His vengeance on those who betrayed Him.

Chancel arch An arch across the east end of the nave which opens into the chancel. The part of a church near the altar reserved for the clergy and choir. It is usually enclosed.

Chancel or Rood screen A screen which divides the nave from the chancel.

Chapter House The administrative office, a building where the Dean and canons (Chapter) of a cathedral or collegiate church meet.

Choir-stall A fixed seat in the choir of a church.

Clerestory or Clearstory A series of windows in the upper part of a large church aisle clear of the roof thus letting in the light to the central part of the church.

Closing ring A circular door handle or knocker.

Communion rail A low rail or rails enclosing the altar. A rail in front of the altar at which people kneel to receive Communion.

Corbel A projection of stone, timber etc.. jutting out from a wall to bear weight. They are frequently ornamented with carvings or may hold a statue.

Cornice A horizontal projection or moulding running round the wall near the ceiling.

Crosier The pastoral staff of senior clergy. An Archbishop's processional cross.

Distaff A cleft stick for holding wool or flax for spinning by hand.

Dragon A mythical fire-breathing monster with a forked tail and a pair of wings. A symbol of Satan.

Dripstone A stone moulding above a doorway, window or arch meant to throw off rain water.

Elbow rest An arm of a chair between the stalls.

Faldstool A chair used by a bishop or other prelate when not occupying the throne or when taking a service not in his own church.

Fetterlock A padlock as a heraldic badge or device.

Finial An ornamental knob.

Font A free-standing receptacle for holy water used in baptism.

Gargoyle A stone water spout draining a gutter generally carved as a grotesque face or animal.

Green Man or Jack in the Green The carved head of a man with greenery issuing from his nostrils or mouth to represent the wild man of the woods.

Griffin A mythical, evil creature with the head and wings of an eagle and the body of a lion.

Kneeler A cushion or hassock for kneeling upon when praying.

Label-stop A boss or corbel generally featuring a carved head or animal on a rectangular dripstone.

Lectern A stand or desk with a sloping front to hold a Bible, book or notes often in the shape of an eagle with outspread wings.

Lectern fall A piece of material falling from the back of the lectern.

Light A window opening or a division in a window.

Lozenge A rhombus-shaped pane of glass in a window.

Medallion A round or oval decorated panel.

Misericord The misericord was a projection beneath a hinged choir stall seat often with entertaining carvings, both sacred and profane, to give support to someone standing.

Mermaid A part human part fish sea creature with the head and bust of a woman and the tail of a fish.

Monstrance An open or transparent vessel for exposing the consecrated Host.

Mosaic The creation of pictures or patterns by cementing together small pieces of stone or glass et cetera.

Nave The main body of a church from the west door to the chancel.

Pew A long seat for a group of worshippers. A bench to seat the congregation.

Poppyhead A finial decorating the top of a bench-end or choir-stall.

Pulpit A raised structure from which a preacher delivers a sermon or conducts a service.

Quarry A small, diamond or square-shaped piece of window glass.

Reading-desk A desk for supporting a book whilst it is being read.

Reclinatoria A T-shaped stick upon which the aged and infirm clergy were allowed to lean during services.

Rebus A representation of a word or phrase by pictures or symbols.

Reredos An ornamental screen covering the wall behind and above the altar.

Rood-screen A wood or stone screen, usually richly carved, across the chancel.It usually bears the rood i.e. a crucifix above the centre of the screen.

Roof boss A round knob at the intersection in vaulting on a ceiling.

Screen A stone or wood partition usually decorated separating the nave from the chancel.

Scrip A small bag or purse for alms carried especially by pilgrims.

Sedile/Sedilia Usually three canopied and decorated recessed stone seats placed on the south side of the chancel near the altar and for clergy use only.

Spandrel A triangular space generally decorated between an arch and moulding, and between adjoining arches.

Stall A fixed seat in the choir or chancel reserved for a specified member of the clergy.

Stall front The front of the stall behind which is the seat.

Supporters Subsidiary carvings on either side of the main subject on a misericord.

Topsy-turvey Inversion of the proper order.

Transept The transverse part of a cruciform church at right angles to the nave.

Tun A cask or barrel for wine or ale.

Tush A canine tooth of a male horse, boar or elephant.

Tushed Having a tush or tushes.

Tympanum A space over a door between the lintel and the arch.

Unicorn A horse-like mythical beast having one horn in the middle of its forehead. It could not be conquered thus symbolising Christ, his passion and incarnation.

Vestibule The entry to a church.

Voussoir A wedge-shaped stone forming part of an arch.

Vulning Self-wounding to draw blood to feed young.

Wall Painting A mural or fresco painted on the wall.

Wodehouse A mythical wild man of the woods dressed in the skins of wild animals.

Wyvern A winged dragon with two feet like those of an eagle, and with a barbed tail.

SELECTED BIBLIOGRAPHY

Anderson, M.D. (1938) *Animal carvings in British Churches.* Cambridge University Press.

Anderson M.D. (1955) *Imagery in British Churches.* Murray.

Anderson, Margaret D. (1956). *Misericords.* Penguin Books Ltd., England.

Carter, Robert. (1976) *A Visitors Guide to Yorkshire Churches.* Watmoughs Ltd. Bradford.

Cowes, Painter. (1985). *A Guide to Stained Glass in Britain.* Michael Joseph.

Degraaff, Robert M. (1991) *Book of the Toad.* Lutterworth Press.

Douglas, J.D. *et al.* (eds.) (1982). *New Bible Dictionary.* (second edition)

Druce, George C. (1914) *Animals in English Wood Carvings.* Walpole Society Vol.3.

Druce, George C. (1919) *The Medieval Bestiaries, and their Influence on Ecclesiastical Decorative Art.* British Archaeological Journal.

Evans, E.P. (1896) *Animal Symbolism in Ecclesiastical Architecture.* William Heinemann.

Farmer, David Hugh. (1983) *Dictionary of Saints.* Oxford University Press.

Friedman, H. (1946) *The Symbolic Goldfinch.* Pantheon Books, Washington.

Friend, Rev. Hilderic (1883). *Flower and Flower Lore.* Vols. 1 & 2. George Allan & Co., Ltd. London.

Gibson, Peter. (1979).*The Stained and Painted Glass of York Minster.* Jarrold and Sons Ltd, Norwich.

Grigson, Geoffrey. (1987) *An Englishman's Flora.* J. M. Dent & Sons Ltd. London.

Grossinger, Christa. (1989). *Ripon Cathedral Misericords.* The Dean and Chapter, Ripon Cathedral.

Hayman, Richard. (1989) *Church Misericords and Bench Ends.* Shire Publications Ltd.

James, Anne. (1989) *Book of Flowers.* British Museum Publications Ltd.

Janson, H. W. (1952) *Apes and Ape Lore in the Middle Ages and the Renaissance.* Studies of the Warburg Institute Vol. 20. University of London.

Kear, Janet. (1990). *Man and Wildfowl.* Poyser.

Laird, Marshall. (1986). *English Misericords.* John Murray, London.

Leach, Peter. (1981). *Saint Mary's Church, Studley Royal.* English Heritage, London.

Mee, Arthur. (1941). The King's England: Yorkshire *East Riding with York City*).

Mee, Arthur. (1941). Yorkshire *West Riding.*

Mee, Arthur. (1941). Yorkshire *North Riding.* Hodder and Stoughton.

Pevsner, Nikolaus. (1997). *Yorkshire The North Riding.* Penguin Books.

Remnant, G.L. (1969) *A Catalogue of Misericords in Great Britain.* Clarendon Press.

Rowland, Beryl. (1973) *Animals with Human Faces.* University of Tennessee Press.

Tanfield, Thomas R. *Beverley Minster. Misericord Seats.* Beverley Minster Parochial Church Council.

Toy, John. (1985) *A Guide and Index to the Windows of York Minster.* Dean and Chapter of York.

Varty, Kenneth. (1967). *Reynard the Fox.* Leicester University Press.

Varty, Kenneth. (1999). *Reynard, Renart, Reinaert and other Foxes in Medieval England.* Amsterdam University Press, Amsterdam.

White, T.H. (1954). *The Book of Beasts.* Jonathon Cape, London.

Pamphlets and Guide Books.

Adel Parish Church. (2000). Leeds Guide Book.

Adel Church Guide (2003).

Aldborough. Church of Saint Andrew. 1989.

Alne. Saint Mary's Church. 1979.

Aysgarth. Saint Andrew. 1987.

Barton, Allan B. *A Guide to the Church of All Saints.* North Street, York.

Bolton Priory.

Leeds. Saint John's Church.

Riccall. Saint Mary's Church.

Ripon Minster. (1985).

The Folklore of Birds. (1997). Compiled and published The Countryside Collection.

West Tanfield. Saint Nicholas Church. York.

Where no details are given none have been traced.
The above is correct as far as is known.

www.ingramcontent.com/pod-product-compliance
Lightning Source LLC
LaVergne TN
LVHW061223100826
845148LV00004B/838
9780954403515